DEMOCRATIC WOMEN

An Oral History of the Woman's National Democratic Club

By Jewell Fenzi and Allida Black

A publication of the WNDC Educational Foundation
Washington, DC

WNDC Educational Foundation Oral History Series No. 1

Democratic Women: An Oral History of the Woman's National Democratic Club
Jewell Fenzi and Allida Black

Copyright © WNDC Educational Foundation, 1526 New Hampshire Avenue, NW, Washington, DC 20036 (202-232-7363); WomansNDC@aol.com; <www.wndcfoundation.org>
All rights reserved. No part of this book may be reproduced or transmitted in any form or by any means, electronic or mechanical, including photocopying, recording, or by any information storage and retrieval system, without permission in writing from the Publisher.

WNDC Educational Foundation
1526 New Hampshire Avenue, NW
Washington, DC 20036

ISBN 0-9705503-0-8 $19.95

Library of Congress Control Number: 00-136032

Design: ExArte Design, Inc.

Printed in the United States of America

CONTENTS

		Page
Acknowledgements		*v*
About the Book		*vii*
Prologue		*ix*
Chapter 1	The Founders	*1*
Chapter 2	The Clubhouse	*17*
Chapter 3	Eleanor Roosevelt: WNDC's First Democratic First Lady	*25*
Chapter 4	World War II and Afterward	*43*
Chapter 5	An Open Door	*61*
Chapter 6	Democratic Renaissance	*71*
Chapter 7	Thoroughly Modern Members	*87*
Chapter 8	Cooking Reagan's Goose	*101*
Chapter 9	Changing Times	*123*
Chapter 10	Task Forces and Committees	*141*
Chapter 11	WNDC's Educational Foundation	*155*
Appendix: Past Presidents		*161*
Bibliography and Sources		*163*
Index		*175*
About the Author, the Historian, and the Editor		*181*

Detail of cover photo. Eleanor Roosevelt with WNDC members at the White House. Rideout Photo, courtesy of WNDC-EF library.

ACKNOWLEDGEMENTS

Scores of generous colleagues, friends, scholars, and institutions helped guide this book from tape to print. I am deeply indebted to all of them. Initial encouragement came from Newell Blair, son of Woman's National Democratic Club (WNDC) founder Emily Newell Blair, who opened his personal papers, made generous donations to the WNDC Educational Foundation (WNDC-EF) oral history program, and became a warm friend. My gratitude to Newell and his wife, Greta, is boundless.

I thank WNDC member Jane Evensen for her early encouragement and support, and WNDC-EF for sponsoring *Democratic Women* as a component of its oral history program. The club fund in memory of Harryette Cohn helped with early transcribing. Bountiful anonymous donations bought state-of-the-art electronic equipment.

Club members Sandra Bieri, Coralee Farlie, Nicki Lagoudakis, and Susan Myrick recorded informative interviews. I am also indebted to Susan for her research on India Edwards; to Kathy Schmidt for her Eleanor Roosevelt research; to David Richardson for taping memories of his grandmother, Frances G. Blake; to Phyllis Fineshriber for her recollections of Olya Margolin; and to Betty Hight for sharing her candid interview recorded for the Eleanor Roosevelt Oral History Project of the Franklin Delano Roosevelt Library in Hyde Park, New York. Dorothy Dillon provided the transcript of her interview for the United States Information Agency. In the 1970s, former WNDC archivist, Margaret "Peg" Colton recorded cameo interviews with India Edwards and club past presidents, Constance Casey, Margo Davis, Marian Driver, Mary Keyserling, and Sherley Koteen. All were valuable resources.

For the prologue, I edited text from the WNDC Diamond Jubilee exhibit, "Where Minds May Meet: A History of Woman's Suffrage and the Founding of the Woman's National Democratic Club." Lou Ann Broad curated the exhibit, emphasizing political sisterhood. Historian Edith Mayo's cyberspace exhibit on the history of suffrage for the National Museum of Women's History Web site also inspired the prologue.

Lewis L. Gould, former Eugene C. Barker Centennial Professor of American History at the University of Texas at Austin, was once again a patient mentor and friend. Always helpful, Dennis Bilger of the Harry S. Truman Library in Independence, Missouri, forwarded India Edwards's papers. I am indebted to the Western Reserve Historical Society in Cleveland, Ohio; to Virginia Laas, associate professor of history at Missouri Southern State College in Joplin; and to Kathryn

Anderson, professor of women's studies, Fairhaven College, Western Washington University, for their help in interpreting the club's Emily Newell Blair collection. Bonny Headley sent information on Head Start from Anchorage, Alaska; and I had several lively sessions with New York independent scholar, Jo Freeman. Assistant Professor Nancy Beck Young at McKendree College in Illinois and scholar Judy McArthur were generous with their research on Texas politician Minnie Fisher Cunningham. From Thetford, Vermont, Phyllis Darling, granddaughter of Florence Jaffray "Daisy" Harriman, loaned Harriman papers destined for the Library of Congress and gave the club her grandmother's scrapbook of the 1912 presidential campaign that details women's entrance into national politics.

Closer to home, Donald Ritchie, associate historian of the U.S. Senate; Cynthia Harrison, associate professor of history and women's studies at George Washington University; and independent scholar, Kristie Miller, generously shared their wide-ranging expertise. Washington writer, Carl L. Nelson; editors, Barbara Lundberg and Mary Muromcew; and publishers, Mary Louise Hollowell, Liz Hill, and Evelyn Metzger were excellent advisors. And I thank William H. Davis at the National Archives for the National Woman Suffrage Association petition.

Always ebullient, Dr. Allida Black came on board as historian. Judy Beck, vice president for professional development for the American Association of Colleges for Teacher Education, was a wise and thoughtful reader. It was my pleasure to record many of the interviews, acquiring in the process an even greater respect and admiration for my colleagues at the Woman's National Democratic Club. I am grateful to all who took part.

I wish to thank WNDC-EF president, Cynthia McCaughan; WNDC president, Anna Stout; and the club's administrative staff for unwavering support. Every oral history project needs a transcriber and discerning editor, and Sally Cutler, a special friend and freelance editor, ably filled these two demanding roles. Sally's encouragement, keen wit, and enthusiasm helped sustain the five-year project. Finally, I am grateful to my daughter, Ruth Reeder, for artistic advice and to my spouse, Guido C. Fenzi, for his wisdom and patience. Any errors or omissions are my own.

Jewell Fenzi
Chair, WNDC-EF Oral History
September 2000

ABOUT THE BOOK

Emily Newell Blair, the original advocate for the Woman's National Democratic Club, was the inspiration for *Democratic Women*. The club's seventy-fifth anniversary was the catalyst. It prompted an evaluation of WNDC's future by visiting its political and social past.

The book was a project of the WNDC Educational Foundation (WNDC-EF) oral history program. It has been edited from interviews with more than fifty club members. Although WNDC extended full membership to men in 1988, the club history was defined primarily by the experiences of volunteer women.

Because of time, space, and financial constraints, only a sampling of WNDC members could be interviewed. Not all interviews could be included in the book, and some received more emphasis than others. In every case, the selection process was undertaken with an eye toward capturing the broader outlines and the common elements of the experience of being a WNDC member.

Some stories could not be independently verified from historical sources. But all of the interviews were taped and transcribed, and all interviewees signed deeds of gift transferring ownership of the tapes and transcripts to WNDC-EF.

The spoken language of the transcripts moved the narrative forward, but was frequently edited. In every case the thoughts and emphases of the interview subject remain unchanged. Unless otherwise noted, interviews were recorded for the WNDC-EF oral history program. A complete list of interviewees appears in the Bibliography and Sources.

National Woman Suffrage Association.

President, SUSAN B. ANTHONY,
　　　　　　Rochester, N.Y.
Ch'n Ex. Com. MATILDA JOSLYN GAGE,
　　　　　　Fayetteville, N.Y.
Cor. Sec'y, JANE GRAHAM JONES,
　　　　　910 Prairie Ave., Chicago, Ill.
For. Cor. Sec'y, LAURA CURTIS BULLARD,
　　　　　85 East Thirty-ninth St., New York.
Rec. Sec'y, MARY F. DAVIS,
　　　　　Orange, New Jersey.
Treasurer, ELLEN C. SARGENT,
　　　　　Washington, D.C.

1873

To the Honorable Senate and House of Representatives in Congress assembled,

We, the undersigned, citizens of the United States, but deprived of some of the privileges and immunities of citizens among which is the right to vote, beg leave to submit the following Resolution;—

Resolved, That we, the officers and members of the National Woman Suffrage Association, in Convention assembled, Respectfully ask Congress to enact appropriate legislation during its present Session to protect women citizens in the several States of this Union, in their right to vote.

　　　　　Susan B. Anthony President
　　　　　Matilda Joslyn Gage Ch. Ex. Com
　　　　　Elizabeth Cady Stanton

National Woman Suffrage Association petition signed by NWSA president, Susan B. Anthony; NWSA executive committee chair, Matilda J. Gage; and Elizabeth Cady Stanton, 20 January 1873. Courtesy of the National Archives.

PROLOGUE

Suffrage Sets the Stage

1840   Lucretia Mott, a wise Quaker minister; Elizabeth Cady Stanton, a brilliant activist housewife; and other women abolitionists are denied seats at the World Anti-Slavery Convention held in London. With women representing half of the world's population, Mott and Stanton feel obliged to promote women's rights when they return to the United States.

1848   Mott and Stanton organize the Seneca Falls [NY] Convention, the first gathering convened for the specific purpose of addressing the rights of women. Stanton writes "The Declaration of Sentiments," a statement of rights for women based on the Declaration of Independence. All twelve resolutions are unanimously adopted except the suffrage resolution.

                 The women and the convention are ridiculed by the public and the press, except for Horace Greeley's *New York Tribune* which treats the issues seriously. The "Declaration of Sentiments" creates the agenda of women's activism for decades to come.

1850   The first National Woman's Rights Convention is held in Worcester, Massachusetts. A strong alliance is formed with the abolitionist movement. Frederick Douglass, William Lloyd Garrison, Lucy Stone, and Sojourner Truth attend.

1851   Susan B. Anthony joins Stanton to lead the suffrage movement, which becomes a lifelong crusade for the two women.

1853   The World Temperance Convention held in New York City refuses to allow women to speak. Antoinette Brown Blackwell, the first ordained woman minister in America, is shouted down when she tries to speak.

1861-65	Suffrage movement efforts come to a halt during the Civil War. Women put their energies into the war effort and are instrumental in the development and advancement of medical and sanitary practices.
1866	Stanton, Anthony, and abolitionist Lucy Stone help found the American Equal Rights Association, an organization dedicated to the goal of suffrage for all, regardless of gender or race.
1869	The American Equal Rights Association disbands over disagreements about the 14th Amendment, which conferred citizenship on all persons born or naturalized in the United States, and the proposed 15th Amendment. The latter would enfranchise black American males while making no mention of suffrage for women.
	Two rival organizations emerge: The National Woman Suffrage Association (NWSA), a radical organization founded by Stanton and Anthony that refuses to support the 15th Amendment; and the American Woman Suffrage Association (AWSA), a more moderate group founded by Lucy Stone and Julia Howe.
1872	Susan B. Anthony and many other women, including Virginia Minor, voted or tried to vote. Anthony was arrested at her home, tried, and found guilty. Minor's case went to the Supreme Court, which decided that citizenship did not assure voting rights.
1878	A woman suffrage amendment is proposed in the U.S. Congress. Called the Susan B. Anthony Amendment, it is finally passed by Congress forty-one years later, in 1919, with exactly the same wording.
1890	Rival suffrage organizations, NWSA and AWSA, unite under the banner of the National American Woman Suffrage Association (NAWSA) with Stanton as the first president. The movement focuses efforts on securing suffrage at the state level. In 1892, Anthony succeeds Stanton. Anthony retires from the presidency in 1900 at the age of ninety, but remains a key leader until her death in 1906.

1890-1914   Wyoming becomes the first state to grant women the right to vote when it enters the Union in 1890. (As a territory, Wyoming had granted women full suffrage in 1869.) By 1912, women can vote for president in five additional states: Colorado, 1893; Utah, 1895; Idaho, 1896; Washington, 1910; California, 1911. Oregon, Arizona, and Kansas give women full suffrage in 1912. Nevada and Montana join the ranks in 1914. By the 1910s, women have partial suffrage in many states

1890-1920   The Progressive Era flourishes as women from all classes and backgrounds enter public life. Politicization of women increases as women's roles expand. The issue of woman suffrage enters the mainstream at the state level.

1912   Woman suffrage is supported for the first time in the national platform of a major political party, Theodore Roosevelt's Progressive (Bull Moose) Party. WNDC founder Daisy Harriman enters national politics to organize the Women's National Wilson and Marshall Association.

Alice Paul and Lucy Burns revitalize NAWSA's Congressional Committee, establishing the first permanent suffrage headquarters in Washington. NAWSA provides an annual lobbying budget of $13, with the understanding that Paul and Burns will raise additional funds.

1913   Paul organizes a historic suffrage parade on the day preceding President Woodrow Wilson's first inauguration. Thousands of suffragists march along Pennsylvania Avenue, diverting public attention from Wilson's arrival at Washington's Union Station.

1914   Alice Paul and her Congressional Union leave NAWSA to organize the National Woman's Party (NWP), the militant wing of the suffrage movement. Paul holds the party in power responsible for passage of a suffrage amendment, and campaigns to defeat all Democrats in 1916.

1916   Jeannette Rankin, a progressive Republican from Montana, is the first woman elected to the House of Representatives. A pacifist, she voted against entry into World War I, and was defeated in 1918 when she challenged incumbent Senator Thomas J. Walsh (D-MT).[1]

At the 1916 Democratic national convention in St. Louis, Carrie Chapman Catt and WNDC founder Emily Newell Blair organize a silent demonstration called the Golden Lane. Dressed in white, with yellow sashes and parasols, and spaced four feet apart beside their state suffrage banners, suffragists form a quiet gauntlet through which the Democratic delegates must proceed to the convention site.

1917 On 10 January, Alice Paul and Lucy Burns organize the first picket line at the White House. Picketing continues into the spring, becoming an embarrassment to the Wilson administration. The women are roughed up, arrested, jailed in unsanitary conditions, and force-fed when they stage hunger strikes. Their plight focuses national attention on the suffrage issue.

1918 To construct an effective world peace, Woodrow Wilson needs the women's vote to help reelect the Democratic Congress. He appears before Congress to announce that suffrage is now an emergency war measure, and makes an impassioned plea for Congress to pass the legislation. The Republicans prevail and retake Congress in the 1918 election.

1919-20 In 1919, Congress finally passes the 19th Amendment, sends it to the states, and the ratification process begins. Three-quarters of the state legislatures must ratify it. Tennessee is the last state, and the amendment passes by one vote.

The 19th Amendment is added to the U.S. Constitution on 26 August 1920. From Europe, where he is heading the peace delegation, Wilson cables his congratulations to Carrie Chapman Catt and NAWSA. He does not contact Alice Paul or the National Woman's Party. NAWSA becomes the bipartisan League of Women Voters.

---

[1] In 1941, again in the House of Representatives, Rankin cast the only vote against entry into World War II. She did not run for reelection.

PROLOGUE

1921-23   The National Woman's Party debates the wording of an Equal Rights Amendment. The ERA is introduced into Congress in 1923. It finally passes in 1972 but is never ratified, failing by three votes. A national campaign to reintroduce the ERA receives wide support in 2000.

Emily Newell Blair, founder and WNDC president 1928-29. Photo by i.f.a. galleries, courtesy of WNDC-EF Archives.

Chapter One
THE FOUNDERS
From the Right to Vote, the Power to Lead

To the women, this casting of their first vote brings the thrill of new, unexpected adventure. To the middle-aged woman to whom life has become a trifle humdrum, a new experience is offered, revealing new worlds to conquer. To the younger woman, the vote appeals with the fascination of the unknown. No wonder that a wave of curiosity and a thirst for specialized knowledge suddenly possess our serious sex!

Emily Newell Blair, "What Shall We Do With It: The ballot, of course! We have it! Now what!" The Green Book Magazine, n.d.

Emily Newell Blair

In 1920, for the first time, American women were eligible to vote in a national election. They did not support Democratic candidates James M. Cox and Franklin D. Roosevelt. Their ballots were cast for Warren G. Harding, the charismatic Republican candidate who, along with his wife, Florence Kling Harding, had vigorously courted the "woman vote" during his presidential campaign.

The Democrats had ignored the feminine electorate even while adopting twelve of the fifteen planks introduced by the League of Women Voters. The Republicans had adopted only five when Harding responded to pressure from Harriet Taylor Upton and influential Republican feminists by sponsoring "Social Justice Day." It called for equal pay for equal work, an eight-hour day, the end of child labor, prevention of lynching, maternity and infancy protection, an extended children's bureau, appointment of women to state and federal employment boards, a minimum wage, national health care programs, and the creation of a department of social justice.

Harding's social justice agenda endorsed virtually the entire program of the League of Women Voters. As a result, the vast majority of progressive women voted the GOP ticket. Harding and Calvin Coolidge won by seven million popular votes and the Republicans controlled the U.S. Congress. The election was a disaster for the Democrats and in the nation's capital the party was declared dead.

In spite of the resounding Republican victory, Emily Newell Blair, by 1922 one of the most prominent women in national politics, had two visions for the Democratic Party: She wanted to organize newly enfranchised women into a partisan voting bloc, and she wanted a Democratic club for women in the nation's capital.

Blair was a writer, feminist, and veteran of the suffragist campaign who had come to Washington committed to reinvigorating and rehabilitating the Democratic Party with the help of women. She had gained national attention as editor of *Missouri Woman*, the state's suffrage magazine. She and Carrie Chapman Catt organized the Golden Lane, the silent protest by thousands of suffragists at the 1916 Democratic national convention in St. Louis that symbolized the absence of women's voices in national politics.

During World War I, Blair had worked in Washington on the women's committee of the Council of National Defense, where her excellent report on the committee's work reinforced her national prominence. Now Blair was again in the capital, at a different, but still difficult time. Harding was in the White House, Republicans controlled both houses of Congress, and women were in transition after ratification of the 19th Amendment. Moreover, Blair was out of favor with her state party machinery after tangling with James Reed, the anti-suffragist Missouri senator. The breach was never healed.

As a result, Emily Blair was existing more or less in a social vacuum, viewing the capital from a bleacher seat, much as she had a decade earlier when her husband, Harry Wallace Blair, had studied law at Columbia College, now The George Washington University. "It is an environment I never enjoy for long," she wrote in her mid-1930s autobiography. "There were available no Democratic hostesses with big houses. But there were Democratic women, wives of senators and representatives and permanent residents who had no opportunity in the voteless District to serve the party. Why, I thought, couldn't they be organized to promote a Democratic women's clubhouse?

"There was also a special reason why I wanted social contacts in Washington," Blair wrote. "I knew how much easier it was to exchange views over a dinner table than a desk, that breaking bread with anyone put him or her on a different footing with you. I felt the need of more information than I was acquiring at my desk. How I was to manage to make the necessary social contacts I did not know, but somehow I must. And then into my office one day walked Mrs. J. Borden Harriman, later to be known to me as Daisy. I told her I had two things in mind. I needed to meet senators off stage and, further, how much it would profit the party if there was some Democratic drawing room where our senators—they were few in number—congregated socially, discussed things informally. I recalled to her Mark Hanna's [Republican] breakfasts and Ruth Hanna McCormick's Saturday evenings."

The skills of the two women were complementary, and by November, Blair and Harriman had rallied a group of influential Washingtonians to organize the Woman's National Democratic Club, the first socially acceptable meeting place for Democratic women in the capital. Blair noted in retrospect: "Only women of more faith than practicability would ever have tried to launch a Democratic women's club at the time. No project could seem wilder in those days of 1922 when publicists were prophesying that the Democratic party was dead, when hardly anyone in Washington seemed willing to acknowledge themselves Democrats, and there were no financial angels to draw on.

"Daisy Harriman discussed the matter with former president Woodrow Wilson," Blair continued. "He took an interest in it (insisting that the club be political as well as social). Cordell Hull, then chairman of the Democratic National Committee, encouraged us. We found a few women to go in with us. Mrs. Harriman says the idea for the club was mine, but the enthusiasm, much of the work, and the prestige were hers. Those were the essentials that made it go. And so we began." Under Blair's guidance the women provided a base for the Democratic National Committee's new and growing women's division.

What motivated Emily Blair to dedicate years of her life to suffrage and the Democratic Party remains unclear. She was a happily married Victorian woman in comfortable circumstances, but she continued to pursue her goals beyond the frontier boundaries of Joplin and Carthage, Missouri.

Blair was born in Joplin on 9 January 1877. A diminutive beauty with a retroussé nose, bright brown eyes, and ladylike demeanor, she also possessed a brilliant, analytical mind. She received scholastic honors in Missouri public schools and attended Goucher College in Maryland for a year before her father's death forced her return to Missouri.

On Christmas Eve in 1900 she married a childhood friend, Harry Blair, who supported his partner's deep need to broaden her horizons. In 1910, after a decade as a young society matron and mother, Emily commented to Harry that she was tired of reading magazine articles about unhappy housewives. He encouraged her to write. The result was "Letters of a Contented Housewife" that Emily sold to *Cosmopolitan,* therewith launching a writing career that would span more than three decades and include a lengthy editorship at *Good Housekeeping.* By 1935 it was estimated that Blair's name was familiar to six million readers.

Emily's writing brought her to the attention of Missouri suffragists, and she worked tirelessly for the woman vote. After ratification of the 19th Amendment she considered becoming a progressive Republican, having been politically "discovered" by suffragist Ruth Hanna McCormick, whom she greatly admired. But Emily wavered, reluctant to join the party of Mark Hanna and big business.

Join the Democrats, her husband urged, and make them more progressive. During her years on the Democratic National Committee Blair traveled throughout the country, helping found hundreds of Democratic women's clubs and setting up training schools for recently enfranchised woman voters. Progress in women's issues, Emily believed, would come only if women exercised their right to vote.

Harry Blair, content to be an influential, small-town attorney, subsidized Emily's political ambitions in a significant way. One of Harry's clients, the Missouri and North Arkansas Railroad, entitled Emily to a "white pass" that enabled her to travel at virtually no cost on all trains. Responding to a request from Eleanor Roosevelt that Blair consider working outside Missouri, Emily wrote in 1932, "If you think it desirable for me to come on to New York to discuss these matters with Miss [Molly] Dewson and yourself, I could arrange it. As I travel on passes—my husband being a railroad attorney—this expense would not be great." Additional trip expenses and her passion for extravagant clothes were largely self-financed.

Recalling WNDC's founding, Emily's son, Newell Blair, said at age eighty-nine, "In organizing anything there has to be a spark plug, a person who generates the energy and direction, a real 'doer.' My mother was a doer for WNDC and she got the idea by herself of having a club because she found that Democratic women needed a place to organize around. It still was a man's world and the men were shoving the women around as much as they could and the women needed a place where they could do their own thing."

WNDC members elected Emily Blair their first secretary. She used the position to formulate club policies and to launch a *Fortnightly Bulletin* at the DNC that in later years was published by the club as *The Bulletin*. In 1925, when WNDC got into financial difficulties, she successfully sought help from wealthy Houstonian Jesse Jones, financial director of the Democratic National Committee. Blair proposed that the committee fund three major expenses for two years: the rent on WNDC's clubhouse at 820 Connecticut Avenue, a salary for Texas politician Minnie Fisher Cunningham to be executive director of the club, and publication of *The Bulletin*. In that way Jones could save the club and the DNC could use it as a clearinghouse for the activities of Democratic women. Jones held Blair in high regard and believed the club served a purpose. With Clem Shaver, chairman of the DNC, he agreed to keep WNDC solvent, and both men made personal contributions. But both felt that the shabby Connecticut Avenue clubhouse presented a poor image and urged Blair to find more suitable quarters.

Blair returned to Missouri from Washington after Minnie Fisher Cunningham, whom she greatly admired, was hired as executive director of WNDC. In 1928, while residing in Joplin, Blair was elected WNDC president. She took the train to Washington for two monthly meetings, then wired her resignation, pleading her continued absence from the District and her principle against absentee officers. At the November meeting of the governing board, the secretary was directed to write Mrs. Blair a strong letter insisting that she remain president because "to resign now would look, we fear, to the public, as if our club were on the verge of dissolution [after Herbert Hoover's election] and at the present moment we must make the public feel we were never more firmly established. With the future of our club at stake we cannot believe that you, a founder of the club, would put us in such an embarrassing position, and we must earnestly hope that you will reconsider. Our first vice president will relieve you of all active duties of course." Emily stayed on as president until the eve of Hoover's inauguration in February 1929.

Although she was a member of the New Deal women's network and was appointed to the Consumer's Advisory Board in 1933, Emily Blair's most satisfying political reward came later that year after she had negotiated Harry's appointment as U.S. assistant attorney general. It is ironic that Emily, after years of promoting women in politics, had to settle for a high-level New Deal position for her spouse. She would always feel that while she had achieved individual recognition for her political work, she had not been able to create a position of power for other women. She believed a "new feminism" was needed to urge women to run for public office and to support them when they did. She also felt that the bridge from Victorian society to the New Deal, slowly and laboriously built by her generation of women activists, had led to a strange new world, "a world so new that the women there seemed strangers, many of them, to the bridge builders."

Florence Jaffray "Daisy" Harriman

Daisy Harriman's stately but faded yellow brick townhouse stood at 2017 F Street NW, a few blocks from the White House in a once fashionable Washington, DC, neighborhood. With her flair for style and a cavalier disregard for mounting personal debt, Harriman had endowed the spacious old house with an aristocratic elegance and during much of 1922 had aggressively promoted it as a Democratic rallying point in the nation's solidly Republican capital.

In the spring of 1922, two years after the 19th Amendment gave women the vote, Harriman had called on Emily Newell Blair at the Democratic National Committee with an offer to help revive the moribund party. Blair had two solutions: Establish a Democratic salon and organize a national Democratic club for women in Washington.

Daisy at once launched her bipartisan Sunday night suppers that would become a Washington institution, and throughout the summer and fall she hosted a group of socially and politically prominent women dedicated to organizing a Democratic women's club. Daisy initiated an intensive letter-writing campaign to attract influential local and out-of-town members.

An early note went to Eleanor Roosevelt, who was among the first women outside the capital to join the prospective club. She had become increasingly involved in New York Democratic politics after her husband had been stricken with polio. Elizabeth Bayard, wife of Senator Thomas Francis Bayard Jr. (D-DE), also responded positively, even though the senator was vehemently opposed to women's suffrage. "What will become of the family hearthstone around which cluster the very best influences of human education?" he had thundered. "You will have a family with two heads—a house divided against itself. You will no longer have that healthful and necessary subordination of wife to husband."

In spite of the senator's apocalyptic prediction, an organizing committee met on 24 November 1922 in Daisy's parlor to establish the Woman's National Democratic Club (WNDC). The autumn day was the type considered good for Democrats—sunny, brisk, an invigorating fifty-five degrees—but more than a few of the women, well aware of Mrs. Harriman's disregard for unbalanced ledgers, privately despaired of the club's future. There was tension in Daisy's fashionable parlor.

Harriman, with her political and social connections, and Emily Newell Blair, director of women's affairs at the Democratic National Committee, were the principals. They were joined by Marian Banister, sister of Senator Carter Glass (D-VA), who would become Franklin Roosevelt's U.S. treasurer; Henrietta Bonsal, "a society matron for whom Democracy was almost a religion"; Ethel Cantrill, whose husband was a six-term congressman from Kentucky (1909-21); Catherine Filene Dodd [Shouse], who almost half a century later would give 100 acres of her Vienna, Virginia, estate for the Wolf Trap Farm Park for the Performing Arts; Antoinette Funk, a feisty Chicago attorney and renegade Republican; Huibertje "Bertie" Hamlin, wife of a Federal Reserve Board governor and a "Democrat to her backbone"; Frances Hull, wife of Cordell Hull who was chair of the Democratic National Committee and later Franklin D. Roosevelt's secretary of State; Natalia Jones, wife of Senator Andrieus A. Jones (D-NM); Eula Kendrick, wife of Senator John B. Kendrick (D-WY); and Isabelle Snell, "a Washingtonian leader of women." They had come together in the wake of a Republican landslide.

A report in the Washington press announcing that "Mrs. J. Borden Harriman Founds Democratic Women's Club" prompted other prominent women to join. Nonresidents sent membership checks but questioned locating the club in the capital. Why not New York, the center of national politics? Dauntless and persuasive, Daisy declared that the center was shifting south.

Emily Blair and Bertie Hamlin noted in later years that the club was not founded without controversy. Two months after being elected president, Mrs. Harriman, to avoid conflict of interest, submitted a letter of resignation. Daisy was an associate of Story and Company, the agent for the townhouse at 1724 I Street, NW, that she had urged the club to rent with option to buy. The board refused to accept her resignation, at the same time rejecting the I Street residence as a possible clubhouse.

Because all meetings had been held in the Harriman residence, another small contretemps had arisen. The ladies felt that "the laws of hospitality would be violated if they criticized their hostess's views," yet realized that differing opinions were bound to develop. The need for a clubhouse was obvious, and a search committee set about finding suitable headquarters for the new club.

In 1924, WNDC opened its doors in an old townhouse at 820 Connecticut Avenue, NW, providing the Democratic Party with a public forum in congenial surroundings. Daisy Harriman organized the initial speaker luncheons that in 1926 became a formal program and, in time, the club hallmark. Individual speakers and panel discussions at luncheons and dinners informed members and the general public of the important issues of the day, while illustrating the evolution of Democratic views and the changing status of women in Democratic politics. In June 1928 the WNDC *Bulletin* listed "Some of the Prominent Democrats Who Have Spoken to the Club." They included Josephus Daniels, former secretary of the Navy in the Wilson administration; Senator Alben W. Barkley (D-KY), who would later become Franklin D. Roosevelt's vice president; and Mrs. Nellie Tayloe Ross, former governor of Wyoming.

Equally important to the club were the bipartisan Sunday night suppers Harriman had launched in the summer of 1922, giving Emily Blair the opportunity she sought to meet with senators. The first guest list included Senator Thomas J. Walsh of Montana, one of Daisy's suitors, who was instrumental in exposing the Teapot Dome scandal.

Society reporter Anne Hard and her husband were frequent guests; and Hard wrote of Daisy's dinner parties: "About the end of wartime [World War I] she took an old house in F Street, whose pale yellow brick walls mask charmingly furnished rooms and a shady garden, and began giving Sunday evening supper parties which are unique in Washington. There are several tables so that during dinner there may be the intimacies of conversation. At the end of dinner some chance remark, some assertion made at one of the tables, will open a sudden field of general conversation. Then the chairs will be pushed back and the cigarette smoke will curl up under the soft light of the candles in their tall glass bell-shades, and talk will flash across the room, interesting, often brilliant, frequently witty. A senator, newspapermen, cabinet officers, diplomats, military men, attractive women—all sorts of types will contribute with apparently complete abandon to the mood which Mrs. Harriman is able to create. It is the only house in Washington where that ideal, the 'political salon,' so often talked about and so seldom existent, is actually found.

"At Mrs. Harriman's, women take a hand in the conversation, not merely in behind-the-fan tête-à-tête, but in what frequently amounts to a debate. No one in Washington could get away with it but Daisy Harriman. She does it, and superbly, because of her own personality, at once engaging, gay and serious, and because of her own genuine and unfeigned interest in public questions, in topics that seem to be concerned with human betterment."

Political activist, social reformer, writer, peace advocate, diplomat, Democratic grande dame, Daisy Harriman was born Florence Jaffray Hurst in New York City on 21 July 1870. The family was aristocratic, rich, Republican. Daisy's mother died when her daughter was three, and Daisy and her sisters were sent to live with their maternal grandfather, shipping magnate Edward S. Jaffray, who gave Daisy her name. She didn't look like a Florence, he said. Through Jaffray's activities Daisy was exposed to political and business leaders of the day.

Her formal education was sketchy: Eight years of exclusive private classes conducted in J. P. Morgan's home began when she was ten. After her debut in 1888, Daisy married Jefferson Borden Harriman, a childhood friend, neighbor, and banker a few years her senior, who was a cousin of railroad magnate E. H. Harriman and statesman Averell Harriman. After a decade of miscarriages—Daisy reputedly refused to give up horseback riding while pregnant—she had her only child, Ethel, in 1898.

In 1906, when her husband disapproved of women staying unchaperoned in New York City hotels, Daisy helped found the prestigious Colony Club, New York's first social club for women. There Daisy was introduced to the National Civic Federation and through that group toured cotton mills in the South to inspect child labor conditions. In 1911 she published articles about her findings in *Harper's Weekly*, the first money she ever earned.

Writing became a necessity after her husband died in 1914 of complications from alcoholism. "Bordie was rich one week and poor the next," recalled Daisy's friend Alice Roosevelt Longworth. "Unfortunately, he died during one of his poor periods, so Daisy wasn't particularly well off." With her fortune in tatters, Daisy turned to other sources of income. She became a realtor and an interior decorator, and later she rented Uplands, her Foxhall Road estate, for special occasions. Years later she endorsed Lucky Strike cigarettes declaring, "I don't smoke…but I used to smoke a great deal…[and] my favorite was Lucky Strike." Frequently in debt, Harriman spent money she didn't have and borrowed with abandon. When Daisy's friend, Senator Thomas J. Walsh, died in the early 1950s, WNDC received a bill from his estate for $4,000 in outstanding loans. "She lived as if she were rich," noted Ann Morin, an authority on women ambassadors. "She knew no other way."

In 1912 Daisy entered national politics, heading the Women's National Wilson and Marshall Organization during the first presidential campaign of her friend, Woodrow Wilson. She was not campaigning for suffrage: Sanctioned by the Democratic National Committee, she was appealing to women to urge their spouses to support Wilson on his progressive record as governor of New Jersey. In *We Have Come to Stay: American Women and Political Parties, 1880-1960,* author Kristie Miller questions Daisy's effectiveness in the 1912 campaign, noting that "it is easier to see that the organization helped Daisy Harriman achieve some of her own political aims. It gave her a forum to promote two of her causes: the use of public schools for voting and civic meetings, and health care reform for children."

Daisy continued to organize after Woodrow Wilson became president. In 1917 she led the New York City suffrage march. In 1918 she organized a Red Cross Motor Corps for the District of Columbia and served as assistant director of transportation in France, where she met and captivated General John J. Pershing. And in 1922 Daisy used her political connections to found WNDC. Acknowledging her leadership, the club unanimously elected Daisy president and reelected her in 1929 and 1947.

Daisy's failure to endorse Franklin D. Roosevelt for the presidency in 1932 relegated her to the political sidelines. For four years she painstakingly built new ties to the Roosevelt team, inviting Frances Perkins, Roosevelt's secretary of Labor and the first woman cabinet officer, to live with her at Uplands. In mid-1932 WNDC published *Democracy at the Crossroads,* a symposium of articles by leading Democrats, authorities in their respective fields. Journalist Ellis T. Meredith Clement provided energetic editorial direction. Daisy recruited the contributors. Among them was Thomas J. Walsh, by then a four-term senator from Montana, who predicted that utility regulation would be a major political issue. Senator Robert F. Wagner of New York wrote "The Right to Work"; William H. Parker, secretary of the Federal Reserve Board from 1914 to 1918, discussed the Federal Reserve Act; Huston Thompson, former assistant attorney general, wrote "The Road Away From Revolution," dealing with the abuses of monopoly; and Newton D. Baker, Wilson's secretary of War, contributed "Democracy Goes to War."

After Daisy's vigorous support in his second campaign, FDR appointed her U.S. minister to Norway, where he assumed that, at age 67 and a grandmother, she would be safe from the impending conflict in Europe and could help persuade the Swedes to award the Nobel Peace Prize to Cordell Hull. On 9 April 1940, Nazi forces invaded neutral Norway, and hours later Daisy followed the Norwegian royal family through the countryside as they fled into exile.

Harriman was only the second woman to head a U.S. legation. Minister to Denmark and Iceland Ruth Bryan Owen, daughter of William Jennings Bryan and a WNDC member, was the first. Daisy's excessive personal expenses as minister to

Norway—she once rented a river for a salmon-fishing holiday—forced her to sell Uplands, her Foxhall Road estate. She moved from one small Georgetown house to another, where she continued her Sunday night suppers and where eventually Averell Harriman supervised her care. Prompted by her friend, Mildred (Mrs. Robert Woods) Bliss of Dumbarton Oaks, President John F. Kennedy awarded Daisy the first Citation of Merit for Distinguished Service in an April 1963 White House ceremony in the Blue Room.

As a suffragist, founder of the Woman's National Democratic Club, Democratic committeewoman for the District of Columbia (1924-55), Franklin Roosevelt's envoy to Norway, and a supporter of home rule for the District of Columbia, Daisy Harriman remained a player on the Washington political stage for almost half a century. When she died in September 1967 at age ninety-seven, 350 mourners paid homage to her at the Washington National Cathedral.

Huibertje "Bertie" Pruyn Hamlin

Bertie Hamlin was a stalwart Democrat whose life was strongly influenced by national politics. Her husband held high government positions in the capital for twenty-five years and Bertie had strong family ties to the Democratic Party. She was born into one of the old New York Dutch families and shared a Hudson River Valley heritage with her childhood playmate, Franklin Delano Roosevelt, who called her "an old river friend." Bertie was born a Democrat, she married a Democrat, she loved being a Democrat. Her home was dominated by politics.

Bertie spent her summers on Cape Cod, but lived the rest of the year in rented houses or hotel apartments in Washington. Her husband, Charles S. Hamlin, was appointed assistant secretary of Treasury in 1913 and a year later, governor of the Federal Reserve Board, a position he held until 1936. He then served as special counsel to the board until his death in 1938. For that quarter-century Bertie Hamlin moved at the center of Washington power circles throughout the administrations of Woodrow Wilson, Warren G. Harding, Calvin Coolidge, Herbert Hoover, and Franklin D. Roosevelt.

In 1904 Bertie attended her first Democratic national convention in St. Louis. Twenty years later she occupied a seat on the platform of the national convention in Madison Square Garden when John W. Davis became the presidential nominee on the 103rd ballot, the longest convention in party history. The New York experience made her aware that coalition-building was essential to unite the varied and often opposed people and principles needed to win a Democratic election.

A prolific correspondent and chronicler, Bertie wrote lengthy letters and kept meticulous memoirs and records. Her Washington diary describes pre- and post-World War I society in the capital: the lack of suitable housing, obligatory seven-course formal dinners, escalating servant salaries, Prohibition, the emergence of the six o'clock cocktail party, and the rigid protocol of social calls.

Bertie's first call after her husband's appointment to Treasury was paid on Nell McAdoo, Woodrow Wilson's daughter and the wife of Secretary of the Treasury William G. McAdoo. A flustered Mrs. McAdoo answered the bell as a commotion raged in the far reaches of her grand Massachusetts Avenue townhouse. Bertie soon learned that Nell McAdoo had locked the butler in the pantry because he had carelessly polished the silver. The unfortunate man, loudly protesting his incarceration, was duly released on Bertie's arrival and tea was served.

The founding of the Woman's National Democratic Club was high on Bertie Hamlin's personal agenda. The club would impart knowledge; be a place where women could meet, listen, question, and discuss the issues of the day; and, equally important, confront the capital's overwhelmingly Republican press. It could also serve to educate newly enfranchised women on one of Bertie's favorite subjects, the influence of Democratic Party policies on American history. But the road to the club's founding would not be smooth.

"I wrote Mrs. Harriman I thought it a fine idea but felt we should begin very carefully—perhaps take a room in a good location and have teas every week in the season and find out what the reaction was before we plunged into any expenses. I met her at the tennis matches in Newport one day—a bastion of Republicans!—and she did not agree with me at all: The dignity of the party called for something much better.

"We had meetings all winter to try to form a constitution and to get members pledged at $25 for resident and $10 for non-resident and $100 for founder. We had pretty good luck and then for some reason we felt we must own a great seal, so we all chipped in money to have one made of a globe with 'Democracy' on it, in spite of having no way to use it. We had subsequent meetings at our house, 919 Farragut Square, as it was convenient for everyone.

"Mrs. Harriman became very anxious to have a house for the club and she set her heart on the Arnold Hague house at 1724 I Street. We all went over the property. I felt it was a hopeless proposition because the house was expensive. We had no money except the dues—none in sight—and no fairy godmother to help us. We had a long and stormy meeting at our house.... Franklin Roosevelt agreed with me that it would tie us up badly, so I was fortified in my stand, but Mrs. Jones and I were the only two to vote against it. Mrs. Harriman felt it very much as the vote had to be unanimous and she was very angry.

"Discussions had been hot and heavy for over a year and when I returned on December 1, it was to find that Mrs. Harriman, as president, had leased a house at $300 per month which seemed an enormous sum as the house was old and not in any good order and unfurnished. But she had had the living room walls tinted a light shade of green, paid for with members' dues. She had donated two pairs of lovely chintz curtains and all that gave great style to our domain."

In 1924, Bertie Hamlin wrote in her diary: "On Tuesday evening, January 15, we opened our Democratic club at 820 Connecticut Avenue right close to our house. Many came to our party, Mrs. Wilson, too, as President Wilson had been much interested in the proposition and had given us an etching of him by a very good artist. We all contributed things and the club money stretched to two sofas and two armchairs from our neighbor the upholsterer.

"Some of the meetings were awfully funny. Mrs. Funk talked right up to Mrs. Harriman who was always quoting the Colony Club. One day Mrs. Funk arose and pointing her finger said, 'Daisy Harriman, if you mention that club again I will leave the meeting.'

"I wish I had written down all the ins and outs of the club's start—they would now be illuminating. Things were made unnecessarily difficult and complicated and any disagreements were looked on as personal which was too bad as we needed free speech. Mrs. Harriman often threatened to resign and placed us in holes."

Bertie soon wrote, "I found the Democratic club quite strenuous as I was chairman of the house committee."[2] In a 1958 letter to then-WNDC president Lindy Boggs, Bertie described the kitchen of the 820 Connecticut Avenue clubhouse: "I am glad to know that you do not have to tackle the always leaking secondhand ice boxes of our early days. The tin cans under the old ones were always overflowing. The small ice box stood on three legs, had a lake under it, and was propped up with a piece of kindling. Pieces of tin were nailed over the mice holes in the floors!"

Bertie Hamlin was elected president of WNDC prior to Franklin D. Roosevelt's first inauguration on 4 March 1933. The Democratic victory bolstered Bertie Hamlin's two-year presidency. Wives of Democratic U.S. senators were encouraged to join WNDC, and congressional spouses were recruited at a reduced fee. Membership chairman, Daisy Harriman, received an anonymous $1,000 for an honorary life membership from "a gentleman interested in the Roosevelt administration." The governing board, by unanimous vote, awarded the membership to Secretary of Labor Frances Perkins, the first woman cabinet member.

When her husband died in 1938, Bertie retired to Cape Cod. Later that year Eleanor Roosevelt wrote a short note urging her, as the club's great peacemaker, to return to Washington to heal a rift in the membership: Two factions, each with a

---

[2] Today's vice president for administration.

determined candidate, were vying for the presidency. Bertie found it difficult to refuse her friend.

In a thoughtful letter to Eleanor Bertie wrote, "As to the Democratic club, I have had several letters in the last month about it. They have excellent timber in their membership and I feel the younger members should come forward as they must run things eventually—we old ones have had our day and must hand on the torch. I think it is a pity, too, to have 'repeaters'—it looks as if they were hard up to have to turn back."

Frances Greenough "Franny" Blake

Unlike her friend, Bertie Hamlin, Franny Blake was not actively involved in politics, but she was an ardent Democrat and she supported WNDC financially. She kept up-to-date on club activities through Bertie, her summer neighbor on the Cape.

"My grandmother, Mrs. Arthur Blake, was a founder of the club," recalled WNDC member David Richardson in a 1998 interview. "She was a nonresident member who contributed a modest amount of money to help get the club started. Granny had an affinity for Washington, having lived here during the Civil War, and I suppose she was eager to help Mrs. Hamlin and the Democrats in anything they did. I don't think she returned to Washington after the club was established.

"My grandmother was Frances Greenough Blake, a born Democrat from a large family of intellectuals and artistic people who lived in Cambridge and were part of the Thoreau-Emerson group. She had lived in Europe, read widely, had many interesting friends, and was very close to Mrs. Hamlin. To begin with, they were both Democrats. My grandmother stayed a Democrat to her dying day, always voting the straight Democratic ticket.

"Women like my grandmother and Mrs. Hamlin *knew* who they were. They never worried about their position; they weren't worried about feminism. They felt they could get anything done that was necessary, and they had the money to do it. My grandmother didn't go out on the streets to march for suffrage. She was very ladylike, but she supported that sort of thing. It seems incredible to me that women only got the vote in the early '20s because all the women I grew up with acted as though they'd had the vote for a thousand years!

"My grandmother's summer house in Mattapoisett, Massachusetts, was next door to the Hamlin house on Buzzard's Bay. The Hamlins were friends of the Delanos, relatives of Franklin Roosevelt's mother, who would come over to the Hamlins' beach on weekends from Fairhaven with a whole bevy of children. I would join them, and I remember a Mrs. Grant, probably a cousin of Franklin's, who was an Edwardian lady in a long white lace gown and with a white parasol sitting on Mrs. Hamlin's beach watching these wild children and me roar around.

"In those days the Mattapoisett summer houses were quite widely spaced and everybody had big, huge wharves. I remember being very impressed one weekend when Mrs. Woodrow Wilson, who was a friend of Mrs. Hamlin's, arrived for a visit. Well, I would have been six years old then. But I remember Mrs. Wilson came from Washington on what appeared to be a small destroyer, and that was very exciting. The destroyer came up to Mrs. Hamlin's deep-water dock and Mrs. Wilson got off the ship all dressed in black and, seeming like a tragedy in a movie, walked up to Mrs. Hamlin's house.

"Then, of course, the next day Mrs. Wilson and Mrs. Hamlin came to tea, so I met Mrs. Wilson. I remember thinking what a nice woman she was, even though she was wearing black. I don't know if Granny had known Edith Bolling Wilson before, but I could see they were having a nice chat. Having the wife of a former president to tea in Mattapoisett was very exciting."

* * *

The founders of the Woman's National Democratic Club were aristocratic or upper middle-class women who had worked for suffrage in a variety of ways. A women's club in Washington became a symbol of their struggle for political equality, and their diverse interests and skills were vital to the club's early success. Emily Newell Blair's organizational ability and Democratic networking gave WNDC sound political credibility. Bertie Hamlin kept the peace while members with conflicting views compromised and hammered out bylaws. Frannie Blake had the means to help launch a club she would never visit and the social standing to give it appeal. And Daisy Harriman led the push to rent an old townhouse that left much to be desired, but was the first step in acquiring the historic mansion that members treasure today.

Equally crucial to the genesis of the club were the organizational skills women had developed during the Progressive Era (1890-1920) when, through their involvement in civic and welfare work to help women and children, they had moved from parlor to politics. They had formed women's clubs, the socially acceptable forum for upper-class and upper middle-class women to move from the private to the public sphere.

Nancy Beck Young, assistant professor of history at McKendree College in Illinois, noted in a 1995 interview: "I see the [founders] as very earnest, very dedicated, very committed people who were trying to achieve a voice in the political process, women who were very involved, women whose husbands were very involved in the Democratic Party, in Democratic policy. They were concerned with the issues of the 1920s, and like their counterparts in the 1950s, they were organizing at a time when the Democrats were out of power. They were very concerned about getting the club on an honest, solid footing, getting the housekeeping out of the way as quickly as possible to enable them to accomplish their political goals. They were very much a part of the heady, post-suffrage days. They were very excited about suffrage and probably saw the vote as just the first of many victories. They expected much more in the aftermath of suffrage than actually happened."

Prominent members in front of the new WNDC clubhouse purchased with a loan from Margaret Meigs. Left to right: front row, Etta Ross Hubbard, Isabelle Snell, Natalia Jones, Frances Hull. Back row, Caroline Thompson, Rose Forrester, Meigs, Eula Kendrick. World Wide Photos, courtesy of WNDC-EF Archives.

Chapter Two
THE CLUBHOUSE
Where Democrats Meet

Those who feared that politics would make women mannish may calm their fears. The Woman's National Democratic Club has reversed the role and put politics into ruffles.

The new clubhouse on New Hampshire Avenue, right in the heart of Washington's most exclusive residential section and itself one of the finest old houses on the street, is the last word in putting "Ritz" into politics, and it is safe to say that never before have political schemes been concocted in such rarefied surroundings.

Here, under high ceilings, before dignified marble fireplaces, in an atmosphere of lovely prints, antiques and all, the "lady politicians" of the party will meet to sway the destinies of a nation.

—*The New York Sun,* May 1927

Minnie Fisher Cunningham

"Oh, Emily, it's grand!" executive director Minnie Fisher Cunningham wrote on 12 May 1927 to Emily Newell Blair on the opening of WNDC's new clubhouse. "It really seems terrible that you and Mrs. Harriman who organized the club should both be absent at this high moment, but be assured that you are both very much in our minds all of the time.

"On Tuesday of this week we moved from 820 Connecticut Avenue to 1526 New Hampshire Avenue. If I went through the dictionary and picked out all of the words that are synonyms of 'thrilling' I could not begin to tell you how I feel about this.

"On Wednesday we held the May board meeting in the drawing room here and in addition to the great ladies who are members of the board, a number of other great ladies came and went, visiting the house. We served luncheon as usual and a great many people stayed....

"Last but not least, Mr. [Clem] Shaver [chairman of the Democratic National Committee] was here last week and I had a short but satisfactory visit with him. He sent the April check for the same amount as he sent last year. And I am hoping for the same good fortune in May. You cannot imagine what a relief this is to my nerves."

On the back of her typed letter Cunningham had scrawled, "This one couldn't be dictated. I've reorganized the house committee and am myself on the steward's committee that has charge of service and meals.... We've gotten to be stylish in this house."

Liz Carpenter, press secretary and staff director to Lady Bird Johnson, recalled at a 15 March 1992 dedication of a Texas state historical marker commemorating Minnie Fisher Cunningham: "What was she like, this remarkable lady? You got notes all the time from Minnie Fish [sic] on little pieces of paper, written around the side, giving you the strongest kind of instructions, like 'Ride to the Alamo!' or something like that. There was no piece of paper too small to write to enlist—or really to demand—your services. I really treasure those battered pieces of paper. Those were the two-cent and three-cent stamp days. Those were mimeograph machine days. And she taught me the first rule of being a political activist. She said, 'Stamp the envelope first, then address it. That way you will write the letter and mail it.' Can you imagine if Minnie Fish were alive today, what she'd do in the computer world, and with laser printouts and fax machines? She would have already staged a coup to take over Washington. She would be a 110-year-old whirlwind of paper and beepers, telling us how we had to save the Republic. And we would all be better for it. And the country would be better for it....

"What did she look like? She was a knock-out as a young woman. Spirited, and described by one Texas politician as a 'whimsical red-headed woman with more than her share of feminine charm to cloak a lucid mind.' Stories about Minnie Fish are legion. When she headed the Texas suffrage campaign she was determined that the opponents not vote twice, and as we all know, that's a sometime habit in Texas. So she guarded the polls with grass burrs, which they slipped onto the coats of voters. And that way they caught the culprits who had two grass burrs on their coats. It's symbolic of Minnie Fish that she not only believed in working the grass roots but with grass burrs."

In 1919, Carrie Chapman Catt, president of the National American Woman Suffrage Association (NAWSA), invited Cunningham to Washington to serve as the secretary of the association's congressional committee. After passage of the 19th Amendment, Cunningham remained in Washington, becoming in 1920 executive secretary of the National League of Women Voters, which had emerged from NAWSA. She coordinated the activities of the League's national office and helped organize new branches throughout the country. Turning to party politics in 1923, she conducted training schools in Democratic organizations.

As executive director of WNDC, Cunningham found furnishing the large clubhouse daunting, but Bertie Hamlin

WNDC's landmark clubhouse at 1526 New Hampshire Avenue, NW, Washington, DC, 16 May 1927. Tenschert Photos, courtesy of WNDC-EF Archives.

brought Empire copies out of storage to help fill the spacious rooms. Over the decades the mansion was further enhanced with antiques, rugs, silver, art, decorative objects, and Frances Perkins's symbolic desk. The club's donor list is a "who's who" of twentieth century Democratic dignitaries and includes Jacqueline Kennedy.

Memorabilia and photographs of party celebrities line the walls of corridors and public rooms such as the First Ladies Room, the (WNDC) Past Presidents Room, and the Emily Newell Blair Room. An Eleanor Roosevelt wing includes the library and features photographs and a bust of the club's first Democratic first lady. The archives contain a historical record of Democratic women's volunteer activities for over three-quarters of a century. The Daisy Harriman Room replicates her Georgetown parlor. Averell Harriman loaned the furniture after Daisy's death in 1967 and eventually helped the club buy it from her estate.

In 1966, Marjorie Merriweather Post donated $10,000 to refurbish the main drawing room. At the formal dedication, Mrs. Post, director emeritus of the giant General Foods Corporation and one of the world's richest women, gave the assembled throng some humble domestic pointers on washing, ironing, and sewing. Mrs. Post had come bearing more gifts, among them table linens of all kinds, "thousands of dollars' worth." She then gave minute instructions on how to care for linens, counseling members that "it is not necessary to wash a tablecloth just because of a few spots....I have cloths which have never been laundered after forty years of use," she said, and proceeded to give tips on ways to remove various kinds of spots. Mrs. Post then invited the club's housekeeper to visit her Hillwood estate, where she would have her staff demonstrate techniques in spot removal.

Since the 1960s, thousands of Democrats have passed through the Post Room and the other well-appointed public rooms of the historic mansion. The residence was designed by Washington architect Harvey Page for Sarah Adams Whittemore, a direct descendant of the Adams family of Massachusetts who distinguished themselves in American literature and politics.

Mrs. Whittemore worked closely with Harvey Page on the design: The house posed some problems because of the triangular lot at the intersection of New Hampshire Avenue and Q Street. A pastiche of Victorian architecture, it was built in 1892 and was one of the first in the District to be wired for electricity. The facade featured a running bond of rare wafer-thin bricks, fired from clay found in a unique New Jersey deposit and ranging in color from deep rose to ocher. Another striking feature was the English slate roof, once described as "a large cape of a roof with an occasional raised eyelid draped down over angular, turreted Roman brickwork."

In 1932, Mrs. Whittemore's son, Walter D. Wilcox, wrote to Bertie Hamlin: "Some years after my mother's death in 1907, I bought my sister's share and made certain changes in the house, such as uniting a dining room and a billiard room to create a dining room capable of seating forty or more people at one table. The ceiling design was worked out by Nathan [N.C.] Wyeth.

"During the years shortly before and after my mother's death, the house was rented to various tenants, among them John Weeks, secretary of War during the Harding and Coolidge administrations, and Senator John Dryden of New Jersey."

With a $20,000 interest-free loan from member Margaret Meigs, the club bought the historic mansion for $100,000. Minnie Fisher Cunningham spearheaded negotiations for the property. At the dedication of the new clubhouse the American flag was unfurled over the balcony with the blue field dangling at the bottom. The flag was quickly righted and ceremonies proceeded, but not before Pathé News had photographed former first lady Edith Bolling Wilson; Ellen Davis, wife of the 1924 Democratic presidential candidate, John W. Davis; and Natalia Jones, president of the club, at a politically awkward moment.

Eventually, two adjoining buildings—1520 New Hampshire Avenue and a house on Q Street—were purchased, furthering the members' unrealized dream of owning the entire lot bordered by New Hampshire Avenue, Q and 19th Streets, and Dupont Circle. In 1967, the less pretentious Q Street house was razed to make way for the Adlai Stevenson dining room and the Sam Rayburn lounge. The club undertook major renovations again in the 1980s, converting the third floor into work space for staff and volunteers and installing an elevator, central air conditioning, and a state-of-the-art sound and video system. The Q Street disability ramp was constructed at that time.

In the long run, real estate proved to be a financial disaster. In spite of a building drive, theater benefits, skits, fashion shows, teas, dinners, galas—the staples of women's club fund raising—red ink flooded the club books during the 1970s and '80s.

Maureen "Molly" O'Brien

"You need two skills for the club's administrative job," said Molly O'Brien in a series of 1990s interviews. "First, you need to know how to manage a house. With five sons—all Dems, married to Dems—I fall naturally into that one. Then, with all the wild things that go on, you have to have a sense of humor."

A Navy wife for over twenty years, Molly titles her curriculum vitae "Experience Gained Without Compensation in Civic, Political and Organizational Activities." A long-time member of the League of Women Voters and a tireless worker for women's and civil rights, Molly O'Brien is WNDC's vice president for administration.

"What do I mainly do? Well, I'm in charge of maintaining the clubhouse. By paying attention to details we accomplish a lot with not much money. During the summer we renovate, repair, repaint, reupholster. At Christmas time I'm in charge of decorations. Christmas trees, garlands and bows on the front staircase, wreaths and swags and lots of poinsettias. It's fun to do the holiday decorations because the effect is so wonderful in this wonderful old house. We always give the decorating committee a free lunch and that helps, too.

"Other committees—mailing, telephone, hostess and lounge, building and grounds—also come under admin. And the arts committee. They mount four art exhibits a year in the Stevenson Room, and keep that low-ceilinged cavern from looking like a church basement. I also manage the Sign of the Donkey boutique for the finance vice president. It is important to develop a good working relationship with both the members and the staff. Even so, things happen.

"When the attic on the fourth floor was being converted into office space, two of our staff set up a little love nest under the staircase there. And, with the cook, they were running a weekend catering service out of the club—we were rarely here on weekends in those days—and they were using club food, utilities, utensils, everything. One of the club presidents happened to drop by on a Saturday and found them busily catering an outside party. Needless to say, they did not last long. On a lighter note, we once had three men named Robert on the kitchen staff. The one who did desserts we called Chocolate Robert. The others were Cookout Robert and Muffin Robert.

"Not so long ago, someone came along in the dark of night and stole our copper gutters. Even though we had insurance, they were terribly expensive to replace: They had to be copper and historically correct. And then some years ago, a truck drove up to the front door and the crew said they were here to take the carpets away for cleaning. They managed to steal two large, expensive Persian rugs. They were going around to embassies and clubs collecting carpets! Fortunately, we have beautiful oak floors. It could have been worse.

"And some years ago, two windows were shattered in a drive-by shooting. That sort of thing doesn't seem to happen any more. The neighborhood has gotten upscale again, and as a result, the club is used a lot for wedding receptions and other events. This is part of our moving with the times. We aggressively market the house and the result is a significant increase in revenue.

"Financially, we've had good years and bad, but we have always been able to adapt and prosper. During World War II, we rented the club to the British officers, the 'British Occupation' as it's known, and we got on pretty solid financial footing. Then when the real estate market was good, and with our unfavorable tax situation, we sold 1520 New Hampshire Avenue, the property next door, to the Jamaican embassy. We paid off the mortgage on this house, bought our famous Wendy's franchise in Frederick, Maryland, and set up an investment portfolio.

"On a much smaller scale, I was able to sell the linens that Mrs. Post gave us. Nobody wants to iron any more, but we did make a nice profit from the linens because they came from her famous yacht. Then we have Joan Millen's legacy and endowment committee and we use those funds to refurbish the house. I call it Joan's committee because a lot of members give simply because of Joan.

"We've come a long way as an organization, thank goodness. We can be very 'tea and cookies,' but now, while we're not exactly reinventing ourselves, we're recollecting ourselves. And I think we are becoming ever so much more action-oriented. The task forces are the heart of the club and that's how I became active and involved. The task forces are wonderful.

"I'm a women's issues person since forever. I joined NOW thirty or so years ago—as soon as it started—and other advocacy groups. For several years I came to the club with a friend before I could afford to join; and as soon as I could, I joined and began working with the new task force on women's issues. Jeanne Simon, Senator Paul Simon's wife, was the chair. Then I took over. Then a friend of mine, who has since died of breast cancer, was chair. Next was an American Association of University Women [AAUW] lobbyist, and she used to take her merry band up on the Hill. That's the type of thing we want to do more of.

"Then I became chair of the public policy committee. It eventually became a vice president's job and creating that position was very important, made a really big statement. I personally think we didn't do enough internal PR on it. But I wasn't quite so mouthy in those days. Now I'm a little more mouthy.

"We used to have a huge governing board—about sixty people—that included all the committee chairs, all task force chairs, just about everybody. It was just wild. All the past presidents used to come and clump together; they would sit right in front of the president, always in the same front-row seats. They tended to be very ample ladies, and they would sit there with their arms crossed. Mention any change at all, and they'd all look at each other, knowing we were on the road to ruin. This group liked to have their little drink and when they surged into the Rayburn Lounge, it was like ships under full sail. We all parted like the seas. One of them was on the finance committee, and she would announce firmly and loudly in the lounge that everyone had to drink because the club needed the money!

"But they were very nice and they were very powerful. They had a lot of friends and supporters who'd been club members for years and years and years, and what they wanted got done. They were long-time Washingtonians, wealthy women who were very powerful in their own right and very intimidating to newer, younger members. No one can ever replace them and the club is a poorer place without them."

The Democratic Bulletin, Election Number, November 1932. Courtesy of WNDC-EF Archives.

Chapter Three
ELEANOR ROOSEVELT
WNDC's First Democratic First Lady

The most remarkable presidential and congressional elections in modern American history wrecked the Republican Party and divested it of national power on 8 November 1932. It is as if a political revolution, and such indeed it is, has taken place...but all is well on the Potomac, and the government at Washington still lives.

Frederic William Wile, CBS, "The Democratic Landslide," 1932

In March 1933, when Eleanor Roosevelt arrived in Washington as first lady, election euphoria had subsided. The climate on the Potomac was tense. General despair hung over the city, induced by the Depression's economic crises and by the many Republicans who had been in power for twelve years and lost. Washington's poor were camped out in the alleys or exiled to the huge ghettos that resulted from former first lady Ellen Wilson's misguided slum clearance. No attempt had been made to eradicate the conditions that caused the slums, or to provide housing for predominantly African Americans who were working as domestics. There were huge pockets of poverty.

The remnants of the Bonus Army, the World War I combat veterans who had been promised a pension in 1925, were camped out on the flats of the Anacostia River. By 1932, many of the men had lost their homes, their jobs, and their savings. They had walked, hopped on trains, hitched rides, and brought their families to Washington to camp out to lobby for their pensions, which they hoped would be paid in 1933. The previous summer President Herbert Hoover, concerned that

Congress might acquiesce to the Army's demands, had ordered the U.S. Army—at that time led by Douglas MacArthur, George Patton, and Dwight Eisenhower—to dislodge them. The soldiers fired on American veterans. Tents were burned. The press reported that one marcher was shot to death by the police and that fifty-eight had been wounded. It was a national outrage. Veterans who had served overseas had been fired on by U.S. troops. It was a volatile time and Washington was politically nervous.

Social Washington was also nervous. The previous Roosevelt imprimatur had been Theodore and Republican. There was tension between Washingtonians and the newly arrived Roosevelts, even though Franklin and Eleanor had resided on R Street near Dupont Circle when FDR was assistant secretary of the Navy in the Wilson administration. Washington women invited to the White House ran their hands down the bannisters to check for dust and gossiped among themselves that Mrs. Roosevelt was a terrible housekeeper. When the first lady hired an all black domestic staff for the White House, she further alienated the old guard. Happy days were not here again for Eleanor Roosevelt, who viewed the move to the White House as a life defined by white gloves and teas and a deep erosion of her independence.

For more than a decade Eleanor Roosevelt had created her own life. She had a huge political responsibility and a career in her own right. That all had to go, Franklin Delano Roosevelt said, with their move to the capital. His wife must resign from the seventeen boards she was serving on. She couldn't teach school, write her newspaper column, broadcast on the radio, be involved in the Women's National Consumers League or the International Ladies Garment Workers Union. She offered to be Franklin's eyes and ears, to help with his mail and his appointments, but was rebuffed. She confided to friends that had she not been married to Franklin, she would have voted for Norman Thomas.

The Woman's National Democratic Club played a role in Eleanor Roosevelt's reinvention of herself in the capital. On 3 March, in the crowded hours before the inauguration, WNDC members honored the first Democratic first lady in the club's eleven-year history at a brilliant reception at the clubhouse. Mrs. Roosevelt and her friend, club president Bertie Hamlin, welcomed the throngs.

On 6 March, in the White House Red Room, Eleanor Roosevelt gave her first press conference for women reporters, just two days after FDR had lifted the nation's spirits with his declaration, "The only thing we have to fear is fear itself." In May, with the public skeptical of Mrs. Roosevelt's innovative press conferences, Isabel Kinnear Griffin wrote an article for WNDC's *Democratic Bulletin*. "The country has a first lady in fact as well as in name. Mrs. Franklin D. Roosevelt is astonishing the Washington newspaper guild with impressive proof that a president's wife who has an exceptionally able mind is not required by law to go into dreary seclusion and hide it. And she is delighting the correspondents with the production of news that is news.

The first lady's press conferences will be historic because they mark a new departure; they constitute a significant and valuable portion of the New Deal." Between September and December 1933 Eleanor Roosevelt received over 300,000 letters.

Press coverage was essential to Eleanor Roosevelt's development as an independent force; it soon played a vital role in convincing the president that his wife could be a political asset.

One afternoon the first lady took Louis Howe, FDR's most astute advisor, for an outing. Eleanor Roosevelt liked to drive, and they rode aimlessly, ending up in Anacostia where the tattered remnants of the Bonus Army were camped out. No major press contingent followed her as she moved among the men, remaining late into the afternoon to talk and share their meager rations. She ate beans from a tin cup with her fingers. Nevertheless, the Washington rumor mill worked overtime. The press demanded to know if were true that she had been with the Bonus Army.

"Yes, and they were fine people."

Headlines trumpeted across the land, "Hoover Sent the Troops. FDR Sent His Wife." With further urging from Louis Howe, who had recognized Eleanor's political potential early on, FDR relaxed his opposition to his wife's involvement in public affairs.

Eleanor Roosevelt became intimately involved in a New Deal network of strong, influential women. They came from a long reform tradition and had real legislative skills. Most notable among them were Mary "Molly" Dewson, Democratic National Committee vice chair in charge of women's affairs, the first woman with sufficient power to dispense patronage jobs in a national administration; Nellie Tayloe Ross, former governor of Wyoming, vice chair of the DNC, and member of the WNDC board of governors; Ellen Woodward, commissioner of Social Security; and Secretary of Labor Frances Perkins, the first woman cabinet officer.

Dewson believed volunteer women in Washington should channel their political efforts directly into the Democratic National Committee. Her decision to move publication of *The Democratic Digest* (formerly, *The Bulletin*) from the club to the DNC outraged WNDC members, who were then restricted to one page for club news. Nevertheless, they continued to support the *Digest* and handle subscriptions for the DNC.

While primarily interested in the work of the New Deal women, Eleanor Roosevelt realized that women's commitments to the party came in a variety of levels and forms. In a 1939 issue of *The Democratic Digest* Mrs. Roosevelt explained that the women's division of the DNC worked to organize Democratic women for effective political action at both the local and the national level. The club, she continued, "affords a delightful place for the weekly luncheon meeting, and supplements the work of the women's division in the regular party organization."

As WNDC's honorary president, Eleanor Roosevelt was tireless. She attended luncheons, teas, dinners, fashion shows, and fund raising galas; she drew door prizes and awarded bridge trophies. At one event, resplendent in furs, she was photographed on a manicured suburban lawn with Queenie, the DNC's female donkey mascot. The press devoted hundreds of column inches to her wardrobe, and on 12 October 1939, *The Washington Post* declared the first lady one of the best dressed women in the world. At the same time, she made the club a forum for her personal reform agenda and a sounding board for FDR's innovative New Deal and World War II measures.

Eleanor Roosevelt frequented the club for more than thirty years (1928-1959). Her major appearances included a 15 September 1939 broadcast to observe Democratic Women's Day, carried coast to coast by the three radio networks—ABC, CBS, and NBC. The first lady urged the country to think about the future and what might be done to bring peace to the world. She urged members of women's Democratic clubs throughout the country to take a greater part in affairs of the party and to aid in raising funds to carry out its political and social program. "[If] we want to be treated as equals in party councils," Mrs. Roosevelt cautioned, "then we must be equal all along the line, and in raising some of the money we will feel that we are discharging an obligation which undoubtedly is ours."

Her final appearance at the club was on 25 May 1959 when, just back from Iran, she advocated self-help assistance for Iranian women in remote villages, a concept later replicated in the Peace Corps. That day in May, the former first lady arrived very late at the club, leaving no time for an introduction by Edith Helm, her former White House secretary. Taking the microphone as Eleanor Roosevelt strode toward the podium, Helm delivered the most succinct introduction in club history: "*She* is here!"

The spirit of Eleanor Roosevelt lives on at the Woman's National Democratic Club. Her portrait hangs in the paneled foyer; the library bears her name. Its corridor walls are hung with photos of "ER" with her family, friends, and political associates. Former WNDC president Esther Peterson bequeathed a bust of Mrs. Roosevelt to the library; and at a 19 March 1996 ceremony at the club she presented an Eleanor Roosevelt mink coat to the Smithsonian Institution. It had been a gift to Peterson from a WNDC admirer. As an opponent of the Equal Rights Amendment, Peterson was quick to point out that the embroidered initials, ER, on the lining, stood for Eleanor Roosevelt, "not for Equal Rights."

Mrs. Roosevelt personally inspired two members to join WNDC: Ellie Seagraves, her eldest granddaughter, and Betty Hight, a student activist who kept the first lady apprised of youth activities in the early 1940s. The two were introduced by ER as young mothers in Paris, where their husbands were working on post-World War II European economic recovery. Seagraves and Hight remain friends today.

Eleanor "Ellie" Seagraves

"When I was a child I had no idea that Eleanor Roosevelt was the most famous woman in the United States, perhaps in the world," recalled Eleanor Seagraves in a 1999 interview. "Eleanor Roosevelt was just my grandmother, a compassionate and indulgent woman who enjoyed her grandchildren. We called her 'Grandmère'; FDR was 'Pa-pa.'

"In the 1930s, when we lived in the White House, we went to the Easter egg rolls on the White House lawn with her. It was a public event. The gates were open to any child who came with an adult, and my grandmother always made the rounds with my brother, Curtis, and me with her. The family called him Buzzy and I was Sistie, or Buzz and Sis. We would have our birthday parties in the East Room, and then the crowd of us would run screaming and laughing down the hall to the state dining room for a light supper of hot cream of wheat and ice cream and cake. We were quite boisterous, never decorous, much to the consternation of the guests' nannies, who hovered on the sidelines. This was before any of us was touched by self-consciousness—that wonderful time between about five and eight years old.

"Winters we went to the Big House at Hyde Park. The National Park Service now calls it Springwood, a very early name for the house, but we always called it 'the Big House,' and we had a number of family Christmasses there in the mid-1930s. There always seemed to be snow in those days; and we used sleds, metal trays, and small toboggans, anything to take us sliding down the big hill that slopes away from the south lawn. This was a normal childhood for us because we knew nothing else.

"I think I was pretty politically aware even at twelve, thirteen, fourteen. Before that, it hardly mattered. I was born in 1927, so by the end of the '30s I had become aware that our family was well-known. But it didn't really matter to me because my brother and I moved to Seattle with my mother and stepfather, Anna and John Boettiger, in 1936, and I was just a regular kid in the public school and some private schooling.

"Oh, yes, we had Secret Service. But only one man on duty. We had three of them and they alternated in the 24-hour day. They took us to school. They had to play the role of chauffeur, almost. I used to feel sorry for them. It must have been very boring. But apparently—and I didn't know about that until later—there were kidnap threats and that kind of thing. There had been in the very early '30s the Lindbergh kidnapping. The Lindberghs were an extremely wealthy family and also one in the news. So even back then, when the population was less than half of what it is today, there were crackpots around. The Secret Service had to be there. You grew up with that and that was the way it was.

"I was a boarder at Sarah Dix Hamlin in San Francisco for two years before going to Reed College in fall of 1945. My grandfather had died that year, in April, so, of course, there was no special security at Reed. I enjoyed college, but was not an academic. I stayed three years and during that time I met Van, who had been in the Navy and returned to Reed after the War. We got married, started a family, and sailed with our two-year-old son, Nicholas, to France, where Van was to be a junior economist under the Marshall Plan. That was 1951 to 1953 and my grandmother was there as a delegate to the United Nations. So we saw quite a bit of her.

"We hardly ever went to restaurants because our second child was born in Paris, so we were busy. Also, we were very junior and we didn't have a lot of extra money. But my grandmother went out maybe once a week, twice a week, not always with us, of course. She had a little more time then, and she liked to relax in the evening and go to a restaurant. She didn't drink wine or anything; she might have had one sip, but I doubt it, just to drink a toast. Her favorite little two-star restaurant—I've forgotten the name—was very simple and nothing terribly glamorous. Once in a while she would invite me to tea when Van was working. She stayed at the Crillon, accompanied by one of her secretaries, either 'Tommy' [Malvina Thompson], or Maureen Corr; and she invited people from the United Nations and different countries, as she was interested in their political situations. I remember discussions about Tito with people from Yugoslavia, and discussions about what was going on in Israel between the settlers and the Palestinians; but I mostly just sat and listened and tried, on the side, to keep Nick entertained. He was a very well-behaved little boy, so I could take him lots of places and leave the baby at home if it was the right day and the *bonne à tout faire* was there.

"My grandmother was not concerned with fashion, as such, not even in Paris, but she was stylish. She paid attention to her clothes, especially evening clothes, which she wore a lot in the White House years. Being tall, she looked wonderful in formal gowns even when she put on weight in later years. When she traveled after World War II, people often gave her, or she bought, handwoven and other native fabrics. She especially liked the silks from India and had several lovely evening gowns made from them.

"As for shopping at home, she did that in a hurry at medium-priced stores like Arnold Constable in New York City. She made an appointment with her favorite saleslady there, who would get out things she thought Eleanor Roosevelt would like. The store handled fitting adjustments and delivered the clothes to her home. Occasionally, after shopping, she would take the elevator to the top floor to see Mr. Lieberman, president of Arnold Constable. They were good friends who could relax together. They talked about their children, grandchildren, and general news. I believe Mr. Lieberman gave her a ten percent discount....

"My mother, Buzz, and I lived in the White House for over a year before my mother married John Boettiger. [An earlier marriage to Curtis Dall, Ellie's father, had ended in divorce.] Even as children, we were aware that a lot was happening, but my mother made a point of not letting us know about the newspaper publicity we got, a very smart move because, as always, there was quite a bit in the papers about children and pets in the White House....

"One of the things that still bothers me is that people like Rex Tugwell, a great admirer of my grandfather and an ardent New Dealer, who occasionally dined at the White House, complained about the meals. My gripe is that they were surprised that wine was rarely served and that the food was plain. But it was nutritious. *Haute cuisine* at the White House, except for state dinners, was not common until probably the Kennedys. People are always challenged to say something critical, even if only to let others know they've rubbed elbows with the famous. And by the time enough people complain about the meals, a great mythology evolves about everybody in the White House having terrible meals. And that was not the case. The food was just too plain for some of the guests. People who came there expecting fancy food didn't get it. Buzz and I spent parts of many summers and long Christmas holidays in the White House with our family until we were nearly grown, so we had lots of time to observe.

"I think many of the men of that period, the 1930s and '40s, were astonished that my grandmother did so many things and spoke out and really had such confidence in herself and her position and was comfortable, more or less comfortable, almost all the time. It was the male guests who had trouble with a woman who had more important things to attend to than their feeding habits! Now, it is true that Mrs. Nesbitt, the cook and housekeeper, was stubborn and by today's standards knew little about exciting meals, but I guess she was efficient enough for my grandmother. I also understand that Grandmère knew Mrs. Nesbitt was from the Hyde Park area and needed the job. A typical lunch for family and guests in the White House when I was growing up might have included French-cut string beans, or peas, roast beef, potatoes, and salad and a mousse or ice cream for dessert. Now, what is wrong with that?

"My other strong objection is to the gossip or personal opinion which fades into a myth about the 'terrible' Sara Delano and the 'embarrassed' and 'inhibited' Eleanor Roosevelt. There are some minor aspects of it which are no doubt true, especially in the first fifteen years of FDR and ER's marriage. But the way people talk about it as the truth, in capital letters, as an ongoing confrontation, is not right. It was the making of a myth. Grandmère was not always embarrassed about this and that and the other thing. Granny, Sara Delano, was not always the dominating, horrid person that she's been made out to be by playwrights like Gore Vidal and others.

"I think there was friction, but that's not unusual between a young wife and a mother-in-law. Sara could be difficult, but she never raised her voice. She was very firm, but I'm sure that was not unusual. As a Victorian woman you just gritted your teeth and bore it and that's what my grandmother did. She herself could be humorless at times; she says so in her books. So there was some family tension, but it shouldn't be part of the great myth. It's really something that was not out of the ordinary. It's just that it existed in this very interesting political and well-known family. That's what blew it up and not that it was extraordinarily psychologically traumatizing. Dramas have been made out of it!

"There were probably other affluent mothers-in-law who 'bought the house next door.' That was done in those days. Sara obviously controlled the purse strings. But I think my grandmother's great concern was to do her duty, and she had no intention of going into her mother-in-law's house and making her mother-in-law a secondary person. That wasn't done in their Victorian circle.

"So, let's see what else Rexford Tugwell says about Hyde Park: 'FDR could just as well be pictured in the dining room that seemed all old polished mahogany and worn silver.... Eleanor, his wife, was never at the table's other end. That was where the grande dame, his mother, sat, plainly resenting some of the crude political guests who'd come to see her son.'

"I think that happened once in a while, but it was not every day. When it did happen, it was noticed and written about. That's how myths are fashioned and they tend to overtake reality and the everyday life that existed, which was, on the whole, a pretty friendly atmosphere where observing proper manners counted for a great deal. Grandmère may have sat on the side of the long table instead of at the head, but she certainly was not embarrassed by anything. If the occasion required her to be there and help officiate at a luncheon for political people, she would be there, but I don't think she was ever embarrassed or tried to make other people feel that she had been imposed upon. That would have been rude And she wasn't timid about running off after dinner, maybe even not waiting for coffee, to do her own thing....

"FDR was my great-grandmother's only child and she was terribly proud of him. Sara had married a man twice her age who already had a grown son from his first marriage. She had a very hard birth with Franklin when she was twenty-seven. It was in the middle of winter; he was born January 30th and the doctor was coming from across the Hudson River. I've read that they used a little chloroform to help labor, which went on for a long, long time. She was advised not to have any more children, and she didn't. So Franklin was the focus of her life. I think my grandmother, of course, understood that....

"Women like Marian Dickerman from the Todhunter School, and Molly Dewson, who was a real political pro, influenced my grandmother and she became, I think, a really good judge of character and of how much she could do publicly and the ways in which she could be effective. For instance, she did write a great many letters, but she had notepaper that was only this big, and her handwriting was very scrawly. She could get a personal letter off to half a dozen people in half an hour just with two or three sentences. She had a very quick mind for saying what she wanted to say succinctly and not having to have it edited. She had a way of dispatching her letters very fast, sometimes forwarding ideas or requests for help to others in government.

"Most of her letters answering requests for any number of astonishing things were very short, so she got off a lot which her secretaries would follow up on. People often used her as a conduit to the president. I even did some of her thank-you notes in 1944, the summer I was seventeen. I knew her style by then and my pay was twenty-five cents an hour. I think she slept about six hours a night: Sometimes she read into the night or took care of personal correspondence. She was very focused….

"Pa-pa worked very hard over a number of years to recover some leg muscle after he was stricken with polio in 1921, but he finally had to accept the paralysis even as he tried to stay politically active. When my grandmother got involved in New York State politics after 1920, Louis Howe helped her a lot. He was wonderful, and she was part of his 'plan.' She could help get FDR back into public life again, and they both wanted that. She did not want to be married to a retired man who lived in the country, because then how could she accomplish all the many things she wanted to do? She also knew that Franklin would not be happy on the shelf. Louis Howe helped her with public speaking, and she had a natural ability to write. She eventually became a very accomplished public speaker. Sometimes good speeches and sometimes not so great, but she generally knew what she wanted to say. You stand up and say it and sit down. You don't ramble. Howe's advice!

"I think the point that Blanche Cook misses is that in the '20s my grandmother became, really, a rather self-assured person. As early as that. She decided she was going to be her own person, but at that point she did not know, of course, that FDR would be president. People like Blanche Cook, who's a wonderful biographer and I generally like her books, are off the mark on certain points because they don't understand, seemingly, this terrific self-confidence, self-knowledge, and social standing, which we're not supposed to talk about in this country. Grandmère did not really worry about what people thought or said about her. She didn't have to. It sounds strange today because it makes her sound like she was puffed up about herself, but she never was. She simply had the confidence to know who she was.

"People today forget that 'class' was real back then, and she had grown up with customs and ways of thinking that gave her real self-assurance. Even during the White House years she knew how to relax with a group of women reporters and other people and get her points across and laugh at her own jokes and those of others. It didn't bother her if someone took a photo of her in a bathing suit even though she might have put on too much weight. And if she wanted to drive off with Lorena Hickok to the Gaspé Peninsula, it never occurred to her that two middle-aged women friends taking a trip would stir comment!

"Today, of course, people put a sexual connotation on all of that. It never occurred to my grandmother that she would be criticized for doing something that seemed to her a very ordinary thing for friends to do, go off on a trip together. My grandmother had also come to know any number of professional and activist women, some of whom, I suppose, were involved in what were known as 'Boston marriages.' But others were just living together because they were intellectually compatible and could share the rent. When my grandmother was young, I think she hardly even knew what lesbianism was because people did not even discuss marriage, let alone sex. Later on, I'm sure, when she found out what it was supposed to be, she didn't care a rap because she didn't have to think about it. She wasn't doing that, and she didn't care what her friends were doing as long as they were friends and intellectually stimulating and doing something for the betterment of humanity, and, as she and they thought then, for progressive social education and legislation.

"That's where these wonderful historians miss the boat. They don't understand that it never occurred to my grandmother that her gushy letters to Lorena Hickok and maybe to a few other people, or her playfulness with Earl Miller around Hyde Park, would cause comment. And Earl was not the only one. With men and women she wanted to show that she was a 'regular guy,' free to put her hand on your shoulder or your knee. She didn't want to be above anybody. She didn't want to be aloof and out of the loop, so her way of showing she was one of the gang on informal occasions was to wrap her arms around someone and maybe give them a big kiss on the cheek. She wanted other people to see her as the human being that she was. She was a very warm person, but at the same time careful not to overstep the bounds of good manners.

"Blanche Cook writes that my grandmother was very 'physical' in her affections. My definition of physical is not the same as hers: She seems to consider physical the same as sexual. I don't. My grandmother was physical. She would give you a big bear hug and a kiss. She would reach out that way, but she was not about to do anything else. She was very Victorian. In our family nobody ever kissed on the mouth because it was considered unsanitary. A cheek kiss. That's all.

"With the way people think today, I understand where they're coming from, but they don't understand where my grandmother was coming from. That is my opinion from actually knowing Eleanor Roosevelt for thirty-five years and being well acquainted with many in her circle of close friends like Lorena Hickok and David Gurevitsch. The whole point of the gushy letters my grandmother wrote, which have had so much publicity—I feel I know her so well—was to reassure people like Hick that she did love them. Those letters must not be misconstrued. Arthur Schlesinger Jr. explained all this in an article in *The New York Times,* on the op ed page, maybe fifteen years ago. This is just a sideline; it's not an important issue, but I think my grandmother would be amazed at some of the new constructions people have come up with in our day. We know that Hick had lesbian leanings. We also know that she loved my grandmother, but she would not have jeopardized the relationship by putting the friendship to a sex test.

"Oh, yes, I'm sure it is true that the Lucy Mercer affair was very painful for my grandmother. It was. Like a lot of people, my grandmother grew up with fairy-tale ideas of marriage. But there was nothing so extraordinary about this flirtation. Probably, because of social restrictions and a lack of contraception for women in those days, the affair never got beyond petting between Lucy Mercer and my grandfather. Lucy Mercer was a wonderful lady! She wanted to 'do something,' and what did a socially acceptable, young Catholic woman who was a bit short of money do? If they didn't get married right away, they became social secretaries. So that's what Lucy did. My mother knew her later when she was Lucy Rutherford and a widow and liked her very much. I think back to the several times my mother arranged for Pa-pa and Lucy Rutherford to get together for a meal when Grandmère was away. FDR and Lucy were old friends by then, and think of the pressures of being in the White House during World War II, for heaven's sakes! But my grandmother was shattered that there was even an exchange of affection, because that ruined her fairy tale. Also, the fact that she was the woman who'd produced six children and had done her duty and all that sort of thing must have hurt.

"She later realized affairs happen all the time, but in her day nobody discussed those things! That certainly wasn't tea party chatter, although there was gossip, I'm sure, because all we have to do is look at Alice Roosevelt Longworth. She loved to gossip and she had a great time exposing people's affairs, I think. But my grandmother was so busy having children the first ten or twelve years of her married life that she didn't even know what was going on in the rest of the world aside from her domestic and social duties....

"Since 1986, I've been an alternate commissioner on the Roosevelt Campobello International Park. It's a very democratic commission and everybody has an equal vote and we have a good time. What struck me while trying to focus on the life of FDR and ER at Campobello between about 1912 to 1921, roughly in there, is that most of the time my grandmother was there alone, providing for children and any number of guests. FDR would come up to stay for a couple of weeks at a time during the summer when he could get away. My grandmother did all the arranging and running things that people just take for granted. The writers who wrote about that later should look at her in her own time.

"She was not a drone simply running a large household. I'm sure she would have been shocked to think of herself as that, although the work was kind of tedious sometimes. She had servants to help her. The staff didn't all live at Campobello: Some lived in the village and came during the day. But it was Eleanor who had to plan everybody's work. She had to plan to get the food out to the house and since there wasn't a bridge, it had to be brought over by boat. There was one telephone on the whole island. And what else? She had to arrange for entertainment not only for the children and their tutors—there was usually a tutor or two and a governess—but also for lots of visitors: tea parties for the adults and maybe some evening entertainment for the young people. So she was not idle, but it was not exactly the kind of work that she felt inwardly she would like to devote her life to.

"When she had to work in the '20s to help FDR recover, she was also recovering herself. She was through her childbearing years. The two youngest boys were still young, but they were in school. She was free. After the Lucy Mercer affair, of course, my grandparents didn't live as man and wife. I mean, they didn't share a bed. I think that's probably true although I certainly never asked her. That's very Victorian, and, of course, then my grandfather had polio. I think he wasn't impotent—but I don't know about that either—because he was paralyzed from the hips down, not the waist, as some people have written. She was a wife, but not a wife, in a way. She became his partner, and she was free of a lot of domestic tasks. She still ran the house and did all those things with family and kids, but basically she was free to cut her own swath. So by the time she got to Albany, and certainly by the time she came to the White House, she knew who she was and what she wanted to do and what she could do. I don't think she was trying to set a milestone by being a very active first lady. She just did what she felt she had to do.

"She saw people she wanted to see; she wrote what she wanted to write. She tried not to contradict FDR's policies. She was trying to actually help him, and she did help him, but she had a lot of ideas of her own. They had some arguments about what was important, what the priorities were and so on, that everybody knows about, especially during World War II. Her intellect interested FDR, and there was also an affection between them that people have written about, but it was a different kind of relationship than it had been in the earliest years....

My grandmother often spoke of change, political and social, but for her, one thing that remained constant, as I look back, was her loyalty to those people she cared about and who she knew cared about her as a human being."

Elizabeth "Betty" Hight

In 1940, Betty Hight was at Douglass College, the women's division of Rutgers University, when she and three student activists invited Eleanor Roosevelt "to lunch or tea or dinner." Hight was president of the campus League of Women Voters, and the foursome planned to attend a Citizenship Institute of the American Youth Congress in Washington. The young women quickly received an invitation from the first lady to "come around to the front door on February 10 to have luncheon." For Betty Hight, it was the beginning of a long relationship with Eleanor Roosevelt.

"Earlier, we had invited Mrs. Roosevelt to a Peace Day we arranged at Douglass, but she couldn't come," recalled Betty Hight in a 1978 interview with Dr. Thomas F. Soapes, oral historian for the Franklin D. Roosevelt Library in Hyde Park. "When we were planning to go to Washington we decided on the spur of the moment to invite her again because she was a great supporter of the Youth Congress. We came down to Washington by bus and stayed at the YWCA annex on E Street at seventy-five cents a night.

"I was at Douglass on a state scholarship—$500 a year and full board my junior and senior years—that required waiting on tables in the school dining room. I was the student manager, and I had to have a substitute while I was away and pay her thirty-five cents a meal. We were all on scholarships, and coming up with thirty-five cents a meal amounted to a heck of a lot of money in those days. But we came to Washington by bus, stayed at the Y, and went to the White House for lunch. If Mrs. Roosevelt had accepted, I don't know where we thought we were going to take her to lunch. I guess at the Y!

"At the White House luncheon the dining room was crowded. There were small tables, with an older person at each table, and Mrs. Roosevelt just moved from table to table. About halfway through lunch she appeared with about twenty little kids, eight or ten years old, and said she had found them making a tour of the White House. It was one of those rainy winter days, and she brought them in to get them warm and dry. They were drenched. Afterward, we listened to the president out on the south lawn. The Russians had attacked Finland and FDR was giving one of his over-the-top speeches on the war. The students didn't really boo him; they kind of groaned, Oh, no, we're going to be hurt! It was a pretty messy day and our feet sank into the ground.

"We had been told early on, and I forget now who told us, to be careful of Joseph Lash, who was very active in the youth groups. 'If he finds you're getting too close to Mrs. Roosevelt, you'll have your throat cut.' And I said if that's the way he plays the game, then he can have it. Joe Lash was a poor, ambitious Jewish boy. We didn't mix at all. I have never read his *Eleanor and Franklin* because I decided I really wasn't interested in his opinions. He always seemed so stuffy, took himself so seriously. We thought Trude [Lash] was a pretty rough lady. On the few occasions that we saw her in operation, the knife always seemed drawn. So I wondered if Joe was really the knife, or if it was Trude. We just stayed out of their way. Well, he was a young genius, but who needed them?

"After the luncheon we all wrote our thank-you notes. Mrs. Roosevelt answered mine with one line: 'I'm glad you enjoyed yourselves.' We returned to Douglass to find that the college newspaper was being suspended. A few weeks earlier, in the letters to the editor column, one of the girls had pointed out that the head of the German department was anti-Semitic. Now, to go back to the Douglass dining room.

"We had a French house for the French students and a German house for the German students. They sat at their own tables in the dining room to converse in their language, except on weekends when there was open seating. The head of the German department told his students that they were not supposed to sit with Jewish girls on the weekends. He was a real powerhouse, who had been at the college since it was founded in 1918; and he got the college administration to agree that all letters to the editor were to be pre-screened from that point on. We immediately jumped on that. An open letter is an open letter. So the newspaper was suspended. The Rutgers guys were all too scared to get involved, but fellows from Princeton came up and said that if we wanted to publish an underground newspaper, they would be happy to do it for us. I wrote all of this to Mrs. Roosevelt on a step-by-step basis: 'Man! Look what happened when we got back here!' She wrote back and said to stay with it, with her blessing.

"About this time the college indicated to those of us who were involved in the underground newspaper, courtesy of Princeton, that by this action we were indicating a wish to disassociate ourselves from the college. Of course, this threw my parents into a real panic. The college had sent letters to them. My parents didn't say anything, but I knew what they were thinking: 'Betty here you are, a senior. Just a couple of months to graduation. Please cool it!'

"We let the college know that we had a continuing interest on Mrs. Roosevelt's part, and it took a little while, but they did back off. We graduated. This was how my relationship with Mrs. Roosevelt developed.

"After graduation, I went to work for Prudential Insurance in New Jersey. I had hoped to go with the Tennessee Valley Authority [TVA]—I had written a paper about it—but that didn't work out. So I started with Prudential at seventy-five dollars a month. Thinking that I was with the TVA, Mrs. Roosevelt invited me to one of her Hyde Park picnics. I refused, saying that I was with Prudential and we wouldn't have anything to talk about. That was one of two refusal notes I wrote to her. She said to come up anyway. She asked me to stay over. So I stayed a day or two and, of course, I wrote her again.

"Then I decided to take advanced studies at NYU after work. They had a new graduate school for public administration, and I took two courses: public finance and public administration. I could walk down through the Newark warehouse district and catch the tube over to Washington Square and go to NYU and then after classes do some street-corner speaking, which I thought was kind of fun. In those times you could wander around at night; but getting back to Bloomfield, New Jersey, was a bit of a chore. It would be midnight or more before I could get home, using the tubes and then taking two buses.

"There was a bunch of us doing the street corners before the 1940 election, students from the NYU grad school volunteering for FDR. We stood on street corners talking up the New Deal, handing out pamphlets on various issues, and listening to New York opinions. It was lively. I wrote Mrs. Roosevelt and she wanted to know about it: How were the street speakers doing? How were the crowds? Did anybody listen? Find out what they are thinking and saying. She loved that kind of minutiae.

"Then I wrote her that I was bringing my sister to the 1941 inauguration as a high-school graduation gift. Good grief! Again, we came down to Washington by bus. We stayed at the Y, but the invitations started rolling in: ceremonies on the Hill, dinner at the White House, the gala at Constitution Hall, tea at the Woodrow Wilson house. All these crested invitations kept rolling in!

"I also wrote to ask what we should wear, and her reply was that it was cold in Washington. My sister and I didn't know our way around at all, and our funniest experience was the dinner before the evening gala at Constitution Hall. Since we'd been told that it would be cold, we had arrived with our winter Sunday dresses, not realizing that all inaugural festivities, especially if you are going to the White House for dinner, involved evening gowns. So my sister, Helen, and I walked in, and there was Mrs. James Roosevelt, FDR's mother, ensconced in a chair like the queen mother. And everybody, everybody, was dressed to the teeth. Helen and I walked in and Sara Delano Roosevelt took one look and you could see in her face, This has to be something Eleanor dragged in! There was no mistaking that look.

"We were seated at a little table with FDR and his mother nearby. Mrs. Roosevelt had apparently put us there. She did that sort of thing for me all the time and I have never been able to understand exactly why. We could watch and see everything. Mrs. Roosevelt had gone off to Constitution Hall to make sure everything was in shape, and FDR was obviously furious. He had been seated with his mother and two of her friends, and there were all those beautiful people around, you know, very attractive women, and he was with his mother. I gather there was a little flack about that afterward. Then we were packed off in a limousine to Constitution Hall, and again we were seated with the Roosevelt family. It was a real gala and everybody who was anybody was there that night.

"I wasn't feeling very friendly toward Prudential and had wanted to leave. During the 1940 campaign I would come into my office in the morning to find that the head of the department had put on my desk some of the most obscene cartoons pertaining to Franklin Delano Roosevelt you ever saw in your life.

"In 1941, I came to Washington to take a job in the Treasury department, in procurement. I was working in a warehouse at 7th and D, with segregated restrooms and cafeterias and one telephone for every eight girls. Malvina Thompson would call to invite me to lunch and my supervisor would take the call. A junior civil servant getting a call from the first lady! That wasn't doing me any favor.

"That same year, I was invited to Christmas dinner at the White House because World War II had started and federal workers were told they couldn't get any vacation at Christmas. I had planned to go home to New Jersey for a day or two, but when all leave was canceled, Mrs. Roosevelt invited me to Christmas dinner at the White House.

"Leave was later approved, and I called Tommy to say I was going home and couldn't make dinner. She said she would pay my round-trip plane ticket so that I could do both because Mrs. Roosevelt wanted me there. It was the first time I ever flew. My father picked me up at the airport and I had a nice family Christmas dinner. Then I flew back to Washington.

"My landlord—I had a room in northeast Washington—drove me to the White House in his Model A. I found myself seated directly across from President Roosevelt and Prime Minister Winston Churchill, who were criticizing each other's carving skill. Each thought he was the expert carver. I think it was the first time I ever tasted champagne. I took one sip and I didn't like it!

"Later, we went upstairs to watch a newsreel. This time I was behind FDR and Churchill. We were watching a film of their press conference held on a destroyer in the north Atlantic. They were kidding each other, acting like a couple of kids just having fun. FDR said he looked better and Churchill said, I sound better. And then a White House limousine drove me home.

"A friend of mine from NYU had accepted a job at the Department of Justice and was living at the Woman's National Democratic Club. She told me they were taking in war workers, so I moved into the tower room with her, in what's now the Eleanor Roosevelt library. That didn't last long because I was dating John. We were wandering the city and I was coming in at all hours and being quiet as could be; but my roommate told me to get out.

"John was very independent and that caused some awkward moments with Mrs. Roosevelt. He said he felt like an interloper and he didn't want to take advantage of my connection with the White House. It got so embarrassing I just had to tell him point blank that I was not going there any more if he didn't go, too. Well, you could hardly blame John. Some of the things he was putting up with! For instance, John in a private's uniform—he was in the Army—was seated next to Madame Chiang Kai-shek. If you knew Madame Chiang, she wasn't about to talk to low-ranking John, who was supposed to be discussing youth in America with her, including dancing the boogie-woogie. That was Mrs. Roosevelt's gentle way of telling Madame Chiang, Don't be afraid of your own young people. When John tried to talk to Madame Chiang, she'd look the other way!

"Then Mrs. Roosevelt would say, Betty, I don't think your John likes me. He never smiles. She was very sensitive on that score. She liked John. She thought he was very bright, but idiosyncratic. I finally had to tell him to loosen up. And to some extent he did. But John and I were at Hyde Park having breakfast alone one morning—wonderful raspberries with thick cream—and he said, 'We're going to pay for this one day.' And he was right, as you'll see.

"Over the years I wrote to Mrs. Roosevelt about liberal organizations I belonged to or thought she would be interested in, all of them jockeying for position and money. I don't know if they all got in touch with her, or how much she was willing to get involved with groups like the Union for Democratic Action or the International Student Services or conscientious objectors, although she supported the American Friends' Service Committee. At times, she would write 'Betty, I don't think you should get involved. Betty, no.' I had to assume that she knew something I didn't and so I behaved myself.

"Later, in my various jobs, I would be her informal communication channel. Today, that could be whistle-blowing, kind of tricky. When I was at the Department of Commerce, at the National Resources Planning Board headed by FDR's uncle, Fred Delano, there was an exhaustive study on local and state welfare laws that no one had sent to the White House. It was too heavy to frank and I knew Mrs. Roosevelt would be interested in it. So I took it over to her; and FDR, I gather, went through three ceilings because the report had been leaked.

"From 1948 to 1954, we were in Paris while John worked on the European Economic Community [EEC]. I had my first baby and became friends with Ellie Seagraves, Mrs. Roosevelt's granddaughter. When we came back to Washington, John and I were desperate for work. I couldn't be rehired at the Office of International Trade in the Department of Commerce. They had contacted an organization that said I was 'liberal to radical.' Suddenly, I was considered a security risk! I finally got a job at the Department of Agriculture, but was later turned down for a confidential clearance—we shipped Food for Peace and I needed a confidential—even though I had had 'top security' during the War. I was a mole in Agriculture? Obviously, there was a file on me somewhere! But I did get a hearing, and they asked me what Roosevelt said to Churchill and vice versa at Christmas dinner in 1941. I had the pleasure of telling them. I don't think they believed me, but I got my confidential clearance.

"John became Mrs. Roosevelt's advance man for Adlai Stevenson's 1956 campaign. We continued to see her until her death in 1962. John was in Pittsburgh on business when she died and I was in Washington. We met in Hyde Park for her funeral service."

British officers and club members celebrate the leasing of WNDC's historic clubhouse to the British Service Club for the duration of World War II, 22 June 1943.

Chapter Four
WORLD WAR II AND AFTERWARD
WNDC Joins Up

WNDC members focused their fund raising energies on defense efforts during World War II. They sold U.S. savings bonds at a Mayflower Hotel booth, raising $350,000 and winning three honorary citations from the Treasury department. Members also signed on to help with air-raid precautions, first aid, knitting, sewing, and the Red Cross blood bank. They visited the wounded at Walter Reed Army Hospital and worked at the enlisted men's canteen in the old Belasco Theatre.

With all volunteer efforts directed toward defense, the club found itself on fragile financial footing when the Dupont Circle neighborhood was rezoned in 1942. The value of the clubhouse jumped to $250,000 from a prewar assessment of $58,540, and taxes increased accordingly. Inconveniences such as sweeping with a broom and ironing by hand had returned: The vacuum cleaner could not be replaced and the mangle was at Westinghouse waiting to be repaired. All able-bodied Americans had gone to war or to work in defense-related jobs.

Office of Price Administration (OPA) ration requirements "provoked passing perplexities." One clubhouse tenant, citing price control regulations, refused to increase the stipend she was paying for her room and board. Despite these annoyances, the higher taxes, and an outstanding mortgage, the governing board fortuitously refused three below-market offers for the house.

In 1943, Washington's booming wartime economy finally benefited WNDC. The British Service Club leased 1526 New Hampshire Avenue for two years and solved the club's financial crisis with a $20,000 rent paid in advance and an offer to manage the clubhouse. President Elizabeth Sayre, at a welcoming reception for the British officers, remarked that WNDC was the first woman's organization to step aside for a men's club. She called the "British Occupation" an experiment in international collaboration. For the duration, WNDC members had use of the clubhouse on Mondays and on alternate Thursday evenings.

After Franklin D. Roosevelt's death and the end of World War II, WNDC experienced further change that reflected the adjustments the country made to postwar realities and the Truman administration. As first lady, Bess Truman had little interest in public policy; she preferred Independence, Missouri, to Washington and was often absent from the capital. Her growing distance from the White House (and from the club) gave India Edwards an opportunity to emerge as a strong force in Democratic women's politics.

India assumed Eleanor Roosevelt's mantle at WNDC. She was the stalwart New Dealer who, like Mrs. Roosevelt, had great social skills, knew how to make it in a man's world, knew how to influence diverse constituencies, and knew how to hold volatile factions together. India had an engaging persona. People liked her and she was fiercely devoted to the powerful men she worked for. She and three other club members appearing in this chapter were career women whose professional skills furthered WNDC objectives.

India Edwards

India Edwards was born 16 June 1895 into a solid, respectable, Republican family in Nashville, Tennessee. Her mother, a suffragist, was the family's only Democrat. Her father endured financial reverses when India was eighteen, making it impossible for her to attend the University of Chicago's school of journalism.

India, highly intelligent, lively, and attractive, went to to work in Chicago. By age twenty-three she had become society editor of the women's page of Colonel Robert McCormick's *Chicago Tribune*. India was soon helping support her unemployed father, her mother, and younger sister, and keeping herself in her signature hats. She had a passion for hats and wore them everywhere.

In 1917 India married a young Army officer who was killed in World War I. She kept her job as society editor and continued to work at the *Tribune* for seventeen years, through her widowhood, second marriage, motherhood, divorce, and happy third marriage. When conservative Republican Colonel McCormick was asked how he could work so well with India, a liberal Democrat, he quipped, "If she can stand me, I can stand her." At the end of her newspaper career, India was editor of the women's page and reputedly the highest paid woman on a major U.S. newspaper.

India moved east in 1942 when her third husband, Herbert Edwards, took a civil service job with the Department of State in Washington. Two years later, she began writing press releases as a volunteer at the Democratic National Committee. That summer India went to the 1944 Democratic convention in New York City as assistant to the director of publicity for the women's division of the Democratic National Committee. As well as escorting VIP women to their radio engagements, she wrote their speeches, invariably ending each with an exhortation to "Reelect Franklin Roosevelt as president and elect Harry Truman as vice president."

Four years later, at the 1948 convention that nominated Harry S. Truman, India gave the keynote speech. With hat firmly in place, she railed against Republican inflationary policies while waving a raw beefsteak, the price of which had doubled in two years. Of that event India wrote, "The photographers yelled so loud and so often for 'Just one more!' that I must have waved that steak under the television lights long enough to cook it!" The election resulted in the great upset of 1948 when Harry Truman went to bed thinking he had been defeated.

India was a tough and resourceful fighter and her success with Truman depended on those qualities. During many of her discussions with the president, India would leave Truman's office without having attained her goal, only to return a few days later to win him over. She influenced the appointments of Georgia Neese Clark as the first woman treasurer of the United States, Eugenie M. Anderson to Denmark as the first woman with the rank of ambassador, and Burnita Shelton Matthews as the first woman justice of a U.S. district court.

In 1951, President Truman asked India to assume the chairmanship of the DNC. She refused, believing that the time had not yet come for women in sensitive political jobs. Her opinion was validated when India's name was put forward in 1952 as vice-presidential candidate for Adlai E. Stevenson's presidential campaign. When Sam Rayburn (D-TX), the powerful speaker of the House, was asked if it were true that India was going to withdraw her name once she was nominated, he responded, "You're damn right it is! I wouldn't let any lady's name be put in nomination!"

In 1953, the women's division was integrated with the Democratic National Committee and lost control of its affairs. The executive director position was eliminated, but India retained her volunteer job as a vice chair of the DNC. She remained active in politics, particularly as a catalyst in placing women in high office. A quote from Washington insider Clark Clifford sums up the contributions of her public life: "You were the most effective woman in politics I ever knew. Your understanding of the political process and the importance of it to our democratic form of government was superb."

India Edwards was one of WNDC's most politically powerful members. Her club membership (1944-86) spanned more than four decades. In 1981, thirty-seven years after launching her career in politics, India recorded her memories for WNDC.

"I was always a Democrat and when I moved to Washington in 1942, I began reading in the paper about the Woman's National Democratic Club and thought I ought to join it. But in 1944, at the urging of Lillian Owen, a Chicago friend and WNDC member, I volunteered for the Democratic National Committee. Lillian convinced me that it would be more fun to work at the DNC than at the Washington office of the United Nations, where I had planned to volunteer. I worked all through the 1944 campaign, went to the convention first, in Chicago, and then went to the headquarters in New York. We had moved the headquarters to New York for the fourth Roosevelt campaign

"In the spring of 1945, just shortly before Franklin Roosevelt died, I was asked to take Lorena Hickok's job as executive secretary of the women's division of the DNC. If I had known what the job was going to be like, I don't think I would have taken it. I really felt that I was not experienced enough in politics. But I went to work at the committee, and it soon began to seep through to me in various ways that there was not a good feeling on the part of the DNC towards the WNDC. Now, I do not know how the club felt about the committee because I had just become a member; I wasn't an officer or on the board or anything like that. But I was very surprised, and it seemed to me that with that powerful club—and it was a powerful organization because so many of the members were wives of members of Congress or former members of Congress—it seemed to me that it and the committee should be working together, hand-in-hand, all the time. But they weren't, even though they had in earlier times before I knew anything about the committee.

"Molly Dewson, who was a wonderful politician and a wonderful woman and had worked for Franklin Roosevelt when he was governor of New York, was brought down here by Roosevelt when he became president. She became vice chairman of the committee and head of the women's division, and she was definitely set against the club. She did not think that women in the Democratic Party should be working in clubs. She wanted them to be active members of the working organizations in the states.

"I think I understand Molly's point of view, but I think she was wrong. I think there is a place for clubs. There are certain types of women who will work in a political club who would never work for the DNC. So I did everything I could to bring about a rapprochement between the two. Anyway, I am sure that the club had worked very closely with the women's division of the committee at one time. In fact, I think they had put on a conference together. We stored things for the committee, too, but that was before my time.

"I became director of the women's division during the Truman administration, probably in 1947. By that time, I had established a pretty good working relationship between the committee and the women's division of the committee and the club. We used the club for press conferences, and almost any time I gave any kind of a function, I would give it at the club. In those days the clubhouse wasn't nearly as large as it is now so that when I would have a large reception or something, it would have to be at a hotel.

"I was not part of the struggle to admit the first black member to the club because my husband and I left Washington in 1953 for California. But I was very proud of the club when they took Gladys Duncan in as their first black member. I moved back at the very end of 1956 and, very shortly after that, integration came up again. I wanted to bring Edith Sampson, who had been appointed a member of the United Nations delegation by President Truman, to the club. She was a Chicago lawyer, one of the smartest, most prestigious black women in this country; and it annoyed me, frankly, to think that when I wanted to put her up for membership—as a matter of fact, she wanted to become a nonresident member—the club said, Oh, no! We have one token member! And that was that. We weren't going to have any more!

"Emily Douglas rather spearheaded Edith's nomination. She was an outspoken, highly effective political personality, a former congresswoman-at-large from Illinois, and wife of Senator Paul Douglas (D-IL). Dear old Daisy Harriman was in on it, too. I imagine she had also been active in the first struggle. A small group of us met at Emily's house and we decided that we were definitely going to push this through. I remember how unpleasant it was because there were still so many people in the club, particularly the southerners, who did not want any black members. Connie Casey was president then and we all felt that Connie was on our side. She made that very plain.

"Because I was a vice chairman of the committee and director of the women's division, I had to appear before a large group of club members who did not want to admit any other black women and tell them why I felt that we should admit minorities. I remember it was a rather unpleasant experience because the women were so inimical and so determined that they weren't going to admit any more minorities. But we succeeded. There were a few well-known women who had influence, and I think they may have voted for it, but they wouldn't come out openly and support it on the floor.

"I resigned from the Democratic National Committee in 1956 and became a board member of the club after that. As I look back, I think that there was a feeling among some of the women who had been members for years, the older women, that they did not want to be associated with the DNC. They did not look upon the Woman's National Democratic Club as a political club: They looked upon it more as a social club. I know I used to have arguments with them. In fact, one of them told me one time, looking at me rather in an uptight way and looking down on me, My dear Mrs. Edwards, I don't think you quite understand the kind of club this is! And I said, I do understand! That's the whole trouble! I do understand that you are not a political club in spite of the fact that you call yourself a political club!

"I now am almost eighty-six years old, but I still vividly remember my seventieth birthday at the club. It was a lovely party and I was very touched by it. The idea of having the party came about when I happened to mention my seventieth birthday, and one of the members said, Your seventieth birthday! You mean you're sixty! And I said, Oh, I know when I was born! I was born in 1895. I never mind telling my age. It was a lovely party. They called it 'The Men in My Life,' the different men that I had worked with: Colonel Robert McCormick at *The Chicago Tribune,* President Truman, and President Lyndon Johnson. It was a lovely party. To me, it was very touching and gratifying. Loved it!

"Then I wrote my book, *Pulling No Punches,* and I wanted to have it come out in Washington rather than in New York. Two or three members, friends of mine, suggested that it should be done at a club luncheon. I thought that was a lovely affair, too. Most of the women Truman had appointed to office came to that luncheon, and it was, to me, a wonderful occasion. My husband died, you know, just a few days after that, very suddenly. So it was very comforting to me to have had the beautiful memory of that party, to have it along with the bad one.

"I always regretted that the club was not financially able to become the nucleus of a really strong federation of Democratic women's clubs the way the Republican women do. If the WNDC had been able to send a couple of women out into the field to do the organizing—and there are some members who are very good organization people—why it would have been of great value to the Democratic Party. Still would be! Even now, when I live in California and I get the newsletter and the list of events for each month, I regret very much that I won't be able to hear the speakers.

"There was a period in the club when it seemed to me they were shying away from controversial things, and they were having flower arranging and things like that. I did not like that at all! It seemed to me that was a complete waste of time. If a woman wants to learn something about flower arrangements, I don't think the Woman's National Democratic Club is the place for her. I hope when they sit around doing flower arrangements or knitting, they discuss politics. I think the classes are very good and having the classes is a good idea, but they sometimes did things that I felt were frivolous and that were a waste of time....

"By dint of great effort on the part of the editor of *The Democratic Digest,* I had, by the time I left the committee in 1956, a complete set of the *Digest,* back numbers in every issue, from the little leaflet that was first published through to when the men took it over. The *Digests* are a history of the party from 1922 until 1953. I had them indexed and gave them to the Truman Library. Most of my papers are at the Truman Library. I'm very pleased to say that I've heard from a fair number of women who do their PhDs going through my papers, and I always tell them to be sure and go through the *Digest.*"

India firmly believed the DNC's credo that elections are won between campaigns. To this end, she traveled nationwide carrying the Democratic message to prospective voters, and she hired journalist Gladys Uhl-Katcher as her speechwriter.

Gladys Uhl-Katcher

"India Edwards was an important influence in my life," recalled Gladys Uhl-Katcher in a 1997 interview. "I was very fond of her, very fond of her. She called me her favorite ghost; and when she autographed my copy of her book, *Pulling No Punches,* she signed it to 'A great gal, and my favorite ghost.'

"I had never written a speech, but in the 1940s, when I heard that India Edwards was looking for a speechwriter, I applied for the job. I consulted with my husband who said, You ought to read FDR's speeches. They're the greatest. So I went to the library and I found a book of FDR's speeches, and then I went to *The Washington Post* morgue and I looked up India's clippings and read all of her speeches and the press about her and then I wrote a speech. She didn't tell me what it was for or where it was going to be given. I was afraid to ask questions for fear she'd say that a speech is a speech! So I wrote about two big issues that she was deeply committed to: a huge hydroelectric project in Maine; and the Tennessee Valley Authority [TVA], which the Republicans were calling socialism and were trying to privatize or not fund because they didn't approve of it. So I used those as the two basic issues, and she liked the speech and hired me. I'm not sure she ever used the speech.

"India was very, very dynamic, enormously strong and a born leader. She had a delightful sense of humor. She was also very warm and sympathetic. Sometimes on a Friday night, if we'd had a big week or a big success or something to celebrate, she'd invite us to her office for a drink. We sat around and sort of let our hair down. We didn't talk about recipes; we didn't talk about clothes. We talked about issues, or we talked about something humorous. We lived politics! All the time. I found it exciting.

"I went out with her one time, I think, to Iowa. It was an invitation for her to speak. The chairman of the group, who was probably the state chairman of Iowa, said, in front of India, Why don't you let Gladys introduce you? And I thought, Oh, no! No! No! India said, Why, sure! You know me, Gladys! You can introduce me.

"I was so nervous about introducing her I just shook all over. I said to India afterwards, Could you tell I was nervous? And she said, Could I? I was sitting behind you and your rump shook! I went to the conventions with her, and I went to state meetings, regional meetings. We had a meeting in Los Angeles at one point, and I went with India when Helen Gahagan Douglas was running for the Senate and McCarthy, Joe McCarthy, was running wild. And he labeled Helen Gahagan Douglas 'a fellow traveler,' implying, of course, that she was a Communist. No, Nixon labeled her 'a fellow traveler,' out of the McCarthy era. And India labeled Nixon 'a Housebroken McCarthy' because he had served in the House before he ran for president. I wonder what she would say about Senator Al D'Amato (R-NY) today. I think she would have plenty to say on his accusations and actions!

"When India became head of public affairs at the DNC, it was heavily weighted on the executive side with men. India pushed for women and minorities. So, I joined the public affairs staff where I did more writing than just speeches. We had taken over *The Democratic Digest,* which had been published by WNDC. It was more sophisticated than the *Digest* the women published. Theirs was a good solid publication, but more like a newsletter. India recommended that I join the club. To me, it was quite an honor to join, to be accepted. I was on the publicity committee and I think I was on membership at one point. But I had a full-time job.

"When India's devoted Herbert died, he was cremated. India called from California—my husband had also died and I was living alone in Georgetown—to say she was coming east with Herbert's ashes and wanted to have a ceremony for him and asked if she could stay with me. I welcomed her. She arrived with a can of Herbert's ashes and put them on my kitchen counter. I took them away and put them in a cupboard. One morning she asked, Where's Herbert? And I said, In the cupboard! And she said, Well, I just wanted to know where he was.

"We arranged for the ceremony. She had an estate in southern Maryland, a country home named Arden. India and I, and a woman from the trade union movement whose name escapes me, went out to Arden with the ashes. I brought a Bible. India was going to sprinkle the ashes. I also brought a hammer and a screwdriver because I knew I was going to have difficulty opening that can. It was very heavy, by the way, not the ashes, but the can. And I brought a spoon.

"India spooned the ashes from the can and sprinkled them into the water. We were on a little bridge over a creek that ran through the property. I read from the Bible and we were all in tears. A car came by and stopped and said, Can we help? And we said, No. Please, go away! They said, But you won't let us help you? No. Please, go away! I don't know what they thought!…

"India and I were very good friends! Oh, yes. She often stayed with me. When I was alone, she would come."

Marian O. Norby

Marian Norby had a different perspective on speechwriting. After World War II, she worked in the Truman White House and traveled on the 1948 campaign train to work on the president's speeches. In later years, she appeared in two PBS documentaries about the Truman administration.

Marian also worked as a government editor and was noted for her ability to convert bureaucratic jargon into "plain English." She was a senior technical editor for the

U.S. Air Force and for the Library of Congress. After retiring in the 1980s, she organized evening events for career women unable to participate in the club's daytime activities.

In 1998 she established the Marian O. Norby Fund with a $50,000 contribution to the WNDC Educational Foundation. The fund supported two law school fellowships for former White House administrative assistants and financed the WNDC-EF Web site. In 1999 she was honored as a member of the Veteran Feminists of America.

"In July or August 1945, a few months after President Truman took office, the White House was still being staffed and they needed secretaries," recalled Marian Norby in a 1997 interview. "I had moved up to personnel training in the Federal Economic Administration [FEA], and I was not eager to become a secretary again. It seemed like a step backward, so I resisted applying. But jobs were getting scarce after the War, so I finally filled out that famous old civil service form 57. I was so disinterested that I made a mistake and checked that I had been a Communist! It took a while to sort that out.

"Eventually, I worked for Mr. George Elsey, who did much of the speechwriting in the 1948 presidential election. President Truman preferred to campaign by train, so we had the White House make a special filing box for those trips. All of the raw data we needed for the speeches at each stop were in those files.

"If President Truman was going to speak in Pittsburgh, for example, we'd have a file on Pittsburgh full of all sorts of goodies: Democratic praise, Republican scandal, anything useful. On the train we would be busy converting that material into a speech for the president, but the local officials would invariably make changes.

"When we got into town we would unload the train and go to the hotel. Everyone else would get all dressed up and go to the banquet hall, usually for a big fund raising dinner. I would go to my little room over the kitchen and start retyping the speeches for tomorrow. Once, when I got a really good room, India Edwards took it away from me!

"We had old-fashioned equipment, plain old manual typewriters. We even had to turn in our ribbons for the supply clerk to check that both edges of the ribbon had been used, that you'd reversed it, you know, before you could get a new ribbon.

"I had my little perch on the train. I had a little table in a booth back in the corner of the work car where I did my typing. You remember those old wax stencils? Did you ever see those, that you run on a mimeograph? That's how we were producing speeches to hand out to the press. So I'd stick a stencil in, then put in an extra sheet of tissue so I would have a black-and-white copy when I got through. Then I gave the stencil to the mimeograph guy. Then I gave the boss the little insert sheet so he could check it; and, believe me, if there was an error anywhere, it had to be redone.

"But we'd be tootling along and going lickety-split on the train, and all of a sudden, we'd go around a corner and the typewriter would slide off the table! I'd grab it and the carriage would slide all the way down and completely destroy that whole line of typing! I had to start all over again with a new stencil! It was lots of work. I averaged four hours' sleep a night because we worked into the night rewriting for tomorrow, and then the next morning there'd be more people protesting, Oh, we can't say that!

"Usually about four o'clock in the morning a porter would be sent to get me out of the bunk. Mr. Elsey would say, Marian, we've got to have such-and-such a speech redone before seven o'clock when we pull in to such-and-such a town.

"There were numerous campaign trips by train. I can't tell you now how many there were. It's all a blur to me, even yet. We'd come home just long enough to get our clothes washed and our hair washed, and go back to Union Station and start out again. It was exhausting.

"I remember the last afternoon on the train before we pulled into Kansas City to wait out election night at the Meulenbach Hotel. Everyone in the work car was dejected. They were recalling the 'mistakes' the Democrats had made during the campaign. Their conversation was full of 'if only' regrets. Everyone left the train with a heavy heart. John Adams of CBS had bet $500 on President Truman, with varying odds: one to ten, one to fifty. That was a major investment in those days and it turned out to be a good one. He won enough money to leave CBS and buy a magazine.

"I went to the drugstore to buy some shampoo to wash my hair for the evening and I asked the clerk how he felt about the election. He said nearly everyone in Kansas City agreed that Governor Dewey would undoubtedly win. I asked him if he had voted for Dewey. Who me? Not me! Back in the hotel I ordered room service while I was working. My waiter also agreed that Dewey would win, but declared he had voted for Truman. Then, to cheer myself up a little bit, I went to a nice shop and bought a blouse to wear that evening. There were no clerks, and after picking out several blouses I headed for the fitting room. They were all there, all four clerks, talking about the election. One woman said if Dewey gets elected, she was just going to take her money out of the bank and put it in a sock under her mattress. The others agreed that a Dewey win would mean financial disaster for them. I quietly counted four more votes for Truman.

"Election night was interminable. President Truman had invited the entire staff to a buffet in his suite, so we consoled ourselves with excellent food—ham, turkey, beef, every sort of delectable—but it was more like a last supper. We decided maybe singing would cheer us up.

"I played the piano; a friend sat beside me and hummed tunes while I picked out all the songs requested. Finally, at four A.M., John Adams, a much relieved John Adams, rushed into the room waving a yellow slip from the teletype to let us know that Truman was winning. He shouted, 'It was an uphill landslide!'

"I walked down the corridor from the president's suite past all the rooms where the radio broadcasters were working. They were all exhausted, stretched out on beds, speaking wearily into their microphones. The NBC broadcaster was the only one still standing and he was pressing his own rib cage, pumping air into his lungs to make his voice strong.

"I still wonder why I never placed a bet on Truman. I had been talking to the man in the street and knew that John Adams was the only boy on the bus who was right.

"By 1960, I was working at the Air Force and belonged to an informal group mainly concerned with how unjust the workplace was: Women would do the work and the men would take the credit. Men would get the promotions. Someone was distributing buttons with '59¢' printed on them because women were making fifty-nine cents to the men's dollar for the same work. It's about seventy-five cents now.

"Then this group spawned another ad hoc group that lobbied on the Hill. I recruited one woman from Virginia who'd been active in party politics. I knew she had a mimeograph machine in her basement, and I thought if we could get Flora Crater to join us, perhaps she would volunteer to do a newsletter. We became known as Crater's Raiders and were a precursor of NOW [National Organization for Women]. I'd get out of work about five o'clock at the Air Force, come home and have a sandwich, look at the mail, and run up to the Hill. We always found a place to meet. The congressional staffers were very supportive. They let us use the WATTS line at night to call all over the country. So we'd pair off and go around the Senate and the House. The congressional offices were just beginning to start their second shift around five o'clock.

"We were trying to get the ERA [Equal Rights Amendment] out of committee where it had been bottled up for twenty-six years. We blanketed the Hill at night. We carried signs. We picketed. We went over to the National Woman's Party headquarters one night to ask to use their restroom in the Sewell Belmont mansion, and they wouldn't let us. The NOW women were too militant even for the NWP. They didn't like our style. They didn't want anything to do with us. In fact, I said at the time that they would rather lose without us than win with us.

"Anyhow, it was a long struggle and we finally got the bill out of committee. But we had to make two runs of it. The first time it went all the way up through the Senate, where it was turned down. And then we had to start all over again. But the final time, Senator Hubert Humphrey (D-MN), the great liberal and one of our great supporters, was disappointing. He was on the floor for a little while and then he left. I went back and spoke to him, I guess. *The Congressional Record* looked as though he were on the floor supporting the bill all the way, but actually, he came out after the vote and put a document on the table. I think he had two papers in his hand, and the one he used depended on how the vote had gone. I loved Hubert Humphrey, but that broke my heart. We still don't have the ERA.

"Many powerful women fought us, Esther Peterson among them. They felt the ERA was going to undo all of the gains they had made for the working woman. Mary Keyserling sent telegrams to everybody in the Congress, asking them to defeat the ERA. Mary had been in the Department of Labor, head of the women's bureau, I believe, and she signed the telegram as head of the women's bureau even though she was already out and was definitely a 'former.'

"We got there early that morning and her telegram was already all over the Hill. I remember we were all just shocked. Did you *see* what Mary Keyserling *did*? And, of course, everybody got hold of a copy of it. But Mary was too late to have any impact because by that time we had friends everywhere, but still, we never got the ERA through."

Agnes "Aggie" Wolf

Like Marian Norby, WNDC member Agnes Wolf had personal experiences during the 1940s, '50s, and '60s that profoundly affected her political and social philosophy. She also transferred her career skills to WNDC where she has served as vice president for political affairs and chair of the public policy committee.

"After I graduated from Vassar, I was one of fifty interns selected by the National Institute of Public Affairs (NIPA) to come to Washington for nine months of postgraduate work and an introduction to government service. It was a wonderful program initiated by the Rockefeller Foundation. They selected fifty college graduates from around the country to be brought to Washington and given an intense indoctrination into how government works, with the hope of encouraging us to become public servants. We met in Washington in the middle of World War II in the Brookings Institution, then on Lafayette Square near the White House. I guess we came in the fall, right out of college, really, and we had to find our own money either through grants or parents.

"As an intern I decided that I wanted to study the relationship between Congress and the Executive. That's how I got to the Hill, through this program. I convinced NIPA that part of public administration was to learn about congressional/executive relationships and how they were managed. I started my internship at the Library of Congress, and it was fabulous. They provide all sorts of information requested by Congress, so I got an overview of congressional operations. Then I interned with the Senate War Investigating Committee, which was called the Truman committee after its chairman, and that was undoubtedly one of the great experiences of my life. I started as an intern at no salary and worked for about three months.

"After the internship was up, I put out a few feelers and got a job offer to stay with the Truman committee as an investigator. They had had only one woman on their investigating staff, who happened to be a Vassar graduate I knew. She was leaving to have a baby, and I came in and took her place, basically. They put me in charge of handling a number of different investigations, including the manpower needs of the war effort. I was investigating all aspects of this.

"One of them led me to meet my husband! I think ours is probably the only romance that's on file in the National Archives, because we met over a cup of coffee in the Senate Office Building cafeteria in the company of the Senate War Investigating Committee's chief investigator, Matthew Connelly. I was there with Connelly and the Navy officer who was appointed to be the liaison to our committee. He had recommended that we talk with Lieutenant Commander Alfred C. Wolf as 'just the man for me' to meet with! I remember thinking when Al walked in in his uniform, I had never seen a handsomer man, and I wished I'd had my hair done. It was hellishly hot in Washington in those days before air conditioning. We talked about the investigation and agreed to we meet later in his office to follow up on this meeting.

"There were several more meetings, and one thing finally led to another. He said he told his commanding officer that he married me in the interest of the Navy, to stop the investigation! And I married him, I said, because I needed to be a mole in the Navy! What I basically did was the research for Truman committee reports, and I was there until the infamous 80th Congress, the 'do-nothing Congress,' came into being.

"My next career progression was to the Democratic National Committee. I applied for a paid job, but there wasn't one available. They were looking around for money, as usual. So I decided I'd volunteer as a research associate or assistant on India Edwards's staff. I decided to work for them for two reasons: Obviously, we wanted Truman to win in '48; and India Edwards was a remarkable woman in every way, shape, and fashion, and it would be fantastic to work for her. In those days she was head of the women's division.

"India said in her book that during the Eisenhower administration, when Steve Mitchell did away with the women's division and integrated women with the DNC, she, along with Eleanor Roosevelt, feared that integration might mean interment. In spite of the progress we had made in the elective field, India felt that women were not as much full partners then as she and others had been in the Roosevelt and Truman administrations. This is, I think, a very important point, because today we have something called the Women's Leadership Forum, which, in effect, is the direct descendant of the women's division. It now has its own budget, however small or large. It has the complete backing of Hillary Rodham Clinton and Tipper Gore, who is the honorary chair. The question in my mind is, is the DNC going to really utilize us and put a lot of effort into getting us back into the fold where India Edwards was fifty years ago, or not?

"I got to the famous 1948 Democratic national convention in Philadelphia where people were pretty discouraged. Only India was optimistic, but then India was always optimistic. I was present when Humphrey emerged from his famous meeting and announced the civil rights plank of the Democratic Party, after which the southerners walked out. So I was there at that historic moment, seeing him interviewed as he emerged in his shirtsleeves. That's a sight I'll never forget.

"The delegates were a dispirited bunch of people. It was hot. There wasn't any air conditioning in those days. We were all uncomfortable and hot. It was after midnight when Truman came, and he gave the speech of his life. He had all of us standing on our seats afterwards, giving him absolutely the most tremendous ovation. That was the beginning of his whistle-stop campaign, and we all know what happened. This is one of my happiest memories.

"I continued to work for India only through the convention, and then I went looking around for a job. My husband was in the Navy—we married in 1945, between VE Day and VJ Day—and I ended up working for *Congressional Quarterly News Features* as one of their reporters. Then, I think it was at the end of that period that I went back to help write the final report of the Truman committee.

"My next job was on the Senate Crime Investigating Committee, nicknamed the Kefauver committee after Senator Estes Kefauver from Tennessee. That was another unique experience. The reason, I guess, I was hired was that the chief counsel had been associate counsel on the Truman committee. My main job there was as an investigator, but I also served as hearings editor. One of my roles was to investigate the infiltration of organized crime into legitimate business as a cover for their activities.

"I will now tell a tale out of school because it illustrates what really happens in political life, and the people are dead whom this would harm. As we got ready to write our final report and our recommendations to the Senate, I got a call from the chief counsel that we were going to hole up at the Shoreham Hotel and do this over a weekend of intense labor. Along with other staff, I was to show up and spend the weekend there, period. Leave home. So I said goodbye to my husband and traveled with my little suitcase and notes to the Shoreham Hotel, where we indeed did hole up. To my surprise and shock, the chief lobbyist for Seagram Industries was in our hotel suite during all this period. It turned out he was a friend and associate or a colleague—I don't know where they joined forces originally—of the chief counsel. But here was the main liquor lobbyist, if you will, on the Hill. He was famous, and his job was to keep us off the neck of the liquor industry, obviously.

"Well, we worked hard. I handed in the original draft of my report. Later, I got it back in galley form to look it over for corrections, and the whole section on the liquor industry had been deleted. So I thought about this long and hard. This was really shocking. I could not prove anything, obviously. I had to do this in some subtle way. So I decided to simply send the edited galley proof, along with a copy of the original draft, to Senator Kefauver's personal attention, saying that I thought he might like to have a look since, 'through an inadvertence,' the section on the liquor industry had been left out and I thought he might wish to make sure it was included.

"I guess I spoke with him on the telephone later, and he said, Oh, yes! Of course, I want it in there. I'll see to it. So that's how it got into the final report. I think for students of political science it is interesting to know that this is how politics actually work. People leak all the time in Washington. People do this sort of thing for what they think are good and sufficient reasons. And I felt it was in the public service to do this and Senator Kefauver obviously agreed with me. But I did it in such a way that it wouldn't reflect on anybody at the time. It certainly was something that couldn't be proved. There were no recriminations. Nobody knew how it happened. So that was the end of that. Never heard anything further.

"I was still working for the Kefauver committee when we moved to Virginia in 1949, and I think that's when I joined the club originally. But the first thing I did in Virginia was join the local Democratic Party and become a member of the Fairfax County Democratic Committee, which I have been a member of and still am a member of, lo, these many years later. In those early days I got involved with the first campaign of the newly created 10th congressional district with Ed Campbell, husband of our beloved Elizabeth Campbell, who ran for the job and lost by 363 votes or thereabouts. I was very active in that campaign, in his campaign office. Then, after the election, I went to Capitol Hill to try to get a recount of that vote and we were turned down because the committee on the Hill could only take four cases within their budget: two that might result in Republican victories and two that might go to the Democrats. They chose two other races over ours, unfortunately, and the rest is history. It took us a long time to get rid of Joel Broyhill, the Republican winner. Those were the days when I was very active in local politics.

"Of course, I also stayed active in national politics. In 1953, when Eisenhower came in, we left Washington and went into exile in Cambridge, at Harvard, along with some other Democrats. We formed a government-in-exile. My husband got his master's in public administration there, but he was mainly working on a Ford Foundation grant to Harvard to develop a five-year plan for the government of Pakistan. That led him to the Ford Foundation. We moved to Greenwich, Connecticut, a heavily Republican town, where I was elected a member of the Democratic town committee in an eleven-to-one vote, my only venture into elected politics.

"While in Greenwich, we had to make some difficult family decisions. Earlier, while I was on the Kefauver committee, I had had great difficulty conceiving, and I had been very lucky after a few years to get into the hands of a prominent doctor, a world-famous doctor who didn't see anything that was preventing us from having a baby. So he sent me to a biologist who was doing brilliant research in fertility as head of the Wistar Institute in Philadelphia. On the recommendation of my prominent doctor, the biologist took us on as guinea pigs. As the result of his research, we ended up with two children, and I later wrote up our experience for *Cosmopolitan* magazine, and they published it as a spur to women not to give up.

"After we had these two children, my husband's seven-year-old niece came to live with us. We were living in Cambridge. I thought, Well, three children! This is a nice handful! Then, unexpectedly, I became pregnant with child number four. I still thought this is a fluke and didn't use any birth control methods and got pregnant again! It was a painful decision, but my husband and I knew that we could not in good conscience do justice to a larger family.

"Nobody wants to have an abortion, and you do it only if you are at wits' end and knowing not what else to do. I went to a renowned doctor who never uttered a word, never said anything. I guess he was afraid that the walls might talk. He wrote a number on a slip of paper, passed it to me, and finally said, Just call this number and take it from there. It's safe, and you'll be in safe hands. And that's all I knew. I've told this to Kate Michelman, and I've told her I'd go on the record any time. I'd lie down on the streets and die for her.

"I called the number. It was like something out of a movie. And I was told they'd call me back. That was the first thing that happened. Obviously, checking me out. So they called back on a safe phone probably and told me exactly what I had to do, which was to appear in a seedy part of New York City in a seedy doctor's office, a front, and I was to come alone with a thousand dollars in cash, *in cash*; and my husband was not to come with me. Nobody was to come with me. I was told that the procedure would take maybe half an hour and I was to leave immediately afterwards. And that was the end of that. I did what I was told. I followed the orders. But I never in my life want to see any woman go through what I did. It was a most degrading, terrible experience.

"Unfortunately, I still thought that pregnancy was a fluke! Like a fool I got pregnant again and went through the same thing with the same person again. It was the only avenue I had in those days. After that I realized that I could not leave this to fate any longer, that I should have had my head examined. I needed to get birth control, which I then proceeded to do, and then had no more children. I thought someday I'd write the sequel to my original article: how to get pregnant and then what I went through not to get pregnant! So I've been on both sides of it, knowing how a woman feels about these procedures. My attitude toward fertility treatments and pro-choice was profoundly influenced by these experiences.

"The circumstances for women have changed tremendously since those days. That generation got older, retired, died; and the next generation entered the work force. Betty Friedan wrote her book in 1963, but it took it seven years, really, to become the bible of the women's movement. We owe her a great debt.

"But that's also when women dropped out of the volunteer sector. Club activities began to fall along the wayside because there were more options for women and much less domestic help. I had competent household help in the '70s. Big item. Big item. So that made a major difference, and I think that is one of the differences between today and when we were volunteers long ago. It accounts for some of the drop-off in membership and for some of the lower intensity of activity now compared with the '60s and early '70s. Parking at the club is also a problem, but that is another story.

"Hillary Clinton just made a wonderful speech to the Women's Leadership Forum. The forum is now five years old, and we hope it will have more clout than the women's division people have had in the past. Hoping for the best. It is certainly my hope, as vice president for political affairs and chair of the public policy committee at the club, to make every effort to get us more heavily involved with the administration offices that are working with women's groups. We need to coalesce. We need to be active coalition members."

WNDC president Ann Chapman shares a reflective moment with Adlai Stevenson at the club's Democratic Women's Day tea, 15 September 1953. Courtesy WNDC-EF Archives.

Chapter Five
AN OPEN DOOR
The Club Integrates

During the early years of the Eisenhower administration, there was no organized women's movement as it is known today, even though women's groups were the base for the continuing struggle for equality: Church Women United, the League of Women Voters, the National Council of Catholic Women, the National Council of Jewish Women, the National Council of Negro Women, the National Federation of Business and Professional Women, women's labor auxiliaries and affiliates, and women in the political parties, including members of the Woman's National Democratic Club. The National Woman's Party played a key role in promoting the Equal Rights Amendment, although Alice Paul had shifted her interest to international affairs.

President Dwight Eisenhower appointed former Women's Army Auxiliary Corps general, Oveta Culp Hobby, to his cabinet, the only high-ranking woman in his administration. Bertha Adkins, former head of the Republican National Committee women's division, received a subcabinet position as assistant secretary of Health, Education and Welfare. With the cessation of World War II, much of U.S. society assumed that women would willingly retreat to home and hearth and yield to returning veterans job gains made during wartime emergency.

Out of power for the first time in twenty years, WNDC elected high profile member Ann Chapman as president. Ann's husband, Oscar Chapman, had served for twenty years (1933-53) as assistant secretary, under secretary, and secretary of Interior in the Roosevelt and Truman administrations. Both Ann and her husband were highly regarded in Washington. Club membership increased as criticism of the Eisenhower administration mounted. Especially disturbing were Secretary of State

John Foster Dulles's atomic brinkmanship and Senator Joseph McCarthy's (R-WI) Communist witch hunt.

Ann Chapman

"I was elected president of WNDC on 4 May 1953," Ann Chapman recalled in interviews recorded in the 1970s and in 1996. "We didn't expect much activity at the club. We thought it would be a holding action and we'd be lucky to keep our membership. And we got seventy-four new members, a very active year.

"As always, we observed Democratic Women's Day in mid-September. Eleanor Roosevelt organized the first Day to commemorate the date women were admitted to the executive council of the Democratic National Committee. It was always a fund raiser and in 1953, at India Edwards's suggestion, the club had invited Dr. Mildred Otenasek, the state vice chairman from Baltimore, to be our speaker.

"Word got out that Adlai Stevenson was in Washington and intended to stop by the club. Poor Dr. Otenasek was lost in the shuffle when Adlai appeared. The cameras came, the press had gotten word, and we had an overflow crowd. Adlai was, of course, greatly honored. He always had a good time when he came to the club, and he was a great wit. He told us that he thought President Eisenhower might make a small contribution to the Democratic Party, because no one in the country was more indebted to the party at that moment. Adlai, of course, had lost to Eisenhower in the 1952 election....

"In March 1954 we did a huge bazaar, the All States Bazaar. The theme was 'Made in America' and each state had a booth. Helen Van Allen, the house manager, and her helpers moved all of the furniture up to the attic for it, a tremendous undertaking. In addition, we had committees from each state that had contacted their congressmen and anybody else they knew who would send items; and as these things arrived they had to be put up in the attic. Then, they had to be brought down in time for the bazaar and the furniture taken up to the attic. We had no elevator then, so it was all those stairs! It was a tremendous undertaking. Every state had unbelievably good things and that was the year we had the bull.

"We had a 700-pound Aberdeen Angus bull calf for auction. It was contributed by the Ralph Gardners. He was a Washington lawyer and the son of Maxwell Gardner, who had been ambassador to England. He and his wife, Fay, were very active Democrats. I believe Sam Rayburn, speaker of the House, conducted the auction. I'm trying to remember where we had the bull stashed even during the auction. I really have no idea where the bull was.

"Then, in 1956, we did a mock convention, 'Jenny for President.' The idea of the contest was to nominate a woman candidate for U.S. president. She would be called Jenny, after the female donkey. The club put a ballot box out and announced at meetings that we should vote for a member for the Jenny role. I was the winner!

"The performance was all done in mime: We pantomimed the words while a voice behind the curtain spoke. In my opening speech I announced that I was going to appoint my cabinet. Each appointee came out dressed to portray her cabinet, and they also mimed their script.

"Instead of a secretary of State I appointed a secretary of Space, and I talked about basketball-sized satellites and going to the brink of space, referring to Sputnik, of course, and to John Foster Dulles's style of diplomacy. I said that the first secretary of Space might become a true symbol of women's freedom and never come home from space at all.

"We took 'Jenny for President' to the 1956 Democratic national convention. In those years there were almost no women delegates. The city hosting the convention always had a women's committee to plan entertainment for the delegates' wives and other ladies attending the convention. So we performed in the Hilton Hotel ballroom. Many of our husbands must have been in the audience because the ballroom was filled. It was quite an experience. It would interest young women today to know that our program assured everyone that 'this is just in fun....'

"I was twenty-seven when I came to Washington the summer of 1932 to visit my uncle and aunt, Mr. and Mrs. Basil Manly, and I've been here ever since. My father was very annoyed with me because I had been teaching school in Brownsville, Texas, and I gave that up in 1930—a terrible time to be looking for a job—and eventually came to Washington. I had never been interested in politics, had never voted.

"The Progressive League had been started during the Roosevelt campaign. It was founded by Senator Hiram Johnson of California and Harold Ickes of Illinois, and was to be a rallying point for people who wanted to vote Democratic for Roosevelt but not be registered as Democrats. They could be members of the Progressive League and my uncle was very interested in that—the Manlys were very liberal Democrats—and he knew the attorney who headed the League here, who asked me if I would like to work for him.

"This was in the middle of the Depression and I was delighted with the offer. I'd meanwhile taken a secretarial course, so I went to work for the Progressive League as a secretary and got interested in politics that way. The first time I ever saw my husband was when he came up to the league's office to ask for the list of Coloradans who were registered as Progressive League people. Then I met Oscar socially through my aunt and uncle.

"After the 1932 election, the attorney with whom I was working at the league said, I'm going to the inaugural committee. Would you like to go with me? and I said, Oh yes! I've never seen a presidential inauguration and I've certainly never seen one put together. I'd be delighted. So I went to the inaugural committee with him. He was chairman of the grandstand ticket sales, so we sold tickets for the parade. Just doing the inauguration was fantastic, a great experience for me. After it was over, I went to work at the Democratic National Committee.

"In the meantime Oscar and I had started dating. He had come to Washington to be in Senator [Edward T.] Costigan's (D-CO) office and then, at age thirty-six, he was appointed assistant secretary of the Department of the Interior by President Roosevelt on 4 May 1933. I became his secretary. I don't know why Oscar and I waited so long to be married, perhaps because he had been married before. I lived with the Manlys for seven years. But in 1940, when Oscar was heavily involved in Roosevelt's campaign and had to travel a lot, we were married. He and a former governor of Wyoming had charge of the campaign in the eleven western states. Oscar was out there for three months…so I began to meet people in public life and become more interested in politics myself."

Ann Chapman was a traditional WNDC president. Politically well connected, popular, and a favorite of the Washington press corps, she raised the club's profile by devoting her energies to customary club activities. But ferment simmered beneath the surface of her presidency and erupted a few months after the end of her term when WNDC voted to open its door to a minority member. The move was vehemently opposed by southern Democrats and resulted in a bitterly fractured membership.

Olie Rauh

"Gladys Duncan was terrific. She loved politics and was very involved in local Democratic issues. That's how we got to know her," recalled Olie Rauh in a 1996 interview. "My husband, Joe, and I were members of Americans for Democratic Action, and Susie Davis worked there. Susie obviously had ideas that integrating WNDC would be a good thing.

"We put up Gladys Duncan's name because we thought it would be easier to have somebody with stature, somebody who had more connection with the world than if we'd had 'Mrs. John Smith.' But we knew there would be opposition. A lot of members were southern Democrats at that time, and if you have southern Democrats, you know there's opposition. So that was no surprise.

"Gladys was an educator, a civic leader, and an ardent advocate of home rule for the District of Columbia. She worked closely with the Democratic National Committee and was a consultant to party officials. She had great poise, great presence and dignity. Her husband was Todd Duncan, the world-famous baritone. He was the original Porgy in George and Ira Gershwin's 'Porgy and Bess' and the first black singer in the New York City Opera.

"My liberal attitude came, really, from imbibing it from Joe. We adored Roosevelt. That was our awakening. [Rauh's late husband, Joseph L. Rauh Jr., was a major influence in the growth and development of political liberalism in postwar America.] But integrating was Susie's idea, and she came to me and asked me if I would join her. I said certainly. So then the problem was, we really needed someone with more stature than a couple of young upstarts. I can't remember who went to Daisy Harriman, but anyway Daisy said yes. That's how it became a threesome. Daisy just lent her name, but that was all we needed. So that is how it was."

The virulent opposition of southern members was a startling surprise to many at the club. At a contentious 19 October 1955 board meeting, WNDC President Alice Hostetler stood her ground, insisting that the bylaws required all applications to be considered and recommended to the board. A motion to delay Duncan's application until the overall question of membership could be reexamined was defeated. There were fourteen votes for Gladys Duncan, eleven against, and one abstention. "She really squeezed by," added Rauh.

Natalie Spingarn

"Well, I was there, and this is what happened," recalled journalist Natalie Spingarn in a 1999 interview. "I went on the board when Alice Hostetler became president, a lovely lady and liberal for those times. But she wasn't a strong president in many ways. Anyway, that was when Gladys Duncan was admitted to the club.

"It was true that Susanna Davis was involved. Susie was surely fervent about integrating the club. I don't know that Daisy Harriman was active, really. She was probably brought into the effort, as we often brought her in, for her name and her prestige. Our aim was to succeed in getting Gladys into the club. You know, as John Kennedy said, Success has many fathers and failure is often an orphan.

"I must have joined the club in about 1955, and then I went on the board and was named chair of the public relations committee. That would be in the club records. Some of the members looked for a person who would be the most prestigious to integrate the club, and that was, of course, Gladys Duncan. I hadn't known Gladys well until we roomed together in Atlantic City at a Democratic women's conference, but I liked her very much. She was such a great person. Remember when we had a women's division at the DNC? They used to have conferences like that. I think there was a certain loss when the women's division went.

"I remember that Gladys and I were lying on our beds in our bathrobes, girl talking, and she told me, Natalie, I'm descended from Thomas Jefferson! Well, that's the first time that I ever heard of the whole Sally Hemmings thing, which, of course, everybody knows about now. But that's all Gladys told me. I guess the story was in her family....

"I had loved working with the WNDC members who were older than I was, who were basically southern women. Lindy Boggs was the most prominent of them, I guess. Some friends and I were discussing this in later years, saying how much we learned from them in how to deal with people, which all politics really is, you know. I didn't exactly have a gauche background and I had some manners, but nothing like they had. Lindy could melt any adversary, or anyone, for that matter. Anyway, I had a certain respect for those women and as a northerner I wasn't naive, but I didn't realize how deeply they were tied to the old southern ways. Essentially, the thing I remember is that we had a vote and that Gladys was approved for membership by written ballot. All the others that day were admitted by voice vote.

"What happened next was—and this is why I'm so specific in my mind and I've never forgotten it—the following morning at about six o'clock I had a call from a very aggressive, southwestern newspaperwoman, who proceeded to call the club's integration a disaster. She said, It's an *awful* thing and *The Washington Post* is going to have a story about it. I want to know what *really* happened!

"I knew the reporter from what was then the Woman's National Press Club, and I thought it strange that she should be engaged in the Duncan story in such a personal way. She said it was going to shake up everything. Later we heard a rumor that Hale Boggs would never be reelected from Louisiana if the club integrated. I mean, all that stuff! Complete idiocy! I suggested that the reporter call Ann Chapman. I knew that the name of a prominent former cabinet wife would calm her down. She did call Ann, who smoothed it over as best she could.

"I've been told that Ann's point of view was that we were ahead of our time. I didn't think we were ahead of our time. I thought we were just *in* the time. As I have said, I was not a naive northerner, but I never thought of us being divided. I was completely taken aback—it might have been my youth—but I didn't know that some leaders of the southern contingent felt the way they did; others I knew felt quite differently. For instance, a lawyer from the South, whose husband had served as an aide to Oscar Chapman, worked with Susie Davis in getting Gladys Duncan in. It was quite disillusioning for all of us that the anti-integration group cared so much. It was never publicized that they asked Alice Hostetler to resign, but they did, and it all could have been handled better. Alice served out her term, though.

"The *Post* did do the story. It would have been my job to smooth things over, but I really didn't want to. I said I would prefer to have them talk to Ann Chapman, who would make more impression on them. I thought it was the greatest thing since sliced bread that Gladys Duncan had gotten in! I thought it was a strike for freedom! Did Ann Chapman tell the *Post* reporter that Daisy Harriman was responsible? Whether it was exactly true or not, it was good image-making. I must add that years later, the reporter who called me at six in the morning had a change of heart, as did many other southerners. She told me she was doing some journalistic project to support minorities."

Opposition to club integration persisted and erupted again at a 17 December 1958 board meeting when the name of an applicant for membership was withheld from the governing board. The candidate, unnamed in the minutes, was Edith Sampson, a prestigious black lawyer from Chicago, who had been appointed to the United Nations delegation by President Truman.

In January 1959, a space committee convened by the governing board to study "crowded conditions at the club," recommended that WNDC membership be closed. Members in good standing had been denied attendance at functions because of limited facilities. The committee recommended that no applications for new membership be accepted until existing members could "fully exercise their rights and privileges." In March, the governing board approved the committee's recommendations.

But, arguing that they had sponsored Edith Sampson before the club membership closed, Emily Douglas, former congresswoman-at-large and spouse of Senator Paul Douglas (D-IL), and India Edwards used their considerable influence to achieve Sampson's nonresident membership.

Lindy Boggs

"Integration took place at the club in 1955, three years before my presidency," recalled Lindy Boggs in a 1996 interview, "and it was very, very difficult for some of the club members to accept. Other clubs that had integrated, that had admitted some black members, were suffering from people being upset and resigning—that was sort of the name of the game. But for goodness' sakes, the liveliest woman under the sun was our first black member, Gladys Duncan. Well, she was such a stalwart, such a thorough lady, beautifully educated and wonderfully refined and smart as a whip—and, of course, Todd [Duncan] was *so* famous.

"I was armed with the knowledge that we were coming into my presidency (1958-59) with black membership assured, with a black member on our roster. Then, a few months later, another remarkable black woman was proposed for nonresident membership. I was determined that the best way to keep our members coming to the club was to have such smashing programs that they wouldn't dare miss one! We had *the* best program chairs you could possibly imagine; and fortunately, our programs were so good, so compelling to the audience, that we had to start serving luncheon upstairs and downstairs.

"And that's when the big move to enlarge the club commenced. We sometimes even had the press people in the basement, looking at the program on closed circuit television. We didn't like to do that to the press; so we then sat them in the front hall. We really didn't make any money because we had very, very low prices for our meals; and, of course, we had to hire extra help to serve both upstairs and downstairs;

and the programs had to be limited to members only because we couldn't accommodate anybody else.

"My program co-chairs were Regina McGranery, whose husband had been the attorney general during the Truman administration; Abigail McCarthy, the wife of Senator Eugene McCarthy (D-MN); and Pauline Gore, the wife of Senator Albert Gore Sr. (D-TN); and I enticed a long list of cultural, journalistic, intellectual, legal, political, and diplomatic figures to appear at our luncheons and press conferences.

"Because Congress convened at noon, there was little other daytime activity that merited press coverage, so our programs were regularly written up in the women's pages. One good speaker led to the next, and people clamored to be on our agenda, turning it into a national showcase for the stars of the party."

Eleanor Roosevelt, Daisy Harriman, and Perle Mesta joined President and Mrs. Truman, Adlai Stevenson, Estes Kefauver, Averell Harriman, Eugene McCarthy, William Fulbright, Paul Douglas, Albert Gore, Hubert Humphrey, Mike Mansfield, John Sparkman, Henry Jackson, Stuart Symington, Lyndon Johnson, and Dean Acheson as lecturers, panelists, book reviewers, debaters, and honorees at WNDC receptions, luncheons, and dinners. Record attendance at these popular events placed a strain on club facilities.

"Then what happened," Boggs continued, "was that there was a study and a change in the membership rules internally. A committee called the Special Committee Studying the Space Problem was set up, and the membership committee was expanded to include some of the people who did the study. That committee voted to close the membership because of crowded conditions at club events. In spite of serious opposition, it all took place in the rather sensible atmosphere of a change in the rules. And what happens in those situations, as you well know, is that you have to have a committee; it has to make recommendations which have to be voted on by the board and submitted to the membership; and that's what was done...."

Constance Casey

An eloquent and articulate advocate of democratic principles, Constance Casey was elected club president in May 1959 at a crucial crossroads in WNDC history. Equally important, she was ambitious, understood politics, and was well connected in Washington political circles. Her spouse, Joseph Casey, a prominent attorney who had been a four-term U.S. representative from Massachusetts, had lost by a narrow margin to Henry Cabot Lodge in his bid for the U.S. Senate. Casey herself, at age twenty-one, had run for office in a primarily Republican district in New Hampshire, losing by only 100 votes.

Connie Casey lost no time in addressing closed membership, her resolve strengthened by a telephone call from columnist Drew Pearson, who had drafted an erroneous column about the club's membership policy. She persuaded Pearson to put his column on hold until autumn.

A study of the closed membership was undertaken during the summer. In a 29 September letter Casey informed members (and Drew Pearson) that "I am happy to tell you that the governing board will resume consideration of candidates for membership at its October meeting."

A compromise was reached to request "each member to propose no more than one candidate annually, to second no more than two candidates annually, and to sponsor no candidate unless the member [herself] had been in good standing for two years."

Twenty-two new members were approved at the October 1959 meeting of the membership committee. The committee, conscientious to extremes, "took the trouble, when data about an applicant were insufficient, to call each proposer and ask her personally to supply more details," adding that the membership committee could not assume that responsibility for future applications. The slate of candidates was posted by committee chair, Frances Scott Fitzgerald Lanahan.

To her report Scotty Lanahan added, "Now, a word about the publicity which followed the membership committee's meeting. I wish to state for the record, and on my honor, that neither I nor, to my knowledge, any member of the committee exchanged a word with…the press following the meeting. The names of the applicants we approved were posted on the club bulletin board…at which point they became public knowledge." The governing board's slate included four qualified black women.

Almost twenty years later in a prepared statement, Constance Casey noted that "1959 had been a watershed year in the life of the Woman's National Democratic Club, an illuminating year in which the club took a strong stand on an important issue that had been exacerbated rather than ameliorated by past actions.

"The club has had—most of the years of its life—a strong influence in this national community because it has stimulated a spirit of learning. It has fostered a spirit of friendship. It has cherished the quality of loyalty to its central purpose, which is working through the Democratic party to make the country a better place in which to live. And it has honored the noble motive of its founding members."

In pragmatic terms, the club leadership and its members had achieved integration by working within the spirit and the framework of the WNDC charter. They had taken an informed, principled stance that put them at odds with the majority leadership in the party in the 1950s. More than a decade later, Dr. Martin Luther King was assassinated, racial riots erupted in cities across the land, and the streets of Washington were on fire a few blocks from the clubhouse.

"Have halo. Will travel!" Former Foreign Policy Task Force chair Dorothy Dillon and her signature hat. Photo by Jewell Fenzi.

Chapter Six

DEMOCRATIC RENAISSANCE
Appointments to High Places

The turbulent decade began with John F. Kennedy's 1960 presidential defeat of Richard M. Nixon by the narrowest margin in U.S. election history. President Kennedy soon came under fire from women's organizations for departing from the traditional method of making federal appointments: He had bypassed the Democratic National Committee and was being charged with neglecting women. Names were not being generated in the same way they had been in the Truman administration when India Edwards, at the Democratic National Committee, helped move women into high positions. John Kennedy turned instead to Ivy League schools, prestigious law firms, and the corporate world to search for "the best and the brightest" for his administration.

Yet, wrote Cynthia Harrison in her study, *On Account of Sex: The Politics of Women's Issues, 1945-68,* "[t]he formation of [John F. Kennedy's] President's Commission on the Status of Women in 1961 resulted in the creation of a national network of knowledgeable women concerned about their status." Unwittingly, the federal government, with the commission and other equity legislation, had helped accelerate the modern women's movement.

"The proponents of the Equal Rights Amendment," Harrison argued elsewhere, "accomplished a legislative coup [with inclusion of the word 'sex' in the Civil Rights Act of 1964] that barred sex discrimination in employment. The derision exhibited by the Equal Employment Opportunity Commission (EEOC), the agency responsible for enforcing the law, spurred the women into establishing a new association committed to fighting for women's rights." The result was the National Organization for Women (NOW), formed at the third annual meeting of state commissions on women that had evolved from the President's Commission in Washington, where

Betty Friedan penciled the letters NOW on a luncheon napkin.

Harrison concluded, "The women's movement ultimately forced federal policy makers to consider action to ameliorate the disadvantages women suffered in virtually every part of their lives. But the federal initiatives taken before the movement's rebirth played a crucial role in forming that movement: They broke a critical stalemate among women's organizations, set much of the early agenda, and legitimated the idea of women fighting for their rights." As a result, women nationwide could be easily mobilized for the cause of women.

Esther Peterson

Esther Peterson was a titan in the movement for women's equity. Although her involvement began from "just being a woman," she recalled in a 1995 interview for *Common Cause Magazine*, Peterson believed that one person could make a difference, and she spent a lifetime proving it.

Peterson's interest in the labor movement began in the 1930s when, as a teacher in an elite private school in Boston, she discovered that the fathers of the children she taught during the day were exploiting the underprivileged garment workers she taught at the YWCA at night. When her evening students failed to appear one night, Esther went looking for them in the poorer streets of Cambridge and discovered they were on strike. The women had been making house dresses, and when company officials changed the pocket on the dresses from square to heart-shaped, the workers couldn't sew them as quickly. Their pay had not been adjusted to compensate for the more difficult work and their earnings declined.

"This was the sweatshop period. They couldn't live on what they were making," Esther Peterson recalled, and the situation made her "furious." She was soon involved in the "heartbreakers strike."

Peterson lived and worked through the Depression, the McCarthy era, the civil rights movement, the women's movement, and the consumer movement. In her various roles as a labor lobbyist; Women's Bureau director (1961-64); executive vice chair of the President's Commission on the Status of Women (1961-63); assistant secretary of Labor for labor standards (1961-69); special assistant to the president for consumer affairs (1964-67, 1977-81); consumer advisor to Giant Foods, Inc. (1970-77); and consumer activist, Esther Peterson was instrumental in bringing about hard-fought legislative victories that today many people take for granted. Among her successes are the Equal Pay Act; the Occupational Safety and Health Act and other job safety provisions; amendments to the Fair Labor Standards Act to raise the minimum wage and expand coverage; and truth-in-packaging, unit pricing, and product labeling of ingredients.

Her determination to improve the living and working conditions of the less powerful in the United States and abroad is seen first in her focus on the trade union movement, then on women and minorities, and eventually on the consumer movement. She described her position as consumer adviser to Giant Foods as "ambassador to the company for the consumer." During her presidency (1968-69) of the Woman's National Democratic Club, Peterson increased minority presence in speaker luncheon programs, drafted guidelines to standardize club operations, and advocated full membership for men.

Esther Eggertsen Peterson was born in 1906 in Provo, Utah, where she grew up in the Mormon church and developed her lifelong theme, "Do what is right; let the consequences follow." She completed her undergraduate studies at Brigham Young University before heading for a graduate degree in education from Columbia University in New York, where she met Oliver Peterson, her future husband, who encouraged and supported her lifelong involvement in the labor movement and consumer affairs.

Esther Peterson had known John Kennedy for two decades when she worked on his 1960 presidential campaign. After the election, the president gave her a choice of positions, and Peterson opted for the directorship of the Women's Bureau, the federal government agency in the Department of Labor concerned with women's labor issues. It was her forte, and she had tremendous support from the entire progressive women's labor community. Arthur Goldberg, Kennedy's influential secretary of Labor, held Esther Peterson in high regard and strongly endorsed her appointment.

After joining the administration, Peterson urged John Kennedy to appoint a President's Commission on the Status of Women. It would "provide cover" for him on women's issues and help advance an administration agenda to enable women, who were plainly going to be a permanent part of the labor force, better to fill their two roles as both wise mothers and wage-earning members of the labor force in positions essential to the development of the American economy.

In 1961, when President Kennedy appointed the members of his prestigious Commission on the Status of Women, he named Esther Peterson executive vice chair. Although she presided at meetings and set the agenda, Esther insisted that Eleanor Roosevelt serve as chair. The Kennedy administration had had rocky relations with Eleanor Roosevelt, and the president was delighted to have a way to bring Mrs. Roosevelt into the administration and smooth troubled waters. (She had objected to Joseph P. Kennedy's financial support of his son's political campaign.)

Eleanor Roosevelt agreed to chair the commission, the last public office she held. Even though she was ill, her presence lent great weight; she was the only person who could have headed the venture. When she died the following year, her chair was appropriately left empty.

After discussions lasting two years, the commission supported equal opportunity for women in the federal government, which President Kennedy instituted in 1962 simply by sending an order to the Civil Service that gender be considered only for a bona fide reason, as opposed to an agency's previous ability to recruit on a gender preferred basis.

Kennedy never overcame the criticism that he did not appoint enough women, although he brought into his administration about the same proportion of women as Presidents Truman and Eisenhower. The women Kennedy appointed tended to be in positions that women had previously held: They were not highly visible. For the first time since Herbert Hoover's administration, there was no woman in the cabinet. When Kennedy was assassinated in Dallas, Texas, on 23 November 1963, Esther Peterson was the highest ranking woman in the administration.

As president, Lyndon Johnson set about fulfilling his pledge to appoint fifty women to high-ranking government positions. He named Esther Peterson as his special assistant on consumer affairs, the single highest post he awarded to a woman. Cynthia Harrison notes: "India Edwards and Liz Carpenter both observed the irony in giving this post to Peterson who already was the ranking female member of the administration as assistant secretary of Labor, a job she retained. Both women pointed out that Johnson would be able to name more women to important jobs if Peterson did not get them all. In fact, Peterson became one of the few Kennedy appointees Johnson continued to trust. Peterson decided to relinquish the directorship of the Women's Bureau, the least prestigious of the three jobs she held, and Johnson replaced her with Mary Dublin Keyserling…a longtime worker with the National Consumers League [who] maintained a firm commitment to protection for working women."

Esther Peterson and Mary Keyserling had differing professional and managerial styles: Peterson was the supreme negotiator, the compromiser who always "compromised up," while conveying an interest in the welfare of others. She left her WNDC administrative duties principally to her vice president, Sherley Koteen. Mary Keyserling was a successful, seasoned bureaucrat, a hands-on president who took great pride in what she did for the club. Yet, while her devotion to WNDC was unquestionable, her aspirations for a volunteer organization were at times unrealistic.

Mary Keyserling

"I became WNDC president in May 1963," recalled Mary Keyserling in a 1970s interview. "It was a very exciting year for me and one of the most rewarding that I can look back on. So many things come to mind that seem interesting and significant that it's almost impossible to put them in simple order.

"One of the most significant things that year was that our President Johnson, who assumed office due to the death of President Kennedy, announced that he was going to appoint fifty women within—I don't remember the number of days he pledged. But he did make his appointments, and they were an outstanding event of 1964. As I remember, on March 13 there was a meeting called by the press women, and President Johnson that evening announced the appointment of…I believe it was more than fifty women, and I was tremendously honored to be one of them. I became the director of the Women's Bureau in March, and I retained the club presidency, having consulted with President Johnson on the appropriateness of this, and with my boss, who was Secretary of Labor Willard Wirtz. And I took time off to run the April and [the] final meeting in May of 1964.

"One of the things that I look back on with particular satisfaction was that when I became president of the club, we set up a community service committee. We had a large membership of extremely able women, and a good many of us felt that we could contribute of our time and our brains and our hearts in our own community. Even though ours was the Woman's National Democratic Club, we were made up primarily of women in the metropolitan area and the District. We committed ourselves to developing projects in the fields of housing, welfare, employment, job training, and education. We called it the Community Service Corps. [The program, announced with fanfare in *The Washington Post,* was ambitious for a volunteer organization and had limited success.]

"Another program was the Democratic Activities Committee. This was, I think, a very successful innovation. We had sent out questionnaires with respect to the interest, skills, and availability of club members in the field of Democratic activities. As a result, we recruited quite a number of volunteers to work at national and local party headquarters and in local precinct organizations. And the committee also enlisted a number of volunteers to help with Mrs. Kennedy's mail.

"Then we set up a library committee, had shelves built in that small upstairs parlor, and attempted to collect books: contributions of books by speakers, books produced by members or their husbands or members of their families. And, as I remember, that committee arranged a book discussion group that met six times during the year to evaluate books of major current interest.

"Of course, the most tragic event of 1963 was the terrible death of President Kennedy. We organized a memorial service and joined together on that sad day, December 2nd, in a tribute to John Kennedy, our beloved president, who meant so much to us all. Mrs. Hale Boggs, our former president, was one of the speakers; and then a second tribute of great eloquence was made by Arthur Schlesinger Jr. We taped that service here at the club and had copies made for purchase. We had requests, I believe, from our entire membership. I can't remember precisely, but I know that we made over 2000 copies to meet the demand….

"There were three money-raising events during my tenure. We realized about

$12,000, which was a very large sum at that time, from a benefit auction we had here at the club. Then there was a ballet, early in the year, 'Swan Lake.' That was followed by a reception and a champagne supper at the club, and Mrs. Kennedy and Mrs. Johnson were the honorary sponsors. And we had a luncheon at a big hotel, with Adlai Stevenson as speaker.

"It was important to raise sufficient funds so that we could enlarge the dining room, increase the club membership, pay off whatever debts we had, and be prepared to assume other obligations if we were to buy the property next door.

"One of the really great events that year was that President Johnson fulfilled his commitment to appoint women to high positions in the government. As I look back on that period, I believe that with his leadership there was a larger percentage of women in top positions in government, in high-level positions, than at any other time before. Esther Peterson was one of his appointees, but she had already been in the Kennedy administration. India Edwards was appointed, and she was a WNDC vice president at the time. India served as an advisor in Youth Corps employment programs in the Department of Labor. When I looked through the club scrapbooks, I noticed that an awful lot of the speakers were stressing women in the working world.

"Another event that I think was outstanding during my presidency was a wonderful tea we had for Mrs. Johnson at the end of the year. I think it was in May. It was a tremendous turnout and a lovely event. Also, we had a tea honoring cabinet wives. We had a lovely dinner one evening to celebrate Mrs. J. Borden Harriman's birthday, her ninety-third birthday. And, as I remember, Dean Acheson paid tribute to her that evening. And she was so beautiful and so alert and so much herself. On another occasion, we had trees planted in her honor here, facing Q Street. She helped plant a dogwood tree.

"Another thing that I'd like to mention. Mrs. Hamlin, an early president, had lent the club a number of charming Empire pieces, which we still have. There were chairs and sideboards, and they were really quite beautiful. And I was going to say that in her will, she left them to the club. But my recollection—and I'm thinking you may want to check on this—is that we were enabled by her estate and by her heirs to purchase these pieces. But the estate did present us with that large sofa that has the secret drawers in the arms.

"I remember with a good deal of humor a little anecdote that is a part of the history of the Hamlin Empire pieces. One day, when we had an event at the club, one of the curators of the Smithsonian was here. He told me that he was a specialist in furniture of the Empire period. He admired the Hamlin furniture, and declared it original. I asked him to look at it very carefully because I, alas, knew that they were not of the period: They were later reproductions. He said, Oh, there isn't the slightest doubt!

And, in fact, he asked us to lend them to the Smithsonian for use at a White House reception. I had the responsibility of having to tell him, toward the end of our conversation, that, alas, we knew they were not originals, that they had been made by a very skilled cabinetmaker, perhaps in the 1880s or '90s. He was very amused and very polite about it, but then said that he didn't wish to transport them to the White House for the reception.

"There were many, many programs that I remember during the year, but perhaps the most outstanding was the very last one to which we invited Adlai Stevenson, who was our representative to the United Nations. It was at the Wardman Park, in those days the old Wardman Park Hotel.

"Adlai was at my right and I was to introduce him. I was really very baffled and bewildered because he had before him a typewritten copy of a speech on international events. But he put it aside, took out some paper and was busy scribbling all the way through lunch. He was writing like mad! It broke my heart because I wanted to talk with him, but I didn't want to distract him. He was obviously concentrating on an impromptu talk. When I introduced him, he didn't deliver his speech on international events. Instead, he paid tribute to about ten of our club members with the parodies of poems that he had been composing during lunch. Mine was a Browning verse, and it's one of my loveliest treasures.

"One other incident that I remember having to do with programs. We invited a senator to speak on Thursday, and I got a call from his office the night before saying that he wouldn't be able to come. Well, there we were on Wednesday evening, and we expected a full house. What in the world can one do at 8:30 at night to get a speaker for the next day? Suddenly, I remembered my good friend, Governor [Averell] Harriman, who had been my boss when he was secretary of Commerce. I remembered having read that day that Governor Harriman had just come back from a trip to Russia, and I knew him well enough, I thought, to call him—it was past nine by then—and ask whether he might come as a pinch-hitter and talk very informally about his trip.

"I reached him and explained why we were asking him at this terribly late hour. He was a little bit distracted, and he said, Mary, are you asking me as a pinch-hitter? I said, Yes, Governor! We would never ask you on a Wednesday night to speak on a Thursday! We would invite you two or three or four months in advance because you mean that much to us! He said, Well, if I'm pinch-hitting, I'll come!

"He spoke informally. He loves us at the club, and he made the best speech I ever heard him make. He didn't have a dais. He didn't have notes. He just spoke easily, and more easily than he does when he's had to worry about it, in fact. And our club just couldn't have been more enthusiastic."

Dorothy Dillon

While Mary Keyserling worked to implement policies benefiting women in the work place, Dorothy Dillon ably utilized the new legislation to advance her career in the United States Information Agency (USIA). In retirement she used her skills and contacts to advance WNDC programs.

Dorothy Dillon graduated magna cum laude from Hunter College in 1939. She received her MA from Columbia University the following year and taught history, political science, and economics at Sweet Briar College and later at Rutgers University.

With a PhD from Columbia she entered the U.S. government in 1948. Her distinguished thirty-year career included appointments to the Library of Congress, Central Intelligence Agency, Department of State, and United States Information Agency, and took her on assignment to Guatemala and the Philippines.

Her last two assignments were as assistant director of USIA's Latin American office, where she headed a staff of 800 in twenty-two regional countries involved in information service programs, and as diplomat-in-residence at American University in Washington, DC.

"I encountered my first taste of gender discrimination at Columbia University graduate school, not by the students, who were mostly men, but on the part of the faculty," recalled Dorothy Dillon in a 1998 interview. When I applied for a fellowship to continue my doctoral studies, I was told that it would be wasted on me since I would marry and not pursue a career. Though I objected strongly to this idea, having already decided that marriage was not my vocation in life, the professor only smiled and probably thought to himself, That's what she says now. Since I had the support of my family, I was able to continue with my studies minus the fellowship.

"During my student days in New York City, one dressed more formally than today. I always wore a hat except in the summer. When I came to Washington, I realized that it was a more informal place, but I continued to wear hats as did most women and men at that time. When hatlessness came on the scene, I just continued to wear hats during the day. I did the same overseas and hats became my trademark. As cultural affairs officer, I was in a high-profile position in Guatemala and in the Philippines, and so was constantly appearing in the newspapers. If the picture was fuzzy or the back of my head appeared, everyone could identify me from my hat! Since I have long hair that I wear in a coronet braid, I have to have my hats made to sit behind the braid in a kind of halo effect. Hence my saying 'Have halo! Will travel!'

"In 1948, I was offered a job by the Department of State to go to Guatemala as a reserve Foreign Service officer. Knowing nothing about government and employment policies, I assumed when I was offered a job, I had a job. But then, I didn't hear anything more from Washington. I was teaching my last year at Rutgers, had indicated I was leaving, and had turned down several assistant professorships because I was going into government.

"When I called my contacts at State, it was to learn that there were terrible budget problems and that they had to withdraw the offer of employment. Finally, in 1951, I was offered a Civil Service slot at State in Latin American intelligence research. Then, in 1953, when the Eisenhower administration came in, two things happened. There was the Wriston program, an attempt to amalgamate the Civil Service and the Foreign Service; and there was a great RIF [reduction in force]. I was holding down two jobs, but I was new in the government and, as yet, had no status. So I was 'RIFfed' out of one of my jobs. The other job eventually moved over to the newly established United States Information Agency (USIA), taking me with it.

"Because of 'Wristonization,' I and many other civil servants were pressured to join the Foreign Service. But for personal reasons, I preferred to stay in Washington at that time. Plus, it was well known that the Foreign Service was very anti-female. There might be discrimination against women in the Civil Service, but it was even worse in the Foreign Service. I eventually joined the Foreign Service in 1960 when my Civil Service career was at a dead end due to gender discrimination. Three years later, I went to Guatemala with USIA. At that time, I was the only woman with a PhD in the country, and they began to refer to me as 'La Doctora.'

"My embassy staff was primarily male, both the Guatemalan nationals and the American assistant cultural affairs officers. I was usually the only woman at staff meetings since I was the only U.S. woman diplomatic officer in the embassy, and we had a large embassy at that time, the largest in Central America, given that the Kennedy administration's Alliance for Progress was at its height in the mid-sixties.

"Being a cultural affairs officer is a very visible position, especially in Latin America, where academic and cultural achievements are more highly valued than in the United States. One is invited to every type of cultural and educational event, generally three or four every day and night. Your picture is in the paper several times a week, and you become very well known throughout the country. If I was at a daytime event, everyone knew that 'La Doctora' had been there if they saw the hat!

"There was only one Guatemalan woman who held a high position in the government in those years. She was head of social welfare and in private life had done a great deal of work with the blind and deaf. She was a wonderful person who, despite coming from a very wealthy and influential family, had a social conscience. We became very good friends, and she began to wear hats to daytime functions!

"As I indicated, I had joined the Foreign Service to escape from a situation in the Civil Service where I had run into what we today call the glass ceiling, even though I knew that I might be going from the frying pan into the fire. However, in 1964, when the civil rights law was passed, federal government employees gained for the first time a possibility of legal redress for racial or gender discrimination. Before I left Manila in August of 1968, I filed charges against my agency.

"By the time I returned to Washington—I spent a month on leave traveling in Asia and Europe on my way back from Manila—I found that I had really shaken up USIA. I was the first woman in any of the foreign affairs agencies to bring charges of gender discrimination, so everyone was taken by surprise. The equal opportunity officer who handled my case did an excellent job and turned up even more instances of job and promotions denial than I had been aware of. The end result was that findings of gender discrimination were placed in my personnel file and I finally obtained my promotion into the Senior Foreign Service.

"I retired from the government in 1978, and the day after I left USIA, I became the founding director of the Washington Center for Latin American Studies, a center representing the Latin American programs of the Consortium of Universities of the Washington Metropolitan Area. In 1984, I was appointed by the secretary of State to the Foreign Service grievance board, where I served as arbitrator for four years. During this period, I joined WNDC.

"I started to attend meetings of the club's foreign policy task force and became involved in the discussions centering on Central America, a hot issue at the time, given the Reagan administration's intervention in that area. In order to help the club come up with a policy position, I recommended that it undertake a study tour of Central America. Human rights violations were committed by all sides in the civil conflicts in Guatemala; El Salvador; Nicaragua; and, to a lesser extent, Honduras, which was a staging area for U.S. intervention in El Salvador and Nicaragua. Even Costa Rica, with the only real democratic government in the area, was being drawn into the conflict.

"The club agreed to the proposal if I would lead the tour and make the arrangements with the U.S. embassies in the five countries to set up appointments with the individuals and groups that we wished to interview. Given the strained relations with the Sandanista government in Nicaragua, I had the Nicaraguan embassy in Washington arrange our appointments with its government officials, while I asked the U.S. embassy in Managua to set up our meetings with the opponents of the Nicaraguan government. On February 3, 1987, twelve of us set out for a two-week study tour of Central America, beginning in Guatemala and working our way south to Costa Rica.

"I had warned the club participants—eleven members plus one husband—that we would be working twelve or more hours a day and that there would be no time for 'tourist-y' things except on the weekend. Despite the long hours we had a marvelous trip. We interviewed over a hundred Central American leaders of various political views and from a variety of fields—politics, economics, labor, culture, education, religion. Fortunately, former colleagues of mine from USIA and ambassadors I had known from my time in the Foreign Service were still around in the countries that we visited.

"Our group received excellent cooperation from our embassies, including embassy receptions, which enabled us to meet many more people than those with whom we had in-depth interviews. We were exposed to a variety of views on what U.S. policy should be toward Central America, ranging from those who expected and hoped that the U.S. would invade and overthrow the Sandanista government in Nicaragua to those who strongly criticized the Reagan administration's intervention in Central America. A high Sandanista official, who had a PhD from Harvard and spoke excellent English, entertained our group at his home and gave us a well-prepared lecture on the evils of U.S. policy and the achievements of his government. I rather startled him with a proposal to demilitarize all of Central America à la Costa Rica. He was intrigued with the idea, but said he would have to think about it. Finally, a question to which he had no stock answer!

"Once back home, our group prepared a paper based on our findings. We made policy recommendations which the club adopted. We strongly supported the peace efforts of the Central American countries that came out of their presidents' meeting in Costa Rica. The meeting took place while we were in San Jose and the presidents stayed at our hotel. These efforts eventually led to peaceful resolutions of the civil wars, democratic elections, and a Nobel Peace Prize for Oscar Arias, the president of Costa Rica, who had called the summit meeting in 1987.

"Subsequent to our study tour I became co-chair, then chair of the foreign policy task force until 1996, when I was elected vice president for programs. During those years, in consultation with task force members, I prepared the club's position papers on foreign policy issues, the foreign policy sections of the club's annual positions-in-brief publication, the resolutions for the club's contributions to the annual meetings of the National Federation of Democratic Women, and the club resolutions submitted to the 1992 and 1996 Democratic Party platform committees preparing for the national convention.

"During 1988-89, I served as chair of the international affairs program committee, an interesting time since it was a presidential election year and we concentrated on campaign issues prior to November. One of the high points was Madeleine Albright's appearance as a speaker in her capacity as senior foreign policy advisor to the Dukakis campaign. We had a great turnout, including the media, both domestic and foreign, who descended on her like a swarm of locusts the moment she came in the door of the club. With my long U.S. government association, I was interested not only in her foreign policy role, but in her career as a woman."

Lady Bird Johnson

While President Lyndon Johnson appointed women to high-level federal positions, Lady Bird redefined the role of first lady. Her approach was more reminiscent of Eleanor Roosevelt than of her more immediate predecessors. Mrs. Johnson had frequently helped with ceremonial responsibilities in the Kennedy administration and had already hired her own personal staff, with Bess Abell as social secretary. In an unprecedented move, she created the position of press secretary to the first lady, and appointed Liz Carpenter.

In marketing her image and in discussing her own political activities in public, Lady Bird Johnson let the public see her legislative role. While ER played down her policy influence, Lady Bird originated the Highway Beautification Bill directly from her office. It was a very controversial position for a first lady to take. The bill extended beyond highway beautification to include land use planning, soil conservation, and restrictive use of billboards and pesticides.

On yet another precedent-shattering occasion, Mrs. Johnson boarded the 'Lady Bird Special' on a whistle-stop campaign to win back the white South after her husband had signed the Civil Rights Bill of 1964. She barnstormed the southern states, making forty-seven formal speeches to an estimated 500,000 people and helping LBJ win six states that Barry Goldwater had considered his own.

Mrs. Johnson kept a careful, detailed diary of her White House years, a portion of which she later published. In 1964, after rereading notes and clippings from her train trip during the campaign, she wrote in her book, *A White House Diary:* "I am increasingly dismayed that I missed recording some very important days and nights.... We were living so rapidly that I was simply too busy and too spent to have an hour or a moment with my recorder.... There were moments of high elation during the campaign. I wouldn't take anything for the Whistlestop through the South—forty-seven stops in four days! [It was a] very special time, those four most dramatic days in my political life."

Lindy Boggs had accompanied Lady Bird on the whistle-stop tour through the South, one of many moments of high drama in her long and distinguished political life. Along with other WNDC members, she was also instrumental in helping Mrs. Johnson organize Head Start.

Lindy Boggs

"In 1960, a group of us very active in the club had been sort of advance people for Lyndon Johnson's vice-presidential train trip. Then, in 1964, we went with Mrs. Johnson on a 1200-mile, whistle-stop trip through the deep South a month before the election. We all learned some things between those years, and by the time of our second trip, the 'Lady Bird Special,' we realized that we should set up in a central location and invite the people from the region to meet with us, at which time we appointed a coordinator there and went on to the next town.

"So, when we were promoting Head Start, computers being less usual than now, Sarge Shriver, who headed the Office of Equal Opportunity [OEO], had his computers punch out for us the 300 neediest counties in the U.S. We had about a month to try to find sponsors for the Head Start program in those particular counties. Of course, a great many of them were in the rural South and Mrs. [Harold] Barefoot Sanders of Texas, one of our people on the Lady Bird advance team, reminded me that we had left a regional coordinator just the year before.

"I was invited to attend the White House tea that announced Head Start, after which Dr. Julius Richmond, the project director, gave me an office in a building on 15th Street from which we could answer correspondence and call our contacts in the South to find sponsors for the Head Start project. I asked for seven tables, two desks, nine unrestricted telephone lines, and a lot of flexibility. A group of cabinet wives, congressional wives, and wives of Supreme Court justices—most, if not all, were members of the Woman's National Democratic Club—volunteered to help. One hundred and twenty-five young federal interns gave up four weekends to travel to these 300 counties in an effort to help them develop a program and an application. They were the content people and we were the organizers.

"Many of these counties in the South had wonderful people who helped us with the Lady Bird train. We called on them again and they were very enthusiastic about the Head Start concept, these wonderful black ministers who knew it would benefit the children in their communities. The ministers had space in their churches that usually had a dining hall, a good kitchen. Many of them had busses; had wonderful volunteer ladies who would conduct the children across the street; examine them to see if their throats, ears, etc. were all right. Our phone calls signed on many of these wonderful people.

"So because of the 'Lady Bird Special' we were able to set up 267 of the 300 neediest counties in the four-week time frame. The campaigning experience was a big help in setting up Head Start because we had recruited all those contacts in the South. Another reason for Head Start's success is because it was seen as Lady Bird's program. She had announced it at the White House tea, to which leading American women were invited, and that made the media decide that we were a 'society' event. Most Head Start stories appeared on the society page, and the public saw Head Start as a nice, acceptable program. Other OEO programs did not fare as well because they were considered 'news.'

"The next step was that Head Start became an ongoing program. At first, it was envisioned almost as a summer program before a child went to school so that children in poverty would be able to be on a par with the other children in their classes:

They would know the stories, the poetry, the songs; they'd know how to use the faucet, how to do all the things that the other children did. Then it became obvious more time was needed with these little children, and so many school districts didn't have kindergarten that that was the reason for making Head Start a year-round program. It grew from there.

"It was an absolutely wonderful experience. Everybody assumed he or she could help a little child. You could get volunteers by the dozens. We could engage some of the parents and teachers to go on field trips and do things of that sort. But we never wanted the parents to feel we were taking the children away from them or from their way of life. We were just trying to give them a head start on what they would need in the rest of their school experience. It's been going almost thirty years now, but Head Start has never had enough money to take care of all of the children. It's been very sad in some places for some of the children whose siblings have been privileged to go and they haven't. We still have work to do."

As a southerner, Lindy Boggs had firm opinions about the role of women in politics, especially when tensions between the Democratic National Committee and WNDC erupted once again. Katie Louchheim at the Democratic National Committee, like her 1930s' predecessor Molly Dewson, felt that women should be allied with the national and state committees rather than expending their energies in traditional women's clubs.

"Katie Louchheim was vice chair of the Democratic National Committee, and she wanted the state party organizations to be much more involved with the DNC. With its affiliated clubs, WNDC had a contact, although somewhat uneven, with the state organizations. Some of them were very, very good and some of them weren't, but we still had a connection with the states. Katie wanted to strengthen and solidify the state organizations, to involve them much more with the DNC. She felt that the club was really diluting that contact, that women were belonging to our affiliated groups instead of backing the DNC. So Katie really was the one who discouraged WNDC's 'state affiliated clubs,' as we called them, and went about trying to form state Democratic clubs among the women to get them to back the national committee.

"Well, that bothered me because I was from the South and I felt that southern women were more comfortable affiliating themselves with the Woman's National Democratic Club, expressing their interest and loyalty by getting the club's literature and copies of speeches that had been given at WNDC, and by feeling that they could come and use the clubhouse if they were in town. Rarely did that happen, but it was available. But there were others in the club who felt that most of the affiliated clubs were just sort of very ineffective and didn't contribute much to the club anyway.

"In any case, the club voted to change the bylaws. For a couple of years after that the women in the states were having trouble getting connected with the DNC. But it's very interesting, because the National Federation of Democratic Women grew out of that decision. The idea for the federation was born at a meeting I attended in Tennessee that was held under the auspices of the state national committee women and state national chairmen of the party. It was there that the idea was born of having the federation, that that type of organization was needed to organize women nationally and strengthen their ties to the DNC. So it's become, of course, a national organization."

Former first lady Lady Bird Johnson at the park named in her honor on the Virginia bank of the Potomac River. In 1973, WNDC raised funds to purchase benches for the park. Department of Interior, National Park Service photo, courtesy WNDC-Archives.

Chapter 7
THOROUGHLY MODERN MEMBERS
"Hair" Raising Programs

Ecology, drugs, welfare, guns—problems, problems, including death and taxes, so many that they seem overwhelming. But never underestimate the power of informed women when they know the facts and swing into action."

WNDC News, March 1973

Throughout the 1970s the nation reeled from the Watergate scandal and President Richard M. Nixon's monumental disregard for the institution of the U.S. presidency. An influential group of women, energized by the legacy of the New Frontier and the Great Society, made constructive use of these social forces to advance the political agenda of the Woman's National Democratic Club. Watergate had mobilized the Democratic electorate. The club became a rallying place. Its goal: Return the White House to the Democrats in 1976. Cabinet and congressional wives and other powerful club leaders supported controversial measures and organized herculean fund raising events. It was a heady time at 1526 New Hampshire Avenue.

But there were dissenting voices when luncheon programs featured feminist speakers and sociologists who explored the new sexual mores. The cast of "Hair," the exuberant 1960s musical, gave a performance at the club, causing at least one member to threaten resignation. The subjects of contraception and abortion were also controversial. In 1996 Olie Rauh recalled, "I had been working for Planned Parenthood, and when I was on the program committee, I tried and tried to persuade the club to let me get somebody from Planned Parenthood to speak. I never could get anywhere and was very discouraged. I was also angry about the committee's attitude toward family planning. There was a lot of talk about abortion at that time, but the club didn't want to talk about abortion. Finally, they agreed to let me bring in the Washington Improvisation Theater, a terrific group of teenagers who acted out situations having to do with teenagers, like pregnancy. Drugs weren't discussed, but they did talk about abortion. That, I think, was the best program I had anything to do with."

WNDC presidents Margo Davis and Marian Driver helped guide the club through the decade, their leaderships bracketing the 1970s.

Margo Davis

Margo Davis, WNDC president from 1970-72, was a 1933 graduate of Smith College with a background in journalism and press relations. Protesting that her talents were few, she nonetheless was a member of the Women's National Press Club and her articles appeared in *Collier's* and *McCall's*.

"I wrote a message in the first newsletter published after I became president," recalled Margo Davis in an undated interview, "that my hope was to provide an open forum for open discussions in which tolerance, courtesy, and good humor would prevail. I tried to inspire or encourage the program chairmen to experiment, to involve the greatest number of WNDC members in the maximum variety of pursuits. I'm sure that I didn't succeed 100 percent, but that was the chief aim of my presidency. I must say that whether I succeeded or not, I certainly enjoyed being president. It was a great deal of fun.

"I have a vivid memory of the reception that we gave for Lady Bird Johnson when her book, *A White House Diary*, was published. It was a sellout event. We arranged for much of the profit from the book sales to go to Mrs. Johnson's favorite cause. At that point, it was the Lady Bird Park on the way to National Airport, the one with the graceful statue of birds and waves.

"Somewhat to our surprise, we were able to donate over $2,400 to help buy park benches. I remember thinking that was a very large sum of money, but, as a matter of fact, it doesn't buy very many park benches. They're more expensive than one would think—another thing that you learn by being president of the Woman's National Democratic Club!

"Somehow or other, as you'll hear over and over again, we're always trying to make money in this club. That's, of course, true of most clubs. But our expenses to run this wonderful, historical building are high; and our dues, as you know, are among the lowest of any club in Washington with facilities like ours. Dues were even lower, of course, in the early 1970s than they are now; and since it's always difficult to raise dues, we were always faced with fund raisers.

"I would like to point out for the record—because I remember all the trouble it caused—that I got the chef's salad on our luncheon menu! I felt that a salad at lunch might enable some of us to get into a size smaller dress. I'm pretty sure I was one of them. You would think all the members would agree, Sure, we can have a chef's salad! It wasn't that easy, but I prevailed.

"What else did I fight for? One thing I remember was the projection screen in the dining room. Films were important, and we could buy a screen for a couple of hundred dollars instead of renting one. It would be a great addition to the club. Well, I had opposition, and it was only when I said I'd pay for it myself that the house committee agreed to get it. I think it has been one of the most useful pieces of equipment that we have. As I look back, it's astonishing that one has to have foolish fights for such good causes.

"The club could no longer afford to run on its traditional summer schedule. That is, we pretty much closed down. Our expenses had increased; taxes and insurance had to be paid year round; and, what's more, our staff couldn't afford to work only nine months a year. We had to have some kind of summer income.

"We evolved the idea of light summer-night programs, most of them centered around films. One summer we got the 'Civilization' series which had been shown at the National Gallery. We rented the films for a nominal sum; and since many members had missed them at the gallery, the films were a very popular series. I think we showed about four, following dinner, of course. Another summer we showed old films: 'The Gold Rush,' 'Casablanca,' and 'Grand Hotel.' They were a lot of fun. That was before the Kennedy Center's American Film Institute.

"Our most exciting programs were the political ones. We had all of the presidential candidates in the fall of 1971 and the spring of 1972. They were great. Maybe we could say Hubert Humphrey was tops because so many of us are so fond of Hubert Humphrey for his loyal service over the years. I remember John Lindsay was a mighty attractive man, and we were so glad that he had decided to become a Democrat.

"There's one program I especially remember: Senator Walter Mondale spoke to us and I had the honor of sitting next to him. There was talk then that he might be running for president; so I just asked him point blank, Would you like to be president? He said he didn't think so because he felt it would require too much sacrifice of his home life. I'm sure he came to that conclusion again when he was running because he said there was just no time for anything else. But, at any rate, now that he is vice president, it's interesting to speculate. I would certainly love to have the opportunity to ask him again, wide-eyed, 'Mr. Vice President, would you like to become president?' I wonder what he'd say.

"In 1971, we constructed a temporary stage in the dining room and had the

Washington cast of 'Hair' perform some of their songs. 'Hair,' you will remember, was a 1960s musical with great freedom of youthful expression—the Age of Aquarius—and not all of our members found it appropriate club fare. But it was one of the gayest, most enjoyable programs I can ever remember. The spirits of the 'Hair' cast were absolutely infectious. Everybody ended up happy, laughing and singing. That will long be one of my favorite memories.

"We had a series of evening programs on the Nixon presidency: his leadership, the economy, and international affairs. I well remember that one of my heroes, James McGregor Burns, was a panelist. Doris Kearns [Goodwin], Averell Harriman, Alice Rivlin, and Henry Royce were also on the panels.

"Another evening series was on the sexual revolution. Milton Viorst and his wife, Judith, were moderators for two of the evening panels. Kate Millett spoke on 'Sexual Politics.' We were probably forward-looking in scheduling that series. There had been a sexual revolution and we felt that the subject should be discussed. Programs are the most important thing about our club, the raison d'être, and the secret of our success."

Marian Driver

"The funniest thing that happened while I was president," Marian Driver recalled in an undated interview, "was a letter from a man in Alaska. I don't remember his name, but here's the letter:

```
Dear Female Democrats,

    In Alaska the female Democrats need a big, female,
Democratic Party club building in the city of
Anchorage, Alaska; and in this building we need a
Democratic civic center with a bingo hall and a dark-
room and a dance hall and a swimming pool and a gym
and a game room for the female Democrats. They need
a convention hall and conference rooms, boards of
directors' rooms, a big committee room and adminis-
tration offices, ticket counters, a dining room and
a kitchen and a sky room and a basement and a first
floor lobby and a big bar for drinking.
    We need a political science center so that the
public can learn to understand their government bet-
ter and a program called Women for Political Action—
all in the female Democratic club building. I am pro
women for politics, and I am a man. In this demo-
cratic society we need programs like that, and I hope
to see more female Democrats in public office.

Sincerely,...
```

"We answered the Alaskan letter and said that while we appreciated the fact that this would be a marvelous addition to the party, we were perennially short of money and weren't sure exactly how we could swing it for Anchorage.

"Like the man in Alaska, I have a dream for the Woman's National Democratic Club and the Democratic Party. We own this house. We own the house next door. And the only thing left in the block is the [old] Dupont Plaza Hotel. I hope someday the Democratic Party will buy the hotel and have the Democratic National Committee housed therein, and then this will be the Democratic block in Washington. Let's do it!"

Sherley Koteen

"When I lived at 1310 New Hampshire Avenue in the 1950s, Dupont Circle was where young mothers rolled baby carriages," recalled Sherley Koteen in a 1999 interview, "and because it was woodsy—there were lots of trees—they made it a sort of playground for the children. Dupont Circle then was still a residential neighborhood. There were some upscale, some downscale residences. The clubs were there: WNDC, the Sulgrave Club. What else was there? The Washington Club. Much, much earlier, New Hampshire Avenue and that area had been known as the 'Champs d'Élysées' because of a Mr. Champs who lived there.

"By the '70s, when I was president of the club, there was, of course, considerable change. There were many more office buildings and it had become a more professional area. Well, back in the '60s, the circle itself had been home to the hippies and the drug culture. They splashed around in the fountain and really changed the whole complexion. But that gradually tapered off and we reclaimed the circle, and now it's an upscale neighborhood. Of course, the District was getting into the high crime era, but I don't believe that kept people away from the Woman's National Democratic Club during daylight hours.

"If anything kept people away from the club it was the parking. Access, as you well know, was getting better with the Metro, which opened in the late '70s. That certainly helped, or I think it helped attendance at the club, but people still wanted to rely on their cars. But the central problem was the changing lifestyles of educated women: So many more were spending their days and their energies in the work place and the professional world. I am confident that almost every volunteer organization was similarly affected by this shift in the focus of women's lives. They just didn't quite have the time, even though they had the inclination and the interest.

"My presidency in 1972-74 was strongly impacted by Watergate. It was Watergate almost from beginning to end. Well, not quite, but that, if anything, mobilized Democratic men, women, and children and had the attention of the whole United States. At the club you could hear what was happening. It was a rallying place. People wanted to come together and confront this terrible situation. So the club was very active during that period. The membership was high. Attendance at luncheons was high.

"I well remember the luncheon when we were expecting Harriet Cipriani at the head table. Harriet at that time was vice chair of the Democratic National Committee. She was very late arriving at the luncheon. Odd, for Harriet, who is always very prompt. When she arrived, I asked Harriet if she had run into traffic. I was curious about her being late because she never was; and she said, Well, the darnedest thing happened today! I went into my office at the Democratic National Committee. Somebody had come into the office and rifled all of the files, broken open the drawers in my desk! I cannot imagine what it was they wanted! We didn't have any money there. We didn't have any expensive equipment, clerical equipment. It was a mess! That was the break-in. At that point, none of us recognized what was happening at all, but that was it.

"Well, the whole country was electrified. The club was mesmerized. As the story unfolded we saw Watergate as an attack on the institution of the presidency. It was a wake-up call that sent us in a new direction. But more on that in a moment.

"I was trying to think back so I can place Watergate in the broader history of the club at that period. We were also somewhat still in the glow of the Kennedy legacy and the Great Society. Many of the members of the board of the club, many of the movers and shakers, were cabinet wives and congressional wives; and their identity and activity with the club, I think, was quite an inspiration and brought others in. Definitely.

"Lady Bird Johnson herself was quite devoted to the club. On one of our anniversaries, the fiftieth, we dedicated the little club garden to her in recognition of her environmental awareness program and I'll have to say the garden dedication was a little bit of a celebrity draw. But almost all of our luncheon meetings were just that. The club was regarded as a major forum where our 'teachers' were practicing experts in their fields.

"Inviting celebrated experts to speak at luncheons on a wide range of issues was highly attractive to much of the membership, but others wanted greater emphasis on planned, in-depth study. For one, Delia Kuhn, who was a journalist and wife of journalist Bernie Kuhn of *The New York Times,* said, What the club's doing politically is just not enough. Our membership wants more. They want better education; more thorough, in-depth education on political issues; and they want to be more active. So we've got to do something.

"It was a struggle to get any kind of political action committee going, for many reasons. One of them was a concern that we would become subject to business taxes. We considered ourselves members of an informal social group, not a corporation or other business enterprise. We had no status of any kind under the tax laws. One of our legal advisors was Carol Agar Fortas, and she hit the ceiling when we said we wanted to do something of a much more active political nature. She said, You can't do that! You can't do that to this club!

"We got other pro bono advice as well. Madeleine Albright met with us several times to try to sort things out, to see what we really wanted to accomplish, how we should organize to accomplish it. She wasn't giving us a legal opinion. We called ourselves a political action committee, which didn't have the same connotation as PAC does today. We could only devote a few programs to the political action committee, but the women who were involved really worked out wonderful discussion groups and panel discussions of all kinds; and again, we had a lot of pro bono authorities on various issues. It was totally issue oriented. We weren't hitting the pavements at that time to support candidates, but we were into issues. That seemed to be the safest way to go. It's one thing to educate your membership on issues and another to go out and raise money or do other things for candidates.

"And that's when the task forces started as part of the political action committee. Well, we very quickly changed political action committee to educational committee! Not so quickly, perhaps, but that was a wise thing to do. We tried to work out some priorities. I can't remember what task forces there were. World food problems. Task force on women's issues. Task force on the economy. Oh, and WNDC officially endorsed the Equal Rights Amendment. The club also set up a talent bank of qualified women, making them available to government or private organizations or committees looking for women to speak or fill positions. I don't think that initiative got very far.

"In the beginning it was a relatively small corps of women, and even as late as the '70s, even within the club, there was some resistance to women getting into all these political activities. So it was a gradual educational process. There were more people who wanted to be active than the other way around. They really did. It was not just something foisted on the membership. Delia [Kuhn] got us started during my presidency, but it just gradually built up and we didn't make any big-time announcement about it. There were meetings and discussions. Much of the time during my administration was spent trying to sort out how we were going to work and how we were going to avoid any problem with our tax status, so we didn't swing into high gear. The (c)(7) tax status gave us a lot of leeway. We are permitted to lobby and to do other things political, but we cannot raise money for or actively support a specific candidate. I think that's correct. We can't contribute to his or her campaign.

"The task forces as we know them now are about twenty-five years old. My sense was that if I did anything for the club during my presidency, it was getting the task forces organized. Not that I did it alone; it was these really dedicated, determined women. I was determined with them, but they carried the ball. What I did was, as I say, worry about the legality of the thing and how to handle it. The club really needed it and just couldn't give up. We'd really had enough! President Eisenhower was neither here nor there as far as moving the country forward, and Richard Nixon we just thought was an albatross. Well, he was the worst person since [Senator Joseph] McCarthy (R-WI)! We were really, really angry about that! So, yes, I think Watergate—you don't like to say something was started because of negative feelings—but Watergate was an awakening.

"When the task forces got started, they had educational programs in some depth. I guess we called them symposiums or some grand name like that. It wasn't really a symposium, but just inviting people from the State department—the civil service or the diplomatic service, from the executive departments and agencies, from the Hill, and from the think tanks, who were experts in the fields that we were studying. It was also the beginning, I think, of interest in the environment. That was very slow to take hold. A lot of people thought that was a nonissue: Why are we spending our energy on this subject when there are so many more pressing things? Lady Bird created the awareness. She didn't like the term 'beautification.' She really preferred 'environmental awareness,' and there was a group at the club who realized that this was the beginning of concern for a broad range of environmental issues. The people I'm thinking of were those who were worried about holes in the ozone....

"Esther Peterson was consumer advisor in the Carter White House and then, during her term as WNDC president, I was her vice president. Esther, of course, was a tremendous inspiration: When she presided at a luncheon or whenever she was there, she was just so enthusiastic. Everybody was with her, and she did a lot for the stature of the club. Esther, however, simply did not have the time to be a full-time president. So that's when I got my feet wet. I really was her backstop and was at the club a great deal. After her presidency I still did not feel that I was ready for the presidency, so Margo Davis said that she would take over. She was only going to stay for one year. Then there was a brouhaha in the club about a successor to Margo. I don't know that we need to put that in, but it is part of the story.

"Well, with good reason the nominating committee thought that the club really needed a sparkling, well-known person after Esther. The nominating committee met at the end of Margo's one year, and to the surprise of a lot of people, nominated Polly Shackleton as president. Polly didn't have any time, and not only that, she really had no real association with the club. Nevertheless, she was nominated. My friends got into high dudgeon and organized a major political fight within the club! At any rate, there was a big campaign. Polly would not withdraw her name. She said, By George, they nominated me and I don't see any reason I should withdraw!

"She was a member of the club, of course, but she just wasn't active. So the ultimate compromise was that Margo took a second term. That's how she got her two years, and then at the end of that time, I was nominated. Nothing much to it except that it was one of the few times when the club got into a political scramble....

"When did I join the club? Lindy Boggs was president. I believe it was about 1958. Much later, Mary Keyserling was president of the club. She was much more of a hands-on person than you would imagine. She outlined a very comprehensive, extensive social service program for WNDC. She really wanted to make a difference in that club, but I don't think it worked out very well.

"On another issue, Mary was against the Equal Rights Amendment, as was Esther Peterson, because they didn't want to jeopardize any legislative gains they'd made for women in the work place. They were very familiar with sweatshop labor and all the things they'd fought to overcome. There was a fairly large segment in the club who really did not support the Equal Rights Amendment 100 percent. But it was adopted as club policy—I won't say it just squeaked through—but it was certainly by no means unanimous. There were a lot of luncheon programs on the ERA. We had a lot of speakers both pro and con, and I think we had more speakers who were against the ERA than for it. It was an odd time, and the club did reflect the change in women's attitude toward women.

"I don't know whether we had as much fun in later years. We had a lot of wonderful events that really raised money and brought the club together in earlier times, particularly in the late '60s. There were the fairs, the all-state bazaars. We had a wonderful play. It was a musical, 'Faze the Nation.' Everybody got involved in that and worked their tails off! Really working themselves to death. I remember the incredibly courageous thing we did in taking a huge block of tickets for the Lippizaners, their first appearance in Washington. Oh, God, we took thousands of tickets, thousands of tickets! With this little membership, you know! By George, it was such a sellout that people were calling day and night! Can we get extra tickets? Can we get any tickets? And, of course, there were a lot of disappointed people. That was during Mary Keyserling's administration, I think. Kay Halle was one of the most forceful personalities in the club.

"Kay was a journalist, a well-connected woman from the Halle department store family of Cleveland. At any rate, Kay would decide that the Woman's National Democratic Club should take 14,000 tickets for the Lippizaners, and she didn't ask anybody's permission. She just did it! She did that kind of thing. But she also knew everybody in this world. She brought Alistair Cook, host of Masterpiece Theater, to the club. She brought John Kenneth Galbraith. Kay was sort of a law unto herself. She decided that the clubhouse needed redecorating and she set about to see that it got redecorated! I don't know what motions were passed or what funds were raised to get it done. Kay was one of the, again, movers and shakers. She brought Pamela Harriman to the club with Averell. That was really a blowout for the 50th anniversary with Harriman and Carol Channing. They were all sitting at the same head table, but who was the big success? Liz Carpenter. She delivered! And that was a day to remember for all of us because they all spoke fabulously. They really did.

"I was chair of the ways and means committee when Alva Dawson and some others started the Clothes Donkey. It certainly was a novel idea at the time, and we didn't know whether it was going to go or not because we weren't sure that people wanted other people's secondhand clothes. It raised a lot of money, and the whole second floor of the club was the showroom. It was just a one-time-only event lasting two or three days.

"I did attend the Carter-Mondale convention in New York, but the club was simply invited to help hostess; and the only reason we were given any kind of role was because Gretchen Poston, a very political young woman although she was a late starter and a late bloomer, knew everybody on the Democratic National Committee. Somehow, she got involved in the convention and then saw to it that we were dragged along. But mostly, as I say, we were hostesses and go-fers. Now, if somebody down on West 12th Street needed some tickets, we would run from 48th Street. I think I spent more time on subways than in the convention hall and not doing anything terribly thrilling except *being* there! Gretchen, as we know, went on to be the White House social secretary.

"After the convention, Joan Mondale was just sort of catapulted into a difficult position. There was no money for a secretarial staff for her. Whatever funds there were, were for the presidential campaign, not for the wife of the vice presidential nominee. After Carter and Mondale were nominated, a flood of correspondence came to Joan and she had no staff to handle it. Bess Abell, who was her exec, said maybe the club can help, and she came over to see what we could do. That's when we had 'Joan's Den' and that really was an episode. We set it up in the basement; about a dozen women were involved. We borrowed typewriters here and there, old-fashioned typewriters, and women came in as volunteers. It was the most primitive operation in the world because half the people who came in really couldn't type.

"We answered each question with a personal letter. The answer depended on who was handling the typewriter that day! In the beginning there were no form letters. Then we figured out we had to organize a little better. But it wasn't all that bad, and I think a lot of good personal responses went out. Joan's Den didn't last forever, but Joan and Bess were very grateful for our getting them out of this bind. The first reception that Joan held after the election, when they were in the vice president's house, was for the Woman's National Democratic Club.

"Later, the idea of volunteers to handle correspondence was picked up by Hillary Clinton. Hers is a big, big operation, but it, too, involves many of our members; and

I think a lot of the things that Joan did, or that happened during her time, were carried over and picked up in the Clinton White House, such as the White House collection on American crafts.

"Joan Mondale was the originator of the idea. Her great support was for the arts, and each year she invited a museum director from each region of the country to bring art from the museums in his region to the vice president's house. She borrowed a collection of Christmas tree ornaments made by American craftsmen from the American Craft Museum, the very same thing that Hillary did, except that Hillary invited the craftsmen directly to make ornaments for the White House permanent collection. So there was a lot of carryover there.

"Well, after the 1977 election I took the job as manager of the vice president's residence for the Mondales. It was fabulous, but whew! They were the first family to live in the official residence. It's an old Victorian heap that had always been sort of managed the way a ship was built and maintained because it was first the home of the chief of Naval Operations and ultimately, the superintendent of the Naval Observatory. . . .

"The mansion and grounds belong to the Navy, and all of the expenses are a line item in the Navy budget, or at least they were at that time and I don't think it's been changed. So I had to go hat in hand and ask the Navy if we could get invitations printed, elegant invitations. But if we needed a new roof on the house, if we needed storm windows for the garden room, or a new lighting system for brightening the public rooms, that had to be approved by the Navy. The FBI decided that we needed bulletproof glass on the ground floor, but upstairs the Mondales needed insulated glass to keep warm.

"The staff was a staff of seven mess specialists, Navy mess specialists, all Filipino. I think each one spoke a different dialect. They sort of communicated with each other, but above all, at the beginning Bess Abell knew that there was going to be a problem because they did not like working with a woman in charge. So that all had to be hassled out.

"Actually, my title was special assistant to the vice president. That was the official title. Bess was, as I say, Joan's exec, and her office was downtown and I had my office out at the residence. When I asked Bess what the duties were she said, Just do whatever has to be done! And when I asked about the hours, she said, Well, they can be flexible. They were sure flexible. At times I'd be there from early in the morning to God knows when.

"I got into contemporary American crafts through Joan's interest in bringing art into the vice president's residence. She herself is a potter, and she always wanted ceramics and other crafts in the collection that was brought into the house each year. Actually, several of the museums that were asked to lend objects didn't know what crafts were, didn't have any, and they had to go out and look around and find them and find out who would donate them. They learned a lot, too, out of that experience. It was a very heady time, I must say.

"Joan had working luncheons. She did a lot of work on the Hill in support of the arts, and legislation and funding for the arts, but essentially legislation. She appeared on the Hill. She testified. She did lots of television interviews from the house. He did, too. So there was just tremendous activity in the house all the time. Some drudgery, but if you like to be a fly on the wall. . .

"Joan also invited the club—I think this was, again, Bess's idea—or anyone who cared to participate to make a needlepoint cushion replicating a work of art at the vice president's house. There is quite a collection of those pillows. There were about six or seven club members who created wonderful needlepoint cushions that replicated major contemporary American paintings. They were greatly admired. One woman wanted to get hers back again, but it belonged to the vice president's house. Couldn't have it! Sorry! But once again, the club was a place that Joan turned to. Quite a few people pitched in, including the man who was, at that time, our bookkeeper. Perrin was his name. He did needlepoint. He was one of the fine needlepoint people in the metropolitan area....

"Again, a personal experience. 'Candide' didn't make much money as a fund raiser. Leonard Bernstein, of course, wrote 'Candide' and he came to the opening. We had taken a block of seats, and his seat was next to mine. So that was in itself sort of an electrifying experience, I should say, because how was the show going to go and how was he going to react to it and all that; and there was to be an after-theater party for him. At any rate, the show got started and it was a disaster, a disaster in terms of the props falling apart, the timing being terrible. All during the first act we were conscious, my husband and I, that Mr. Bernstein was going like this in his seat, slumping further and further down. At the end of the first act, before the lights even went up, he's gone. He never reappeared, at least not in that seat. I don't know where he was in the theater, if he was even in the theater. Eventually, he showed up at the post theater party, but at that point, everyone was leaving. It must have been midnight when he showed up with a companion. I think they were both higher than kites, you know.

"But that was quite an experience, that opening night. 'Candide' has a wonderful overture, but the rest never took off. The music was dull, certainly not 'Bernsteinian' in any way, and maybe it hadn't been sufficiently rehearsed. I remember at the end of the first act the hero and heroine are embracing, and all of a sudden—and he's there on a sort of platform—the platform splits apart. Oh, it was just awful! It was so awful it was just funny!

"I've made a little note about Gretchen Poston. I just couldn't resist putting that down. It just indicates how far Gretchen came. There was an auction at the club, obviously a fund raiser. I can't remember precisely when it was. But one of the auction items was contributed by Marian Burros, who is now senior food writer for *The New York Times* and has spoken at the club. Marian offered a dinner for twelve. She had just written a book called *Elegant, But Easy,* which tells how you can prepare a dinner that can be frozen and then brought out and reheated in your oven before serving. Gretchen was the high bidder. So Gretchen decided to have a little dinner party using Marian's dinner.

"The day of the party we, including Gretchen, were at the club trying to do the seating for 'Candide.' Gretchen just wouldn't quit because she kept thinking we're almost through. It was six-thirty and the guests were coming at seven. We kept saying, Gretchen, go home and get your dinner ready! It wasn't that she didn't have advance warning: We advised her to go home and get dinner going. But she didn't leave the club until six-thirty, at which time she went home and took out this *gigantic* casserole to defrost for the seven o'clock dinner. This was pre-microwave! She did put it in the oven before seven, but to make a long story short, the guests arrived shortly thereafter. I don't know how much we had to drink. Nobody knows how much we had to drink because we couldn't remember the next day. At eleven-something, dinner came out of the oven, still half-frozen! That is a young woman who became a very effective social secretary in the White House!

"I've been thinking of the women who were very active members of the club from the cabinet, from the Hill, who were the magnets for other members. We don't have that any more, and that's because, as we said right at the beginning of this interview, women have so many more options now, so many other places to go. They're working. Hillary Clinton is very receptive and certainly went all out for the club, but not with any interest in promoting it, just doing her duty. Of course, she's a very busy person.

"Maybe it's up to the club to make contacts. Also, the DNC should be letting the club know what Democratic people are coming to town. There should be more coordination between the Hill and the club, and, when we're in the White House, between the White House and the club.

"The young people are the ones who can get the club back together again. Our daughter, Lisa, can come to lunch when she's motivated to and she can bring her friends to lunch, but she has to have a sense that she isn't the only young person. Lisa suggested we take part of the basement and put a gym down there. There are young people living in Dupont Circle condos, and there are a lot of offices there, and I would wager a lot of them would come for a workout before they go to work or during lunch or after they get off work. Well, if we're trying to attract—if we are—and we *have* to attract the young people, that certainly is an ace in the hole if there ever was one."

Left to right: Shirley Henderson, B.A. Bentsen, Kitty Dukakis and Jane Freeman at WNDC's 13 July reception to launch Democratic women's activities in the 1988 presidential campaign. Michael Geissinger photo, courtesy WNDC-EF Archives.

Chapter 8
COOKING REAGAN'S GOOSE
The Club Reorganizes

President Reagan and his fellows have produced the most unethical cast of characters assembled in one administration in my lifetime. The numbers alone are staggering. The National Journal *lists forty officials touched by scandal.... This administration has a penchant for putting foxes in charge of chicken coops.*

Joseph Rauh, 28 June 1984

The Reagan presidency that prompted Rauh's remarks led to an increasing seriousness about politics at the Woman's National Democratic Club. In 1986, longtime club member Olya Margolin launched a series of workshops on the Hill on "How Our Laws Are Made." WNDC became more serious about itself when an embezzlement and real estate dealings threatened the club's stability. Volunteer jobs gave way to paid staff positions, changing forever the character of the club. Escalating operating costs and a financial crisis led to a reorganization of the club's administration.

Jean Jensen

"When I was installed in office in June 1983, I was very excited and very enthusiastic because I had an opportunity to be involved in the club a year before the national election," Jean Jensen recalled in an undated interview. "However, this was also such a critical, unfortunate time in the club's history that I think the following incident must be recorded.

"One of the things that happened soon after my election was that Tony, our accountant, did not have the records ready for an audit. He had called the auditors and postponed the audit date. The volunteer treasurer came in to the club and tried to find out exactly why we were not ready for audit. Concern over Tony's lazy work habits and poor accounting skills turned into a graver concern, and finally the executive committee made the decision to give the accountant an opportunity to resign immediately, and that happened.

"We then called in a special audit team and immediately began to discover that not only did we have improperly kept records, but money was missing. So we embarked on a very arduous task of reconstructing bank statements, checkbooks. The sad thing for the club was that a large amount of money was missing. I think one of the hardest things for us to deal with was that he had been misrepresenting on paper how much money the club actually had.

"To backtrack and accurately analyze how that affected us—we were making decisions to go forward with club renovations on the fourth floor on the assumption that we had money in the bank that we actually didn't have. If I could just pick a figure out of the air, I would guess that he was probably misrepresenting on paper about $150,000. In other words, we were under the impression at the beginning of the renovation period in '81 that we had $150,000 more in the bank than we actually had. So, feeling that we were in a sound financial position, we had made plans to go forward with the renovation and the new costs that would be involved afterwards, only to find out that our calculations were based on inaccurate figures.

"That was the long-range implication. But the reason we had such a struggle to dig out of the embezzlement was that it went back even farther. Tony had embezzled money by not paying employee taxes: He wrote checks for payment of taxes and never mailed them. Also, he was probably taking the cash that was coming in for lunches and bar chits. When we cleaned out his office in preparation for the 'fraud audit,' we found unopened bills from the IRS, notices that we were delinquent in our tax payments. We found them between the pages of telephone books, under the blotters in his desk. We found a cardboard box under the desk that was full of canceled checks, and the checkbooks had never been reconciled. It was just a disaster. The process of preparing for an audit and reconstructing what he had done took almost a year. It was not until the end of that fraud audit, in the spring of '84, that we were actually able to say publicly that money had been embezzled.

"It's very difficult to judge exactly how much he got. We were able to substantiate about $60,000, and that is what we filed a claim for and were reimbursed by the insurance company. But the insurance agent told me he would imagine, in most situations like ours, that the amount actually stolen and the amount actually proved to have been stolen is different, that probably three times that amount had been embezzled.

"One of the important decisions that the club made was to be very forthright. All of this information was presented to the membership at the annual meeting in '84. I knew members were very concerned with what we had been through, and we tried to anticipate all of the questions they had about how he took the money and how we were dealing with it. We simply began the meeting with thirteen or fourteen questions that we felt the membership must certainly have about the situation, and proceeded to answer them in orderly fashion. Then the club made the important decision to bring charges officially and to prosecute, and I think that's one of the most important things we have probably ever done because, in many cases, an organization doesn't want to admit publicly that their systems could have been such that a serious embezzlement could happen.

"It later turned out that Tony had embezzled money in the past, but the people he had embezzled from had never prosecuted and the charges had been dropped. He had been allowed to repay what he had taken, and he had no police record. When he showed up here and applied for a job, he was able to present clean references. He could have gone on forever, moving from one job to another, just quietly embezzling money.

"I think the club made a very courageous decision when the membership took the vote that summer. It was not an easy one. There was controversy in the meeting when that vote was taken. Many people did not want the publicity; they just wanted it to be handled very quietly, thought it would be a very bad reflection on the club. But fortunately—and that's my personal opinion—the majority of the membership felt that it was very important that we bring charges.

"Tony was found guilty of embezzlement and put in jail. He was given an opportunity for parole if he immediately got a job and began a method of repayment. He did not do so. He failed those terms and was put in prison. I don't know what the current status is, but I am very comfortable that we prosecuted.

"The taxes took a lot of reconstruction and negotiating with the IRS. We were fortunate to get some pro bono legal advice. I'm sure that, with the amount of money that was stolen and the kind of precarious financial situation that it left us in, and with the cost of a fraud audit, which was much larger than a regular audit would be under normal circumstances, if we had not been able to get some pro bono help with the legal fees, it would have been very difficult for us. But we were lucky to get some help, and the IRS negotiated. We did have to repay most of the taxes, of course, but our attorneys were able to negotiate most of the penalties and accrued interest.

"Now, on a more positive note, in September 1983, with the help of two other organizations, the National Federation of Democratic Women and the women's council of the Democratic National Committee, we planned a three-day leadership conference. We held it here in the club, and we invited Democratic women from all over the country to attend. We arranged with the [old] Dupont Plaza Hotel for the women to stay there. We just opened up the club for this conference for three days, and it was a session of speakers and seminars on important campaign issues and fund raising. Just getting together was wonderful.

"One of the days was spent up on the Hill. They arranged for the Democratic women in Congress to talk to us. We had a luncheon in one of the large dining rooms in the House, and each one of the Democratic congresswomen came in and spoke for a few minutes about the particular issues that they were working on at that time. It's probably one of the most creative things the club has done in a political sense, and I'm sure that in the future a similar leadership conference will be put together....

"The club's no-smoking policy came about in September 1983. Over the years nonsmokers had expressed their discomfort at being in situations where people were smoking. Then finally, one member took the time to sit down and write a letter to the executive committee, requesting leadership in establishing a no-smoking policy. When the executive committee discussed that letter, we all began to remember a comment here or a comment there suggesting that we should take some action. But it was one member's letter that sparked the executive committee to discuss fully a no-smoking policy and try to come up with a plan. Several proposals were presented to the governing board, which responded very enthusiastically. There was a lot of discussion, and a variety of plans evolved on how we could handle smoking in the club. In the end, it was decided that on speaker luncheon days there would be no smoking at all on the first floor of the club, and that on a sellout day, when members would have to be seated in the lounge to watch the program on television, that there would be no smoking in the lounge. There were two dissenting votes on the board, but otherwise it carried. We removed all of the ashtrays and put 'Thank you for not smoking' signs on the dining room tables....

"In April 1984, twenty WNDC members went to Europe to visit Democrats Abroad. We started in Germany, where the key officers and representatives from various countries were meeting in Heidelberg to write platform testimony for the Democratic convention. Democrats Abroad has about nine votes at the convention and a seat on the DNC council. It was a very exciting experience. We thought we would be bringing them all of the latest up-to-date news on the issues, and it was rather overwhelming to find out the lengths they went to to be well informed on U.S. politics. Sometimes their newspapers are a couple of days late with the news, or they don't get TV coverage of current political events. We stayed in Heidelberg for a few days and then we went by train to visit the Democrats Abroad in Paris.

"We then went to Spain. The Democrats in Madrid were just starting to get organized. We were able to meet with just a few of them, but, they were a wonderful group to be a part of. It was a fantastic experience. We will continue to meet with Democrats Abroad over the years, I'm sure.

"While I was in Europe, I had to miss a tea in honor of Rosalynn Carter. She had just completed her book, *First Lady from Plains,* and the club held an afternoon book signing and tea. The club vice president presided, and it was really a very successful event. A lot of people attended. In fact, later, when we talked to Mrs. Carter's press secretary, she had almost become alarmed at one point because there were so many people in such a small space, and there was the pushing that goes on even among ladies dressed to the nines trying to get close to Mrs. Carter. But it was a very successful event....

"We have always tried to have one or two really strong programs when the club opens in September, a technique to get our members excited and interested in coming back to the club after the summer. In September 1983, one of our very popular programs was Governor and Mrs. Averell Harriman, who had recently been to Russia to meet with Yuri Andropov, secretary of the Communist party from '82 to '84. Between the time we invited the Harrimans to speak and the time they actually were to appear, the Russians had shot down the Korean jetliner. The Harrimans contacted us and said they wanted to keep their commitment, but change their topic and not dwell so much on the meeting with Andropov, but to talk instead about U.S.-U.S.S.R. relations, and specifically about this incident.

"So they came to a sellout audience. Clark Clifford was the introducer. We were upstairs in the lounge during cocktail time when a member of the hostess committee came rushing in to say that one of the secretaries of the Soviet embassy had just appeared at the doorway and wanted to come in, and she didn't know how to handle it. I discussed it with Governor and Mrs. Harriman and with Clark Clifford. Governor Harriman was outraged that someone from the Russian embassy had shown up unannounced and uninvited, and wanted us to politely ask him to leave. Calmness prevailed, and Clark Clifford and Pamela Harriman very quietly told Averell that they felt that much more of an incident would be made if the Russian secretary was asked to leave instead of graciously inviting him to come in and offering him a drink and giving him a seat at the press table. So, it was very nicely resolved, but it was a behind-the-scenes story that only those few people standing around the table in the lounge knew about.

"Another behind-the-scenes program story. In March, Ambassador Clovis Maksoud, who was the chief representative to the United States for the League of Arab States, spoke on 'Prospects for Peace in the Middle East: An Arab Perspective.' When we went to lunch, our very creative chef had prepared stir-fried vegetables on rice, and in front of each plate there was a little brown wooden bowl of Chinese noodles and a little bottle of soy sauce. The ambassador looked at the food, and he looked at me, and he said, This is what I love about Democrats! Only Democrats would serve Chinese food to an Arab!

"The chef included a fortune cookie for dessert! When the ambassador opened his fortune cookie, it said, 'Romance for you tonight could be dangerous.' Well, sitting on the other side of the podium was his beautiful wife, who was, I believe, working on her doctorate in mathematics at Georgetown. The ambassador said to me, Please pass this fortune cookie note to my wife. So I leaned behind the introducer and handed the note to his wife and watched her read it, and then she leaned forward and said to the ambassador, My darling, romance for you *any* night could be dangerous!

"I could probably just continue to tell stories about the wonderful programming, because it ranges over such a wide variety of issues: international, national affairs, liberal arts programs, legislative, all on very timely topics with the best speakers possible available. I was once asked, How much do you have to pay those speakers? It just must be so expensive to have all of these program! And I said, We don't pay our speakers. They come because it's a prestigious podium, and quite often, if they are going to make a really strong, good speech, we get outstanding press and television coverage. C-SPAN broadcasts many of our programs, the national networks, too.

"At the end of a program that has been televised over C-SPAN, WNDC is included in the credits. When I was president, on many occasions in the afternoon after a speaker program there would be a phone call from someone across the country who had seen the program on C-SPAN. A man in Reno, Nevada, called the club on almost a regular basis because he saw so many of our programs. Knowing that they were at the Woman's National Democratic Club, he got in touch with the local Democratic club and found there was not a club for men. So he joined the Reno Democratic Women's Club....

"In early April 1984 the club presented oral testimony to the Democratic platform committee. We had prepared written testimony that was submitted in advance to get us on the schedule. Five task forces of our public policy committee—the economy, education, environment and energy, foreign policy, and income maintenance task forces—had prepared position papers; and we had condensed the long, written testimony into about a ten-minute oral presentation.

"Five or six of us from the club went in and registered and were told that they were running behind time and that we should just go sit and wait in a little lounge area. We did. We went back to check on our time, and they told us that the platform hearings were running so far behind that we needed to condense our ten minutes of testimony to five. So we took our copies of our oral testimony and got away from the crowd and found a little table in the outdoor bar, sat down and put our heads together, and with a red pencil very quickly reduced our ten-minute testimony to five. That was really an interesting experience. I was very nervous about presenting testimony as it was, and then to have to reduce it at the very last minute!

"Another important event in 1984. We were invited to participate in a televised presidential candidates' debate. We gave financial support. The debate, filmed in New Hampshire, was telecast on 23 February, with Barbara Walters moderating. That was the first time, I believe, that the club had sponsored a bipartisan program of that nature. It was good publicity because at the end of the telecast, the name and address of the club and the fact that we had sponsored the bipartisan debate were in the credits.

"In August 1984, after the national convention, the Democratic Party's nominee for president was Walter Mondale, and for vice president, Geraldine Ferraro. One evening, about eight o'clock, I received a frantic phone call that Gerry Ferraro's staff was just overwhelmed by the volume of mail she was receiving from men and women across the country who were very excited about having a woman candidate for vice president. They just simply couldn't handle the deluge of mail. The caller had heard that the WNDC was a very active organization with a lot of good volunteers. Could we possibly help them? To make a very short story of a lot of phone calls, club members ended up being indispensable volunteers for Geraldine Ferraro. She later mentioned our work in the book that she wrote about her experiences as a candidate. I know that she expressed her personal appreciation to one of the members for all that we had done to help her campaign.

"Interestingly enough, the next spring, the board of governors, because of Gerry Ferraro's important place in history even though she and Mondale did not win, chose her for our Outstanding Democratic Woman of the Year award.[3] We held a reception in May 1985. It was a champagne reception and very elegant. The only bad thing that happened was that it ended up being an unseasonably hot day for May in Washington; and because of Secret Service restrictions and the large number of people who turned out to see her, we had to have the members line up outside of the club and not let them in until she arrived, and then only in small groups.

"She arrived late, apparently because she went to Dupont Circle and shook hands with everybody there before coming to the club. And our members...I mean, talk about difficult security! Our members were all standing outside! Of course, those of us who were involved in setting up the reception inside were unaware that it had become unbearably hot and that members were still lined up outside. The reception was successful, but there were repercussions. Many of our members felt that it had not been 'democratic.' That word came up over and over.

"In October 1984, the club celebrated the anniversary of Eleanor Roosevelt's 100th birthday with two events. At the first, James Roosevelt, a grandson of Franklin

---

[3] Ferraro was first proposed as a candidate for vice president by then representative Barbara Kennelly (D-CT) at the 9 April 1984 WNDC speaker luncheon

and Eleanor, was joined by Trude Lash, Robert Nathan, Esther Peterson, and Mary Keyserling, who shared personal memories and little vignettes of experiences they had had with Eleanor Roosevelt. Ellie Seagraves, Eleanor Roosevelt's eldest granddaughter, who's a very active member of our club, also shared some of her thoughts. It was a day of warm remembrances.

"The next week we had a very special celebration. Ruth Morgenthau, daughter-in-law of the secretary of the Treasury during Roosevelt's administration, and her husband, a very distinguished prosecuting attorney, had made a wonderful film of Eleanor Roosevelt that they showed at a club luncheon. The program was repeated that evening, also to an overflow crowd. One of the people who joined us at the head table that day was Mrs. Edward R. Murrow. Eric Sevareid, who narrated the film, was there; he had been one of 'Murrow's Boys' at CBS.

"In 1984, we published, as a fund raiser, a cookbook entitled *How to Cook Reagan's Goose* and subtitled *Political Cookbook Serving Up Democratic Delectables and Republican Indigestibles.* Club members solicited favorite recipes from about 110 prominent Democrats, including Rosalynn and Jimmy Carter, Senator [Edward] Kennedy, Senator [Fritz] Hollings, Pamela and Averell Harriman, Mayor Dianne Feinstein, Muriel and Hubert Humphrey, and Jeanne and Paul Simon. It was an interesting mixture. And really! The crab cakes! Barbara Mikulski's Maryland crab cakes! I still use that recipe. It's one of the best for crab cakes."

BARBARA MIKULSKI'S CRAB CAKES

1 beaten egg
1/2 cup mayonnaise
1/2 teaspoon Worcestershire sauce
1 tablespoon parsley flakes
1 teaspoon Old Bay seasoning

1/2 teaspoon salt
1/2 teaspoon ground black pepper
1/2 teaspoon dry mustard
6 finely crumbled saltines
1 pound crab meat

Mix together all ingredients except crab meat. Blend crab meat in with a fork. Brown the cakes in butter in hot skillet.

How to Cook Reagan's Goose, New York, Karz-Cohl Publishing, Inc., 1984

"We launched the cookbook at a book-signing party and invited as many of the recipe contributors as possible to join us. Members could buy a cookbook and then have the recipe autographed by the author. It was a great success. We made a lot of money on the cookbook, and we also got a lot of press coverage. There was a large article with photos in *The Washington Post,* and there was even a piece in *People* magazine. Republicans weren't crazy about our cookbook, but the Democrats thought it was a great idea. We ended up selling it across the country. In the back was an order form that created a wonderful problem we hadn't anticipated. Once we sold the bulk of our cookbooks, we thought the project would be over. Instead, we couldn't get rid of the job because we had orders coming in from all over the country for years! As a matter of fact, this was in 1984, and I can remember that for at least five years we got requests from people in other parts of the country, Do you still have the Goose cookbook? We negotiated a legal agreement for a reprint and got a little bit of money by selling the publishing rights. They were going to give us a percentage of all the books they sold, but the timing wasn't good. By the time the New York publishing firm took on the project, interest had waned and it just didn't sell.

"For financial reasons we, with the governing board's support, voted to make all luncheons prepaid. In the past when you received a club calendar, you could just fill out a reservation form and send it back in. Because of our 'first-come, first-served' policy, members would get a calendar and be attracted to six weeks of programming and want to attend as many as they possibly could; so they would make reservations for three, four, five, sometimes six or seven luncheons. Then, if they found that their schedule was busy and they couldn't attend, they'd either call the day before, or the day of the luncheon, and cancel. Or just not show up at all. We were wasting a lot of food on 'no-shows,' and we were also hiring too much labor. We would sometimes have fifty and sixty no-shows at a luncheon. During this '83-'85 period we created a prepaid luncheon policy and a cancellation policy that made you financially responsible for your luncheon reservation unless you called by a cut-off date....

"In January of 1985, Paul Kirk was elected chair of the Democratic National Committee, and the members of our program committee extended an invitation to him to speak to the club about what he planned to do as chairman of the party. He accepted the speaking date in March 1985. We had a sellout crowd, more than 350 reservations. They were very anxious to hear what direction he planned to take the party. I had a feeling when he arrived that he really didn't know anything about the Woman's National Democratic Club. Over the years we had had a less and less formal relationship with the Democratic National Committee, and his staff was all fairly new in their positions. But, quite frankly, I think he came unprepared, unprepared from the point of view that these were really active, participating, knowledgeable Democrats. He seemed overwhelmed when he sat down for lunch and looked out at an audience of 350, at C-SPAN and at all the reporters. I think he probably was most uncomfortable that he had not prepared a more substantial statement. He had very brief notes on a three-by-five card, and he made a fifteen-minute speech. Generally, speeches begin at one o'clock, the introductions last five or six minutes, and then the speaker is told to speak for twenty or thirty minutes. That leaves fifteen minutes for questions. With Paul Kirk we had thirty-five or forty minutes for questions! Then he became even more aware of what an astute audience it was because our members are known for their probing, timely questions. Every speaker comments on it.

"He was invited to come back a year later, and this time he knew where he was going. He came with a really wonderfully prepared text, and copies were available afterwards. So I know that it was a good experience for him, and I think it was the beginning of a new working relationship between the Woman's National Democratic Club and the Democratic National Committee.

"A somewhat controversial situation came up when one of the program committees wanted to extend an invitation to Arturo Cruz, who was a well-known Nicaraguan opposition leader. He had served in the Sandanista government as president of the central bank, and he was going to be in Washington, lobbying. A club member had access to invite him to speak. Two different factions of our membership were opposed to him. One, simply for security concerns. They thought that his life was probably at risk at times in Washington and really didn't want the members of the club exposed. Another faction felt that we were going to give a forum to someone who espoused the Reagan administration position on Nicaragua.

"The compromise struck behind the scenes was that we would invite someone who would represent the Democratic position to introduce him. Unfortunately, that did not work out. The person who was planning the program invited someone to introduce who had been at the State department, and who, quite frankly, could possibly have shared the Republican point of view. So the decision was made just to go ahead and let that program carry itself out, and then we would come back later with another program in response to it. That ended up being a very strong program. In June of that same year, in answer to Arturo Cruz, Representative Tom Foley, who was at that point the majority whip and would later become Speaker of the House of Representatives, presented the Democratic position on Nicaragua. We had wonderful attendance, and I think the members of the club who were most concerned about Arturo Cruz were satisfied that our members had had a chance to hear the opposite point of view."

Marelyn Tank

"I was president from 1985 to '87, and those were very exciting years," recalled Marelyn Tank in a series of interviews in the 1990s. "A lot was going on that took a long time to come to fruition.

"One thing I remember most vividly is that the board had sixty-eight members. Sometimes there would be as many as seventy-five people at a board meeting. Every committee chairman was on the board. The vice chairs of the committees came, and the committees almost all had vice chairs. Past presidents came, and, of course, the executive committee. Task force members made up a big part of it. The board voted on every single thing, and we didn't have as many unanimous votes as we have now. We would have policy statements that task forces wanted to have approved, and we would even have opposing points of view presented, which doesn't happen now. Opinions and feelings got aired a lot. We ended up doing an awful lot of committee work that the board should never do. It was like holding a general business meeting every month. It took a great deal of preparation. In some ways, it was wonderful because it produced a camaraderie and a knowledge of what was going on and people felt much more involved. But I must say it got to be sort of a joke. We finally moved the board meeting up to ten o'clock and I would insist that we begin it on time because we had so much to cover and our aim was to finish at twelve-thirty. Yes, that was rushed. When you've got seventy people and at least sixty-five of them want to say something, there was almost nothing discussed that didn't have a lot to be said about it, for or against. In a way, it was good; in another way, it was exhausting.

"The board is much more manageable now. It has twenty-eight members, maybe: the executive committee and the governors and the chairs of the nominating committee and the Educational Foundation. But I think we lost something when we made the board smaller. This is a strong word, but people feel 'excluded.' I think some people feel you get involved in the activity you're interested in. The *News* carries information, of course, but that's slightly different. And, yes, we have a Web site. But still, it's not the same as word of mouth. It's not widely known that anybody can come to a board meeting. And we've got to find a way to bring in all these committee chairs.

"We added two new committees in 1985. One was a publications committee, and the other was a committee of which I was extremely proud: a liaison with the Democratic National Committee. We've had our differences with the DNC over the years but we did a lot of liaison with them. In a way, it was good; in another way, it was bad. It turned out that, oh, yes, they would love our help; but what they really remembered was our work for Geraldine Ferraro. After the election they would send us things that they wanted folded and stamped. We sort of became the secretarial …the 'temps.' I guess we did that for a year and then members got restless. Paul Kirk, who was then the head of the DNC, came and talked to us a couple of times. He muddied the waters by talking about 'you women.' It wasn't what he said so much; it was that term 'you women' or 'you ladies.' He may not have meant to be patronizing, but it came across that way.…

"We had a big reception for Barbara Mikulski in 1985, Outstanding Democratic Woman of the Year. We had about 400 people. The biggest headache was figuring out how we could get a sturdy-enough stand behind the lectern so that she could get up on it. One of the husbands built a stand that folded up into the lectern. Mikulski was wonderful....

"It's interesting to note that our membership in those days was 2,600. We were doing very well! The program committee didn't have as much work getting speakers because people often would call and say they would like to come and make a speech at the club and present this or that idea. Teddy Kennedy was one of them. Gary Hart another. Jay Rockefeller. Now that doesn't happen any more because they already have media saturation. But we had a lot of press in those days and it would get on the evening news if they were prominent names.

"What else were we doing? All through those two years we had constant discussions. One was about young people and, a word that was just getting used a lot fourteen years ago, 'networking.' It was not in the vocabulary of this club. But we had somebody on the executive committee who was very much interested in opening the club in the evening so that young people could come and network. Well, it wasn't that we were opposed to this. We had some evening programs and we did have some young people. We quickly learned that what they really wanted to do was to come after work and meet each other and leave their business cards, and they wanted telephones. Well, that isn't the kind of club we are. We talked it up one side and down the other. I remember for two years talking about this. We never did it, never got the telephones, but we did have a series of evening programs. We tried social hours. We tried cocktail hours. We opened the cocktail lounge from five to seven or eight, something like that. It never worked, but it was a constant discussion.

"Now I'll tell a funny story. When Jean Jensen was president, she threatened to give me the names of the people who fall asleep in the front row at speaker luncheons. One day, our speaker was Ellie Smeal from NOW. And she speaks loudly and makes her points forcefully. Well, we had a raised dais, and there were some members who had had their lunch and were dozing peacefully. Ellie made an emphatic point and pounded on the lectern! Two people jumped so that they knocked over their coffee cups! It was most amusing!

"Then we had an ongoing discussion about getting a 501(c)(3) [IRS tax-exempt status] for the club. There were committees to study it, and it would be discussed at board meetings, the pros and cons. It was finally passed in October of '91 when the WNDC Educational Foundation [EF] came into being. That was an ongoing topic and a very hot one. It was very hard to make people understand the concept of EF, and the biggest fear—and it still exists today—is that EF would become the dog and the rest of us were going to be the tail. It was a terrible fear and we never succeeded in completely allaying it, and we're still learning how to use EF.

"Oh, yes, and we had a mixer stolen from the kitchen! When I think about these things that became issues! We had to have all the locks on the doors changed. That's why it became such a big issue: How much it was going to cost and who was going to have keys and who would come in at what hour and would they sign in and sign out or not? That was just a big problem.

"Then, in June, I guess, of '86 we put out a position paper that was a big deal on the right to choose. It was interesting to me the problems that came up at this time. You would have thought that basically the whole club would have been in favor. That was when I first discovered we have a lot of Catholic members who would call up and say, Marelyn, I'm a good Democrat, but I'm also a good Catholic, and this is agony for me. I just want you to understand why I'm not voting for this policy paper. It passed, but it was an eye-opener for me.

"We also decided it was time to stop being so much a volunteer club, that we were becoming more professional. At that time we had a so-called club manager, but *volunteers ran the club*. They really did! So we decided that what we needed to do was investigate hiring a more professional staff and an administrator instead of a manager. Somebody had come pro bono to evaluate the club, and we were taken aback by her report that pointed out that we were lax even in our reservations and our publications. She said that the responsibility was too much for volunteers who weren't in constant touch with one another, that we needed a coordinator, that we needed an administrator who was going to look after the house—the security, the staff, everything.

"Well, we met every single day for three or four weeks, discussing all of this, and then presented it to the board. The board agreed, though not without a lot of agony. It didn't happen in one sitting, I may tell you. Giving up responsibility to a salaried staff was very difficult, and it still is. And it was difficult to understand, as we still have to understand, that each one of us cannot go in to the staff and say, I want this done today or I want this done now.

"We hired the woman who had done the evaluating. In retrospect, that was a terrible mistake, and it set the concept back. She didn't have the personality to run this club. She was very authoritarian. One of the things she decided was we wouldn't have a cook; we would have caterers. We would have the cocktail hour. Her ideas were wonderful and they could have worked had they been presented differently. This was such a huge transition that I blame myself for a lot of it. I had a better knowledge of this club than she did. I remember going to her house several times and talking to her. Ultimately, we fired her with much acrimony, though not on her part so much. She agreed she was the wrong person for the job, too. The next person we had was very good, and we know now that we must have a financial manager and an administrator.

"You know, I'm eighty-four. It's time for me to stop. Since my husband died, it's been my life, this club, and I really devoted myself to it. I had joined in '77, as I told you, as soon as I could. I filled in for a very close friend right away, practically, as chair of the *News*, so I got to come to board meetings. I got a very quick introduction to the club. So it has been my life, and it still is, but I think it's time for new people and new ideas. I don't know who and where they are, but if the club is going to survive and not turn into a place like the Shakers, you know, all those little old ladies who just died out, we're going to have to change. We all have to face that, don't we? I feel encouraged because we are getting younger members. But I think the spirit of the club will survive.

"Anyway, I think those are the highlights. I learned a lot about people's capabilities and willingness to work and enthusiasm. Also, I just enjoyed watching. I've always enjoyed that, just watching people as you look out at an audience from a dais and suddenly see a person's facial response that says, Of course! Right! You know that feeling, and that you could get it twice a week at the speaker luncheons was pretty wonderful! Anyhow, the club is exciting and I think it's going to go on forever."

Olya Margolin

WNDC's Olya Margolin was an advocate and lobbyist, who believed that all club members should understand the legislative process.

"Let me talk about our memorial symposium for Olya," said Phyllis Fineshriber, longtime Margolin friend, in a 1996 interview. "It was a very special event at the club. By working as a volunteer at the White House, I got Alice Rivlin for the symposium for Olya. I had known Alice before, not well, but somehow or other she trusted me. That was nice. I didn't know what I had done to deserve that, but I was happy with it. I first got to know Alice through Olya, who was her next-door neighbor. At the memorial symposium, which we called 'Advocacy and the Public Interest,' Alice recalled that her first conversation with Olya was about trash. They were neighbors, and there was a little alley between their houses in Cleveland Park, where the rattly old trash cans went. Alice and Olya developed a relationship while chatting over trash cans. Alice said that out in the country good fences make good neighbors, but in the city it's good alleys!

"I had gone to Olya's funeral, and as we were leaving, I said to Shirley Henderson, who was the club president, that we shouldn't just have the usual memorial for Olya because she was one of the few members of the club who really understood Capitol Hill. She did things like fight Richard Nixon's nomination of two southern nominees, Clement Haynsworth and G. Harrold Carswell, for the Supreme Court; and she worked hard for Title IX banning sex discrimination in athletics at schools that get federal funds. Olya would be thrilled if she could see how successful women's basketball and soccer are today because of Title IX.

"She was adamant that every club member should understand the legislative process and was very upset at times when members didn't seem to understand it. Olya could be testy about that, but she always made you feel good after she had been cross by giving you a big hug. She had organized the 'How Our Laws Are Made' workshops on the Hill in 1986, and I said we should think about a memorial symposium for Olya related to that topic. We got in touch with all the speakers who had taken part in the workshops, and we got our beloved crusader for civil rights, Joseph Rauh, to be the master of ceremonies. Joe set the tone by saying that public interest was the central part of Olya's solar system. Mary Keyserling came. Esther Peterson came. Both were WNDC past presidents. Journalist Sarah McLendon came. Ralph Neas, a great coalition builder. Carmen Votaw, outstanding activist for Hispanic women. Mary Jane Patterson. All of them had known Olya. Alice Rivlin was the luncheon speaker. It was an all-day session and I moderated some of the time and got to recognize all of those wonderful people.

"Their tributes to Olya prompted the club's oral history program. We had lost Olya's personal memories, but Carmen Votaw urged us to tape the recollections of our other members. Ben Margolin, Olya's husband, who is a member of the club, gave us a videotape of the symposium that was transcribed for the club archives. I took notes of the 'How Our Laws Are Made' workshops, and with all of that we have a good record of Olya's contribution to the club."

When not organizing symposia or WNDC speaker luncheons for the legislative program committee, Phyllis Fineshriber is a volunteer receptionist in First Lady Hillary Clinton's office. She also crafts needlepoint pillows.

"When Hillary Clinton spoke at the club after publication of her book, *It Takes A Village*," Fineshriber recalled, "I did a needlepoint reproduction of the dust jacket. I learned soon afterward, through my volunteer job in the White House, that when Hillary Clinton received a gift, the president wanted one, too. So, taking inspiration from a photo that hangs in the first lady's office, I designed and sewed a needlepoint pillow for Bill Clinton. The theme is 'A Bridge to the 21st Century,' and I have been told that that pillow is now in the Oval Office."

Jane Freeman

"In 1961, President Kennedy asked my husband to come to Washington to be secretary of Agriculture," recalled Jane Freeman in a 1995 interview. "He accepted and we moved. It was a very difficult move for our daughter and son, particularly for her. She was starting high school. However, in coming to Washington we were also fortunate because the cabinet was composed of several people we knew who had been active in the Democratic Party and because they, like Orv, had been governors, congressmen, or senators before. President Kennedy's cabinet was a very close group. Most of them stayed on through his entire time in office and well into the Johnson administration to keep it operating.

"President Johnson told my husband while we were sitting around the pool at Camp David many years later, Orville, if I hadn't been chosen by Jack Kennedy to be the vice president, who do you think would have been chosen? You, because Jack Kennedy told me so. Well, President Kennedy had spoken to Orv about being considered, and he did call us over to his suite just before he made the announcement to say that he had chosen Johnson, who was then the majority leader in the Senate and who he felt would be an important help on the Hill in drawing the South, which, of course, you have to accept.

"It was a great opportunity coming to Washington with that group, though it was very difficult for us because we had almost no money and we were having trouble selling our house. The cabinet wives were very active. Dorothy Goldberg, wife of Secretary of Labor Arthur Goldberg [later, ambassador to the United Nations and a Supreme Court justice], had lived in Washington for some time. Her husband had been very active in the labor movement and knew a lot about the needs of the city of Washington and particularly of the city's young students, who did not have many opportunities to participate in and appreciate the advantages of living here. She organized some of us into a group called 'Widening Horizons.' We organized programs for schoolchildren to help them understand more about government.

"I became active. I joined the Woman's National Democratic Club and found a great many friends of like mind. That was wonderful. My big problem was not having time because of heavy cabinet duties. In those days, none of the cabinet wives worked. Dorothy Goldberg did a good deal of painting, so Margaret McNamara, Lee Udall, Jane Wirtz, and I and other cabinet wives did charity work and, as I said, participated in the club.

"When President Kennedy was killed, we were on a plane en route to Hawaii with a group of five cabinet members and three top members of the president's staff going on to Japan for an exchange with the Japanese cabinet. We turned around and went back. Everyone was very worried, particularly [Secretary of State] Dean Rusk because everybody thought it was a major plot against the president and vice president. It was a tragic, difficult, horrible time. But I must say that the funeral and the whole process helped you see the grandeur of the American people when they face a major tragedy and how they do indeed come together. It was a good lesson.

"President and Mrs. Johnson ran a quite different operation than the Kennedys had. Mrs. Johnson, for one thing, had been very active as a Senate wife, a very 'political' wife, much more so than Jackie Kennedy had been. Mrs. Johnson and her staff really got busy and organized what became known as the beautification program. I was quite active in that with Mrs. Johnson, speaking across the country and working particularly with youth groups to organize community improvement projects to 'clean up, fix up, plant, and conserve.' It was a very broad program, far beyond what was happening in the capital, though Washington served as an example. Mrs. Johnson wanted people to start their conservation and beautification efforts in their own communities, so she started in Washington.

"Because the Forest Service was part of that department, it was natural for the wife of the secretary of Agriculture to participate. I found Mrs. Johnson absolutely magnificent to work with, and Liz [Carpenter], too. Mrs. Johnson was such a gentle, warm, caring, understanding, and *perfectionist* kind of person; and Liz's great good humor and creativity just added to the fun. We had a very good, active group of cabinet wives, and I organized a lot of the Agriculture wives to participate in many of these programs that spread out across the country quite a bit in the various field services. So it was a good experience in organization, too.

"Meanwhile, a good handful of us were quite active in the Woman's National Democratic Club. Whenever they had a big fund raiser or they needed to have some cabinet wives or some cabinet members to participate in something here, we managed to 'get the bodies' here.

"But, we were still living in very limited circumstances. My husband and I and two other cabinet families were people without private income of any kind, so even though the salary had gone from $19,000 to $25,000 for a cabinet member, it was a tough squeeze with two teenage kids preparing for college and the more expensive living conditions here. I was tremendously tempted several times to take on paid employment, but my husband always preferred that, if we could, we would live on what he made so I could take part fully in community and volunteer activities. I've always been grateful that I could, because I could do the things we both cared about.

"In '68, when Humphrey was a serious contender for the nomination at the Democratic convention in Chicago, he asked me to help organize hospitality at the convention. In those days, candidates had hospitality headquarters, the idea being to get the delegates to come in so you could urge them to support your candidate. Many delegates, you see, still in '68, came to the convention uncommitted, and some delegates were committed to favorite sons who would eventually pull out, so we were trying to get them behind Humphrey. And though Humphrey was the heir apparent, there were others who were equally excited about becoming the presidential candidate, particularly Gene McCarthy, who had been very disappointed when President Johnson did not select *him* as his vice-presidential running mate in 1964, but instead selected another Minnesotan, Hubert Humphrey.

"[McCarthy] was very upset about the Vietnam War, so he had launched a campaign and arrived at the convention with a large number of young people who were not delegates, but were there to make themselves heard. It was those very difficult days in the '60s when civility at the conventions disappeared. There was the very difficult scene at that convention when Chicago police used force against the demonstrators. We were staying in the headquarters hotel. McCarthy headquarters were two floors above us, and through our windows we saw the excrement and *stuff* being thrown onto the police below. It was happening very nastily. Several times visitors planted stink bombs in Humphrey's hospitality suite. McCarthy was not controlling all of that behavior.

But, to go back to organizing the hospitality, I turned to my good friends at the Woman's National Democratic Club and asked for help in making the plans and arrangements. There was lot of advance planning to line up the volunteers to staff the headquarters. Nancy Stevenson, Adlai Stevenson Jr.'s wife, helped organize a lot of volunteers in Chicago. We were eager to have a diverse group, a mixture of people, in Humphrey headquarters.

"Just getting all the equipment and supplies together, the refreshments, the buttons, the balloons, the stickers! I really came to appreciate the organizing capabilities of the WNDC volunteers who put all this together. Their know-how was a godsend, because in addition to all this, that was the summer our only daughter was married. Her wedding was on Saturday, August 25, and the very next day Orv and I boarded a small airplane with Hubert and Muriel and several staff people to fly to the Chicago convention! So it was a summer to end all summers, and besides which, one of the hottest summers we've ever had. After Nixon's victory, which was devastating to us, we moved to New York, where Orv became president of Business International. It was a dramatic change for me. We had to move from Washington, which I dearly love, with many friends and lots of politically oriented people, to New York, which I dearly despise—the noise, the dirt, the crowdedness—where I knew very few people. In Manhattan, we were thrown in with people who were very wealthy, very business-oriented, *very* few Democrats. So it was hard on this political wife to make the shift....

After we came back to Washington, the first thing I did was to get my little self over to the Woman's National Democratic Club, reestablish old friendships there, upgrade my membership to resident membership, and join the international program committee. That began a wonderful relationship with the club. In these last ten years that we've lived in Washington, this club has become very important to me and to my husband. He has loved coming to the programs. He's been an associate member ever since I gave him the membership as a Christmas present when a special promotion for associate members was started a couple of years before we left New York. We've found the club a rich resource for friendship, mental stimulation, and outreach.

"Now we'll talk about my years at the club from 1985, and then the presidency, '88-'89. Let me just say I had a lot of good help and that's the main thing. When I came back to Washington late in '85, as I said, one of the first things I wanted to do was to come back to the club because I always found it so stimulating and I knew I'd find lots of good old friends here. I was disappointed to find the club in a period of great divisiveness and uneasiness. I think the defeat of Mondale for president in 1980 had left people very disheartened. Joan Mondale had been an active member of the club and had involved the club members. They had Joan's Den here, and had really actively worked and supported and felt a part of the process.

"In 1986, '87, members were very divided and disheartened. I was disappointed and tried to help out a little bit on the hospitality committee, to make friends. So I was really overwhelmed and surprised when the nominating committee talked to me in early spring of 1988 about wanting to nominate me for president. I felt that I did not know enough about the club's procedures and its government because I'd not participated in it. I'd been asked once before, in 1969, the year after Orv had left office and we were still in Washington, to agree to be nominated for president and had had to turn it down because I doubted we'd be staying here. So I was amazed, but flattered, and I thought about it quite seriously. Jean Jensen had been an excellent president and had done a lot that year to get things back on track. She had set up a planning session that spring to look into what the club wanted to do, where it wanted to go, and how to get there. They'd lost a lot of members. There were financial problems. They were beginning to have trouble collecting the rent on the building next door. So there were monetary and management and membership problems.

"Anyway, the important thing to me was whether I really could handle the job and get the support. The nominating committee assured me that a fresh face was needed, somebody who'd not been involved with the club's governance, to help pull factions together, and that they would supply me with an executive committee of highly skilled, knowledgeable and experienced, competent people. They did indeed do so. It was the very strong executive committee that made it possible for us to really move forward that year in some very creative ways. It was an important year because it was a presidential election year. Dukakis was already leading in the primaries.

"I was elected at the annual meeting in early June, maybe on a Wednesday, and on the following Monday two things happened. I walked upstairs and on the president's desk was a summons to court from that character, John F. Banzhaf III, who's now professor of law and legal activism at George Washington University, suing us for not having men as full members. The truth is that earlier that year the board had already voted and gone through all the necessary procedures for the male nominees to become full members, not just associate. And at the same annual meeting where I was elected president, the new male eligibility had been passed by the membership. So although we were already in compliance with the law, we had to spend a lot of time, money, and effort to respond to the suit. Madness to spend your time on that when you wanted to be working on getting new male members!

"On that same Monday I realized the full strength of the organizational ability of the people in this club. I had a call from Gretchen Poston saying, Jane, congratulations on being president. Would you like [the wives of candidates Dukakis and Bentsen] there tomorrow afternoon for a reception? Michael Dukakis had announced that day that he was choosing Lloyd Bentsen as his running mate.

"It's now four o'clock on a Monday afternoon. Could we do a reception for them the following afternoon? I said I'd call her back in a few minutes. Luckily, I had already chosen almost all the committee chairmen before I became president, so we were ready to start moving. First, I called the officers and committee chairs, and they activated a telephone network to reach all active members. I knew there were a lot of lifetime members from the Kennedy-Johnson years who weren't really active in the club any more, but whose noses would be out of joint if they weren't notified; and we tried to reach them all.

"I said that we'd just do it simply, nothing fancy, so we wouldn't have to spend a lot of money and we could put it together quickly. If we didn't charge people, there wouldn't be the problem of collecting money at the door. All we'd have to do is give out name tags, get the crowd in here, and keep it very informal. So I called Gretchen back. She was delighted.

"Meanwhile, the staff from the Democratic National Committee were coming over to make arrangements: The Secret Service wanted to be here Tuesday morning, and so forth. I sat down with members and staff to work out the logistics. That was when every bit of experience in my life came into play. Handling the Secret Service people and the Democratic National Committee staff was difficult, but I'd had experience with them in the past and was able to work things out satisfactorily.

"Then I began thinking about the integration picture, because although the club was integrated, not many minority people regularly attended. Shirley Henderson, who'd already given me such good help getting started and organized, was vice president for development, a job that included membership and outreach. Normally, the vice president for administration would have accompanied a guest of honor, but Shirley seemed more appropriate for the occasion. So I called Shirley and asked her to accompany Mrs. Bentsen, and I would accompany Mrs. Dukakis. I asked Jean Jensen, the previous president, to open the meeting. So Jean was pleased, Shirley was pleased, everybody was pleased.

"It was an exciting day. We had over 400 people here. We had telephoned members late into the night, even that morning, and people came, just thrilled to death, and it was a great success and a great start for a new president's year. I think the wisest thing we did was just to invite everybody and finance it out of club funds. That was possible because we did it so simply, with cookies, not a whole big spread, and with only two or three bouquets. As a matter of fact, I think we even got the food and beverages at half price because our suppliers understood the importance of the event. We did have to move the furniture beforehand, but we had staff to do that, and volunteers came in afterwards to tidy things up. The house didn't look its best anyhow because it hadn't been well cared for in recent years.

"That was the beginning of my presidency, and it made me realize the need for getting a lot of people involved. The main thrust of my tenure was to include everybody I could in every event. I was determined to do that."

Carol Channing and Averell Harriman celebrate WNDC's 70th anniversary, January 1992. Mel Chamowitz photo, courtesy WNDC-EF Archives.

Chapter 9
CHANGING TIMES
A Minority and A Boomer

Progress in causes cherished by WNDC members accelerated during the Clinton administration. Bill Clinton, the first Democratic president to be reelected since Franklin D. Roosevelt, advanced more women to executive positions and to the cabinet than any of his predecessors. He doubled the number of women justices on the Supreme Court. He made political sacrifices to block efforts to erode women's hard-won reproductive rights. He secured passage of the Family and Medical Leave Act of 1996. His administration increased funding for battered women's shelters and for law enforcement efforts to prevent crimes against women.

President Clinton and First Lady Hillary Rodham Clinton also championed the welfare of children, another cause high on the WNDC agenda. The Children's Health Insurance Program (CHIP) broadened medical coverage for poor children. Head Start funding grew by more than $600 million, the largest increase since the program was signed into law in the 1960s. The Clinton administration presided over the biggest drop in child poverty in nearly thirty years: from 22.7 percent in '93 to 18.9 percent in '98.

The 1990s were also a decade of progress at WNDC, although, like President Clinton's, the club's pace was uneven. Civil rights and the women's rights movements helped shape the personalities of the two club presidents who would bracket the 1992 election. Shirley Henderson became WNDC's first minority president. Sacha Millstone was its first baby boomer. Both were reformers.

Shirley Henderson
"I was president at the best of times and the worst of times," recalled Shirley Henderson in a 1998 interview. "I was president during the club's seventieth anniver-

sary (1992), a great time to be a Democrat and a member of WNDC. Let's talk about the good times first. We had some really great events for the anniversary.

"The first was a serious symposium on women's rights, very well attended and with a stellar group of speakers. We had Esther Peterson, past club president, labor leader, and consumer advocate; Goler T. Butcher, Howard University law professor; Lynn Cutler, DNC vice chair; Carmen Votaw, Hispanic women's rights activist; Julia Walsh, investment expert; and Mary Lou Friedman, past WNDC president. Sarah Booth Conroy covered the symposium for *[The Washington] Post* 'Style' section.

"She wrote in her article that, 'The speakers called for sharpening the difference between Republicans and Democrats and for the election of a Democratic president and Congress, of course; and made equally adamant statements on equal rights for women. The problem with social programs today is they are being administered, to a great extent, by people who don't believe in them. The Republicans have become the Republi-can'ts, said Peterson.' Esther was marvelous, as always.

"Another outstanding event, a fund raiser, was a retrospective fashion show chaired by Amanda MacKenzie [Hobart]. Members brought out clothes that, for the most part, they had worn to significant Democratic events, or they had a younger member wear them. Jane Freeman modeled a 1960s yellow suit she had worn to one of the Kennedy inaugural events. When she got it out, she discovered a diamond pin that she had thought was lost all those years!

"Peg Colton had two gorgeous gowns from the 1950s that a couple of younger models looked fabulous in. I forget the occasions Peg wore them to, but the gowns were still absolutely beautiful, one orange chiffon and the other rose satin.

"Amanda did a remarkable job with the script. She didn't just have models 'on the runway.' She narrated at length about what was happening politically in the Democratic Party—and in the nation—at the time the clothes were in fashion. All in all, it was a good year.

"Early on we developed, as one of our goals, a two-year strategy to get the club credentialed at the 1992 Democratic National Convention. One of the first things I did was to buttonhole Ron Brown and say, Listen! We have to have credentials for the convention. And he dared not say no! I made him put it in writing in case we met an obstacle, because competition for seats at the convention is very, very keen and at the club we don't have the two things that will get you credentialed: We don't have a lot of votes and we are not deep-pocketed contributors. So we were swimming upstream.

"The other strategy was that we had two members who held important positions at the DNC: Lynn Cutler, who was vice chair; and Claire Apodaca, who was assistant to Ron Brown. During 1991, before the election year, I invited one of the two to be at the head table over and over again whenever we had 'important' speaker luncheons, much to the dismay of some of our members who did not understand the reason behind it. Molly O'Brien's official assignment was to 'schmooze' these two ladies.

"By the time we got to the convention we had a pretty close relationship with the two. So much so, that when Lynn Cutler was married a few months after the election, she had her wedding at the club. She simply walked in and said to the general manager, I don't have time. Do my wedding! And he did! The other thing we did was to get ourselves appointed to the committee planning for the women's activities at the 1992 convention held in New York City.

"We knew we couldn't compete with the larger organizations for the very visible roles at the convention; but we decided we would try for something that would be significant that we could do ourselves and that there wouldn't be much competition for. In fact, I selected the role of handling registrations at the women's caucus, which meant that we could put out our literature and be very visible and participate at the same time. So we were credentialed for eight people the entire time; and for one or two days we were able to get about twenty people on the convention floor.

"After we went to the convention, I decided that the club could benefit from its association with Ron Brown. Alma, his wife, was a member of the club at that time also. So, I knew that if we won the election, he would be in so much demand that we would really have to fight to get him; but if we secured him for a date prior to the election, we would have a better chance. So it could be a big success if we won the election, or it could be a nice little dinner in his honor if we lost. Fortunately, he said yes. Fortunately, we won that election. And fortunately, he was at the height of his popularity at the time. So Sacha Millstone and her *incredible* ability to bring people together and to do fund raising made it the most successful fund raiser that I think we ever had at WNDC. They raised slightly over $100,000; and again, much of that was in the clear because they personally secured the donations of food....

"Shortly after I became president, Pamela Harriman had collapsed her political action committee, her Dems for the '90s PAC. I asked her if we could use that name to encourage young members to join WNDC. At the time of the [Averell] Harriman centennial one of Pamela's friends from New York had contributed $25,000 to be used to promote WNDC membership among young people. So we had a Dems for the '90s kickoff event. Ron Brown and Senator Bob Kerrey from Nebraska were, I think, the speakers. It was such a successful event. I would estimate that we had about a thousand young people in the club that night. They were all in the streets. You couldn't even get in the building.

"The leadership that emerged from that group had, shall I say, goals that were not quite compatible with the goals of WNDC, so the first year or so of Dems for the '90s was pretty rocky. We spent about a year negotiating and trying to work to a point where both groups would feel comfortable in the relationship. I think many of the young leaders of Dems for the '90s had in mind a totally separate organization that would use our facilities and resources for free, that would be financed by Pamela Harriman and not really associated with the Woman's National Democratic Club. On the other hand, the Woman's National Democratic Club saw this group as being a part of the membership, and we had no intention of having it be anything other than that. Also, there was a lot of resistance among some of the older members to what they called 'giving our club away to young people.' What these members didn't take into account was that we had lost money subsidizing their life memberships. As you know, to underwrite club renovations in the 1980s we had offered $1000 life memberships which, in the long run, was a costly mistake. In order to compensate for those losses we either had to increase dues or increase membership numbers. I suppose that whole business of younger members has been a disappointment.

"Pamela Harriman had made significant contributions to the club, being available for speaking engagements and contacts. But during the two years of my presidency we were able to bring her into a closer relationship with the WNDC, largely because of her assistant, Janet Howard.

"Pamela had been a member of the club ever since her marriage to Averell Harriman. In fact, one very famous quote of hers in *The Washington Post* was that when she was invited to join the Cosmos Club shortly after they admitted women members, she said, 'Well, I already have a club. When I need a club, my club is the Woman's National Democratic Club.' She also coined another famous statement about the club, that the WNDC was the Democratic Party's 'living room.'

"In any event, she was very helpful to us during these two years. Whenever we needed a speaker she was willing to help us find someone who could be a good fund raiser. She was at the club quite a bit, and even presided at one speaker luncheon and enjoyed it tremendously. She also wrote letters and made personal phone calls to leading congressional Democrats on our behalf. And she gave the club its podium.

"When we were seated at the Harriman centennial, she looked at me and said, You know, we really do need another podium. And I said Yes, we do. I waited a respectable length of time, and then I called her and reminded her about the podium and asked if she wanted to help us get one. She referred me to the Harriman foundation, and they provided the money for the podium through the WNDC Educational Foundation.

"Here's the story behind the Harriman centennial event at the club. Through Janet Howard I set up an appointment to talk to Pamela about it. We sat in her office while she read speeches that Averell Harriman had given, and cried. I found out later that she was given to doing that frequently. So we both cried together and at the end she said, Well, I think it would be wonderful to have a fund raiser at the club and we'll see how it works out.

"Well, Janet and I and the committee got right to work on a luncheon, and it was a very, very successful affair. I think we raised $97,000 through gifts from Pamela's friends and associates. There was a variety of speakers: John Kenneth Galbraith, Ron Brown, several congressmen and senators. It's funny now, but the Harriman family was all there. The family was united at that particular time.

"Pamela Harriman, I thought, was a unique person. Much has been written about her and the way she achieved her goals, but underneath it all, I felt, was a woman of incredible focus and determination; and I'm not making apologies for her. I think she was the kind of person who would be able to utilize the opportunities and resources that came her way under any set of circumstances. I had the greatest respect for her.

"During my tenure, Harvey Gantt, who was running for the Senate from North Carolina against Jesse Helms, had an event here that's one of my fondest memories. We experimented with a type of programming that could be a model for the ways in which the club could become more active, even though we have a 501(c)(7) tax status and cannot do direct party fund raising.

"I found out that there was a North Carolina club on Capitol Hill, and I called the officers to talk about ways we could raise money for Harvey Gantt. I knew that our membership would be really thrilled to be able to contribute. We formed an organization called 'Friends of Harvey Gantt,' sponsored by the North Carolina club. They mailed out over 500 invitations.

"Prior to his luncheon speech we had a coffee—nothing was served other than coffee—in the library. And it was amazing. In less than half an hour $17,000 was raised for the Harvey Gantt campaign, which technically had nothing to do with the club. It was a private fund raiser and I think I paid fifty dollars out of my pocket for the coffee. Governor, later Senator, Terry Sanford from North Carolina was there. A number of our nonresident members lived in North Carolina, and I asked to have members from North Carolina stand and we were all amazed at the number of people who drove up just to be here when Harvey Gantt spoke at the WNDC.

"Five or six years later, I ran into Harvey Gantt in an airport somewhere in Europe. I went over to speak with him and I said, I know you won't remember me. And he said, Yes, I do. It was that club in Washington. And he remembered how much had been raised and said that was one of the best days of his campaign. He had wonderful memories of the Woman's National Democratic Club.

"Another event during my tenure that I remember very well was when Jesse Jackson came to speak. I think it was done very much on the spur of the moment. I know it wasn't announced in the *News*. One of our African-American members knew someone who worked with his scheduling, and she found out that Jesse Jackson was going to be in Washington. It was during the summer, in August. We simply sent out post cards about four days in advance and scheduled the luncheon, and it was a sellout. I have to say also we had lots of sellouts in those days.

"So Jesse came to the club. We had a reception first. Jesse, John Hechinger, and I were receiving. But the thing I remember—and I find it very humorous—is that Jesse came in asking how long it was going to last. He said he was only able to stay a few minutes, and he wasn't very pleasant about it. I said I was sure that his staff understood that the luncheon programs usually run until about two o'clock, because it's always in our communication to them. He was a little antsy and didn't seem quite happy with it *until* he saw the audience come in. He changed completely! He was a candidate at that time for president, and this would have been one of the few times, early on, when he would have been able to speak to an audience of such diversity. You could see it registering on his face. He told me he could stay as long as we liked!

"Another amusing thing was that a number of our members had planned to come to express their displeasure with Jesse Jackson. They couldn't stand Jesse. They came early and took the tables across the front. They wouldn't actually boo him: They're too gracious for that. But they were not coming to support him. It was something to behold to first see Jesse change, and then to watch Jesse change their views as they sat there. They went from glum-faced and not responding to standing and applauding and laughing. It was quite a day at WNDC!

"I remember his speech—it's probably classic Jesse Jackson—starting off very slowly and then just rising to a real crescendo. At the end, everyone was so worked up, and it was so humorous to watch the people who had come to be the opposition becoming part of the standing applause! True Jesse Jackson....

"I'm ashamed to tell you, but my father was a staunch Republican. I'm not so sure about my mother. Blacks in central Florida were allowed to vote, but they were not active participants in the political process. Rather than being a Lincoln Republican, that is, a Republican based on the fact that 'Lincoln freed the slaves,' my father was a diehard conservative who believed that anyone who wanted to could get ahead, even though he was surrounded by evidence of a different sort.

"I was born in Florida, in a city now known as Winter Haven, but called Florence Villa when I was born in 1929—a real Depression baby—a few months before the stock market crashed. I grew up in Florida. My father was a Baptist minister and a contractor; my mother was a nurse. I had five older brothers and no sisters. As a result, I spent a lot of my time reading since I couldn't be expected to play football all day long. I became interested in government and history, which led me into a history major in college.

"Being a Baptist minister's daughter, I always understood that I would attend Spelman College in Atlanta, Georgia. So, although I was accepted at a number of schools—I think mainly because of my extracurricular activities, which had always been more important to me than my schoolwork—I decided to go to Spelman. I was president of my class; president of the glee club; president of the YWCA; and, during my senior year, president of the student body. I knew Martin Luther King Jr. and his brother.

"I sang in the Morehouse/Spelman glee club for four years and in a smaller ensemble called 'the choir.' Seated behind me for three years as a member of the choir was Martin Luther King Jr. If anyone had asked me to predict Martin Luther King's future, I probably would have said he would be the pastor of a small, insignificant church. He was painfully shy, smiled a lot, and could tell a good joke; but he was regarded as a nerd although we didn't use that word then. Nice, but no one would date him. Ha! On the other hand, his brother, A. D., was the outgoing, extroverted life of the party. I believe A. D. was younger, and we would have chosen him to have been the great leader because he demonstrated what we thought of as leadership ability at that age.

"We knew Martin Luther King's father even better. His father was an extraordinarily gifted speaker and he often spoke at chapel at Spelman and Morehouse. I knew his sister, Christine, and his mother. His mother was a magnificent organist who played the organ in the church and directed the church choir. They were an unusual middle-class family. I often laugh when I hear people describe Martin Luther King as having come up in a very poor Southern family under dire circumstances. That, in fact, is not the case....

"When I arrived in Washington a very prominent socialite took me under her wing, and one day she said, You know, everyone really should have an intown club. Next week we're going to the Woman's National Democratic Club, chauffeur and all! And that's how I got here, and how I became fascinated with the emphasis on the political. Although I'd been involved in local politics in Pittsburgh, Washington would be an opportunity to explore ways I might be helpful in national politics. It seemed a good fit for me, so I joined. Those first years I simply came to programs occasionally. My children were still in school and I didn't have time for many outside activities. Eventually I dropped out of the club, but in the '80s I renewed my membership and met Jean Jensen, who was determined to get me further involved, and she did!

"When I became president in 1990, even though we had elected governors and elected officers, there was no set number for the board: Basically, anyone who wanted to be on the board was on the board, including the committee chairs. We didn't have a fixed number for a quorum. The composition would change so much from meeting to meeting that we spent a lot of time going back over information that had been presented at a previous board meeting. There was just no set pattern to it. We spent a lot of time spinning our wheels.

"Members seemed to feel that if they were not there when the decision was made, it really hadn't been made. So we found ourselves reconsidering issues quite frequently, and my own view was that it was an unmanageable process. We spent an inordinate amount of time doing committee work at board meetings, and the board was not really focused on its three primary responsibilities: policy, management, and finance. As a result of a strategic planning session, we recommended that the board be reduced to a definite number. Governors would carry out their functions as governors. The board would have a more formal, structured way of operating. We also increased the annual membership meetings from one to two.

"The other thing was that members who had never been elected were serving on the board and making decisions. Some of those women had been on the board twenty or thirty years and felt that they had the right to be there. As I say, to make any change was a very controversial move. The decision involved understanding that people wanted the right to be on the board and to make decisions. Because that desire was so ingrained in the corporate culture, it took time to change, but change finally occurred in May 1992.

"As I said earlier, it was the best of times, and it was the worst of times. And the worst of times had to do with 1520 New Hampshire Avenue. During the first month of my presidency I received a letter from the nine attorneys who had remodeled and were leasing 1520 New Hampshire Avenue, the building we owned next door. I don't know when the club acquired it and I don't recall the purchase price, but it was an incredibly good buy. For a number of years before the attorneys took it over it was rented by the Children's Defense Fund [CDF] as their primary office space. When the CDF moved out during the real estate boom in the early '80s, the building was left in disrepair and the club did not have the money to renovate it because we were just about to renovate the clubhouse. So, we rented 1520 'as is' to a group of lawyers for twenty-five years at $2,500 a month.

"By the way, I'd always heard that we mortgaged 1520 to pay off the $620,000 debt for renovating the clubhouse. In fact, we discovered later that it was not 1520 that was collateral for the loan, but the clubhouse itself!....

"My second month in office I received a notice from the attorneys that they would not continue paying the $2,500 a month, and we desperately needed that income for our operating costs. We negotiated with them for about six months, trying to get them to pay. Their response was that they'd pay only if we would renegotiate the lease for ninety-nine years and become a partner with them in a losing deal: They had 'over-remodeled' the building and had a $2 million loan outstanding. Because of the real estate market downturn in Washington during the early '90s, they couldn't find tenants to cover their expenses. So they were really in a bind.

"We, too, were in a bind and we couldn't afford to allow them to renegotiate the terms of the lease to their advantage, nor to become a partner with them in a losing venture. A further complication was that the mortgage on 1526 New Hampshire Avenue had a balloon payment coming due in 1992. About three months before that payment was due, I received a call from a young woman vice president of the bank that was handling our account. The attorneys had notified our bank of their demand. She threatened to call the loan unless we renegotiated our lease. Our pro bono attorneys urged us to take a conciliatory approach, but we couldn't afford to back down. So I turned to my friend Bardyl Tirana, whom I had worked with at national YWCA. He had given us extraordinarily good advice in a similar situation involving a much larger sum of money, and I knew his reputation. He advised us to take a more aggressive approach, and amazingly, the board and membership agreed.

"Bardyl advised us to 'throw dollars' at the courts because the only way we could outwit nine lawyers would be to keep them very, very busy and wear them down rather than their wearing us down. I think we filed at least five different suits in five different courts. We kept filing until we finally found a judge who agreed that we could break the lease, that the lease did not exist because they had stopped paying the rent. We lost several times before we finally won.

"The lease was declared null and void, which meant that WNDC could take over the property. We began shopping for a loan from another bank. The first bank's vice president told me that no one was going to refinance us. In her words, You are marked, and unless you refinance with us, you will not be able to refinance anywhere. In fact, the Dolley Madison Bank came to our rescue.

"During the process we had to get a bridge loan. Our original bank gave us the bridge loan, but charged us points as if we were getting a new traditional loan. When I talked with them about it, they said we were going to have to refinance with them anyway after we renegotiated our lease, so we might as well pay it now. Well, I had to do it! But I did get a letter from the bank vice president, stating that if we received permanent financing from another bank, they'd refund our money. So, Sacha Millstone, who became president after me, took *great* delight in presenting them with this letter and getting a full refund, small as it was, on all the fees we'd paid for the bridge loan. And it all turned out well except, as you know, we didn't have the money for legal services and I'd negotiated an agreement with Bardyl that he would do whatever he had to do, but wait for his money until we had some. We paid off the mortgage on 1526 when we sold 1520, and I think that pretty well deals with the financial situation. But I don't think most people realized how close we were to losing the club.

"I was the first African-American president of WNDC. I've been involved since the '60s in many organizations. In fact, I have integrated—it seems like a quaint word now—but during the late '50s, early '60s, I integrated lots of organizations. It was sort of my mission to break down barriers and to work with women of different cultures. It's my YWCA background. I've held leadership positions in many organizations, most of them integrated. This was the first time I'd led an organization or been invited to leadership in an organization in which my race was not a factor one way or the other. In fact, I refused to serve as president for three years. Each time the nominating committee had asked me to serve as president, I refused. I don't remember why. I guess I was involved in many other things. I was also fearful that we had not been addressing certain financial problems that, frankly, I didn't want to fall on my shoulders. I think there were some other issues that needed to be worked through in the club that I just didn't feel like facing. Inevitably, I had to. I was really testing to be sure that the resolve was there. And I must tell you that I had a number of not unsettling, but sometimes rather strange, occurrences, and had they happened anywhere else and at a different time I would have been offended. But I was comfortable enough at WNDC not to have to feel offended. I think it is a great, great tribute to the membership.

"During my presidency, Wynn Newman, who was the first male member of the club, was on the governing board. He joined in 1988 shortly after the vote to admit men, and was elected to the governing board in June, 1989. Wynn was a leading attorney in the movement to achieve pay equity for women, but I'm hazy over how he came to join the club.

"Also in 1988, when Jane Freeman was WNDC president, John Banzhaf at The George Washington University Law School filed suits against women's clubs, including WNDC, that were relegating men to associate memberships and not permitting them to hold leadership positions. He visited WNDC several times prior to filing. But we had Wynn on the membership roster, and when *The Washington Post* called we were able to say that we already had a male member and would be happy to have many others! The *Post* apparently asked to talk to Wynn, and he ably handled the press for us."

Sacha Millstone

Sacha Millstone's vision for the future of the Woman's National Democratic Club mirrored Shirley Henderson's. Both were advocates for change. Both confronted a membership resistant to change, one that liked things just the way they were. "I was elected president of WNDC in 1992," recalled Sacha Millstone in a 1996 interview. "I would say that my time as president was probably the most 'revolutionary' of the club's existence. Quite a year!

"Basically, we hoped to extend the membership, really reach out to younger professionals. We needed to raise a lot of money to bail the club out of its precarious financial position. It just so happened that there was an exciting presidential election then, too, which worked to our advantage. Our efforts created some controversy among the membership, but ultimately, we reached the goals we set.

"We started off by doing some market research. Almost the first thing I did was contact professional PR women in town from an organization called, I believe, 'Women in Communications.' I asked for volunteers to work on PR and outreach. Three people responded, all of whom were fabulous, so I took them on. That led to the first controversy. Basically, what I wanted to do in exchange for their time was allow them to be members. I told them, they could be members if they'd help me. Immediate outrage! Members saying, Oh, you can't give away a membership! I said, But these people are going to give us hours and hours of time! We *all* give hours and hours of our time and *we* don't get free membership! I just thought it was logical that you take a really talented and excited young person—they were all well under thirty-five—who is willing to give her time, but can't afford to be a member, and make her one. No! The membership would not allow me to do it.

"So I ended up paying my own money so they could be members and we got these wonderful women on board anyway. The most exciting and helpful to me overall was Suzanne Turner. She had *great* ideas, really brilliant. She said that first we needed to do a marketing survey to see how young people perceive the organization. Once we find that out, and what it would take for them to join, we can draft a plan.

"I thought that was a great idea, so Suzanne got Democratic pollster, Peter Hart, to volunteer to conduct the survey. You would think everyone would have been thrilled, but no-o-o. This was not something, I guess, the membership wanted to hear. Of course, the survey wouldn't be entirely flattering. We didn't plan the project so that we could hear wonderful things about WNDC. We wanted to know what the community thought about us, both good *and* bad!

"The focus group we assembled consisted of a great mix of neat women from all walks of life, all under fifty. I think some were as young as early twenties. Suzanne led them in a fabulous session. She got great information. Peter Hart had his firm transcribe the session for free and analyze the results so as to tell us what we needed to do to make a plan.

"Next, I decided that we needed to really work on fund raising because the club had no idea how to raise money. The next controversy came up because I wanted to pay a member's daughter to raise money for the club. That idea just did not go over *at all!* I wanted to pay her a percentage of what she raised. What's the big deal? I thought. Everybody I know gets paid for raising money. I didn't even think about it, but it turned out this was so offensive that there was a major sort of coalition that really worked against us. I was very naive: I didn't understand how everything had to go through this, that, and the other committee. I was thinking, Let's get this done. We only have a year. We don't have six months to be going through committees!

"I got it approved, but we stepped on a lot of toes and made people really mad.

Because of that, they *purposely* did not support the fund raising event. So even though we ended up having *the* best fund raising year the club had ever had, we were prevented from putting on many of the fund raising events we wanted to, say, one or two small ones a month. Not major fund raisers, but exciting. Club members were convinced this would fail, and most of them did everything they could to make sure it *did* fail. Not everybody, but it was hard. There was an undercurrent of controversy.

"Despite that, the first event we put on was a wonderful jazz evening. It was just great. We got the Keter Betts Trio and a performer named Betty Martin, who rejoined the club after I became president. She had owned a place called Charlie's of Georgetown, a very classy jazz club. She was so excited. We tried to do a regular jazz cabaret. It didn't work out, but the first night was really fantastic. The club was full: over 200 people, all of them young. That was our first recruiting event. We put out membership materials and got a whole bunch of people that way. In October we did the jazz night; in December we had a really fine Christmas party. We tried to make it more fun: Do the political stuff, but also make it a more 'meet-the-people' event.

"Then the national campaign started and we got involved in that. We changed the club's newsletter, changed the calendar format, tried to make it more exciting. Tried to see which members were working on the campaign and have them report back to the club. Make it seem like a really alive and exciting place.

"So, we were raising money and we were bringing in new members: We had over 1,700 members that year. Certainly, the national election helped. We ended up raising some money early on for Clinton. In May, before the convention, when it wasn't at all clear that he would be the candidate, we were able to have several members, including me, invited to a private fund raiser for Clinton. That was really good for the club. Several of us went to the convention and were fairly visible there, which was also a good thing: We could participate in the women's caucus, etc. So we did a lot of outreach that year. It was really fun. Wherever I would go, people would ask, You're the president of WNDC? People really knew about us.

"The fact that I was young made a difference in people's opinion of the club, but I became president so fast that the members did not know me and I certainly did not know our membership. If I'd known the bureaucracy and how it worked, things might have turned out better in the end. But unfortunately, I felt that we just didn't have that much time. This was a narrow window of opportunity. It was an election year. We had excitement going our way, and I just really thought, You people need to lighten up and let us experiment! Of course, that was very threatening. Many people felt I was trampling on, sort of, 'the way it was, the way it was supposed to be,' and not giving them enough respect....

"I was born in St. Louis, Missouri. My father worked for *The St. Louis Post-Dispatch.* He was transferred to the Washington office when I was very young, so he covered the Kennedy, Johnson, and Nixon administrations and the Supreme Court. He also covered many of the civil rights issues, protests, and so forth. So I'd say I grew up in a political environment in Washington during the '60s and early '70s. Our house was always full of people talking about politics from the time I can remember.

"During the Vietnam War, whenever there would be a protest march here, my parents would put up protesters at the house. They were my heroes, the Vietnam War protesters. I was about eleven or twelve years old then, and I was so fascinated. These people seemed so romantic and exotic. My ambition was to grow up and be a hippie, but it wasn't possible by the time I got old enough to be one! So I had to turn to more mainstream approaches, I guess.

"Both of my parents were Democrats. They didn't get involved in party activities because my father was a journalist. They never actively supported a candidate by working on a campaign or anything like that, but my father made no pretense of being other than a Democrat. He was very much influenced by the civil rights struggle, and certainly a lot by both Martin Luther King and Bobby Kennedy.

"My parents were the primary influence on my becoming a Democrat. Definitely, my parents. You know, the big thing during my childhood was Nixon. My dad was on the Nixon enemies list. Watergate was a big deal, obviously, with my father in the news business. It was a big topic of conversation. I remember watching the news and I remember the whole Watergate story unfolding, and definitely, I remember Nixon's resigning.

"I was at Earlham College in Richmond, Indiana, and there's not an awful lot going on there politically. So at the earliest opportunity I did a semester in Washington and an internship with Common Cause. I always wanted to come back and work on the Hill, but after that I didn't do anything political. My father had a very broad definition of the word 'nepotism.' He didn't believe in helping his kids, which is weird, but he really didn't. It has dawned on me in recent years that all I had to do was call up his friends, but I didn't do that.

"After college I had no idea what to do. I didn't have any contacts at all, no guidance. So I ended up at the General Accounting Office. It was a terrible job. I hated it. I did that for a little while, and then I got a job in a bank, whatever way I could figure out to earn a living. Then I went to graduate school and got an MBA in financing investments and got into the investment world.

"All this time I had been trying to figure out how somebody who doesn't work on the Hill or as a lobbyist or isn't an attorney gets involved in politics. How do you do it? I didn't know, so I kept looking around for different things. I probably joined EMILY's List first, but, of course, there's nothing much to do with them except write checks. I guess when I started to make enough money that I could give a little bit away, I got involved with EMILY's List.

"I don't remember what brought the Woman's National Democratic Club to my attention first, but I think my boss at the time thought it was important to be involved in the community in various ways, and she had some clients who were members of the WNDC. She thought it would be a good thing for me. At the time I was really involved in a business and professional organization called The National Association for Professional Saleswomen, and I was in some leadership roles there, including program chair.

"Anyway, what happened then was Anita Hill. I was a member of the club about a year before that. I was probably the finance chair at that time, and I was going to some programs but wasn't really that involved. Then the Anita Hill episode occurred. I was attending a meeting of the National Professional Saleswomen and the speaker one night was talking about women's networking. But I couldn't let the night go. I felt the Anita Hill event was having an effect on everybody. I needed to say something. I was the introducer, so I made a sort of political speech, the most political thing that had ever happened at this group's meetings. I don't know why, but that was a real turning point for me. People really responded to that introduction, and as a result I got more involved in WNDC with my heart, not just for networking....

"Another thing was the wonderful fund raiser with Ron Brown on December 3, one month after the election. It was certainly the best thing I'd ever done at the club. We actually *netted* over $100,000. We had a lot of help from Pamela Harriman and Janet Howard to make that happen. People like Mickey Kantor and Alexis Herman were there. [Washington] Mayor Sharon Pratt Kelly spoke. Lots of people came who had known Ron during all stages of his life. The club looked fantastic. The atmosphere was very electric.

"I forgot to mention that during the whole year we had great press. We were in international papers. We were in *Jet* magazine, in *The New Yorker*. The party for Ron Brown got a big play. There was a big story on Pamela Harriman. We had all kinds of wonderful press, not only about parties but also about substance.

"We were really good about identifying hot topics, like NAFTA, and weighing in on them. We had lots of sessions about campaign finance reform. We were actually having enough influence that we made EMILY's List mad. I thought it was great, but I was the only one.

"We had a great group that worked together. We were able to raise money. We were able to get WNDC on the map again and make it a forum for discussion of issues. We attracted a bunch of new members. It was a very alive time, I think.

"There were so many people at our election eve party they were coming out of doors and windows. It was very exciting and exhilarating. We had over 400 people in the house; and, of course, every time we did that, one of the old guard would say we couldn't accommodate that many people or she didn't like it when it was too crowded. But we did it anyway. We had TVs in every room. I'm pretty sure we even got a big screen for that election eve night. We brought in life-size cutouts of Bill and Hillary so people could have their pictures taken with them. We charged them, of course. I think there was entertainment. We had food, balloons. We were packed.

"The other thing we did was for inaugural night. We sold tickets for fifty dollars. We should have charged a hundred! We had 600 people; we had to actually turn people away. Pamela Harriman's fund raiser, Janet Howard, used to tell me, 'Never, ever, turn anybody away!' But we couldn't, really, contain more than 600 people. Inaugural night was the best party. People came back from the inaugural balls because they were boring and crowded and there was nothing to eat. We ran out of food, and artists, too, I think. But we had a great band. People were dancing. I mean, it was a blast! It really was.

"Actually, we did one more fund raiser after that, a small one. We called it 'Shattering the Glass Ceiling.' We were trying to establish a type of fund raiser that could be carried forward year after year after year. By this time, however, there was so much animosity. It's amazing that there was. To this day I can't even believe it myself. People were so angry that the organizer was making a percentage of these deals that they didn't want to support anything she did. I think it wasn't only that she was making money that was a big problem. Her personality is sort of like mine: We just were going to get this done! If people wanted to object, they could object, but we were going to do it anyway.

"We weren't as sensitive as we could have been and I think there was a lot of backlash. Anyway, when we did the Shattering the Glass Ceiling fund raiser, it was a lovely program, really; and, again, we were trying to have substance, as well. But the theme did not appeal at all to our membership. I don't think we sold more than maybe five tickets to members. So we had a really hard time. I think we only raised $30,000. We got money from corporate people. That was our last event. And the whole time people were saying, This is going to fail. This is going to fail. Of course, it didn't fail, but it didn't do as well as it could have done.

"For that fund raiser we had the woman who made the 'shattering the glass ceiling' pins that were very popular at the time design a special award for us to present. *That* could have been carried forward, could have been something really good for the club, something it could have gotten known for, could have gotten press coverage for, something that could have reached out to different parts of the community. But nobody was interested. And that was the last event.

"So, basically, what happened then was WNDC elections, and they decided not to renominate me. There was a whole contingent that decided they were going to write me in as a candidate. Truthfully, I didn't want that, but quite a few people who'd never been involved before had spent a great deal of time and energy on trying to make these changes. They felt that without me as president those changes would disappear, and given the slate that was nominated, I agreed. This group asked me if I would accept a write-in petition, and I said I would.

"Anyway, I did run because they did a write-in. I lost pretty badly, I think. That wasn't good. I kind of wish that that part hadn't happened. All the other parts I think were great. I don't regret a single minute of it. I had a great time. I learned a lot. I met a lot of great people and have a lot of wonderful friends to this day from that time. There are, maybe, things I would have done a little differently, but, I have to tell you honestly, not the major ones.

"What I think is we shocked the hell out of people. We created some opportunities and we made a lot of progress; and I hear through the grapevine from people I still know who are active at WNDC that much of what we talked about is starting to actually happen. So maybe someone just had to be there to do it the first time and be sort of a lightning rod. But the ending was very unpleasant for me. I felt that I had given the organization my best. I really did give it a lot of time and energy. I basically worked there as much as I worked at my job.

"I may be the only president who had a full-time job. I support myself completely; I don't have anything else. So I really gave the club a lot, and I felt that I'd done what I needed to do. So I let my membership lapse.

"I ended up going over to the Democratic National Committee and joined the people who were starting the Women's Leadership Forum, which is part of the Democratic National Committee. That wouldn't have happened if I hadn't met Lynn Cutler and Claire Apodaca through WNDC. We just started saying in 1992 that there was all this energy from women, and we didn't want to see it die. So in the summer of '93 we decided to start the Forum. It was very successful and exciting. *This year [1996] the Women's Leadership Forum raised $5 million for the Democratic Party, starting from zero three years ago. Almost 30,000 people came to events that we had in nineteen cities all across the country.*

"I always seem to have two jobs: one that I get paid for and one on which I spend my money. I feel every single person can make a huge difference, and we all should, in whatever way we possibly can. Well, this is the way I know how to do it, and so, the way I'll do it.

"Oh, the other thing was that when I was president, there was a big argument about whether we should be more political. Now, a huge majority of the members thought we were a *social* club. Well, the time for a social club has passed. It had passed when I was president and it has totally passed now. There is no need for a social club. The last thing women need is a social club. Nobody has any time. So you have to figure out some way to grow which will allow people to be involved in some way where they think they're making a true contribution, give them a structure in which they can make a contribution and have an influence. They will pay for that. So it needs to be a political club that is legal. You know, there is a fine line you must tread. But as we said then, and as I'll say now, if the Christian Coalition can do what they do, if the club is going to be a little bit political, it's certainly not going to be the major scandal of Washington. Nobody's going to attack it. So, go for it! That's what I say. Other than that, I just keep my own counsel.

"The other thing that WNDC has which I think is so wonderful, and that we did publicize a little bit, is all the historical material in the archives. We got that on TV a couple of times. We did a whole thing on Channel 8. They went through the entire house. The history in that house should be shared with the public. For instance, I wanted to make a big deal about that one page from the Kennedy speech that's been framed. I wanted to lend it to President Clinton to hang in the Oval Office during his time and make a ceremony of it. Members of the club were afraid that if someone found out we had it, it might get taken away from us. Again, I'd say, go for it! I think the president would absolutely love it. He probably doesn't even know that thing is in Washington!

"When I left the club I got a huge number of letters that were incredibly supportive and thanking me for everything. I do feel good about the whole thing. In fact, it was what needed to happen at the time both for the organization and for me, so I'm glad that it was possible. That's about it."

Sponsored by WNDC's Public Policy Committee, marchers gather for the Million Mom March to promote tighter gun control, 14 May, 2000.

Chapter 10
TASK FORCES AND COMMITTEES
Working Together

"If you can read, thank a teacher," said Esther Glasser, chair of the Education and Children's Issues Task Force, one of nine WNDC study groups that formulate club policy on political and social issues. Glasser, a passionate advocate of public education, shares the club's leadership with elected officers, including the governing board, twenty-two volunteer committee chairs, and eight additional task force chairs.

Committee chairs report to the club vice presidents for administration, finance, membership, programs, and public relations. The exception is the chair of the public policy committee who is also vice president for political affairs. Committees assume both major and minor roles in the club's management, and their activities account for many of the recorded recollections in the book.

Ola Reeves, as chair of the telephone committee, embodies the dedication committee chairs bring to their jobs. Reeves made a routine committee essential to the club by dramatically increasing attendance at WNDC events. When a low turn-out was projected, the telephone committee went to work urging members to swell the ranks. Reeves drew on organizational skills developed during her years in employee and labor relations: For twenty-six years from Alaska to Washington, she received merit, outstanding, and exceptional performance awards from territorial and federal agencies.

The public policy committee is an umbrella for the nine task forces. With governing board approval, task force chairs release the club's policy statements to the membership, to Congress, to the administration, and to the media. In 1974, at the end of her presidency, Sherley Koteen organized a political action committee (PAC) to shelter the wide-ranging activities of the task forces. Years later, Koteen noted, the club's PAC had wisely changed its name to public policy committee. A capable salaried staff completes the club work force, serving as a support system for committee and task force activity.

The Task Forces

Task force issues range from the global concerns of the Environment and Natural Resources (E&NR) Task Force to local matters confronting the DC/Metro group. The goals of the E&NR task force are formidable and its policy positions ambitious. E&NR supports adequate funding of the Environmental Protection Agency; strict enforcement of the Clean Air Act; international cooperation to protect air quality (acid rain, greenhouse gases, ozone); strengthening of the Clean Water Act and Safe Drinking Water Act; ecosystem preservation in public land management; lower world fertility rates and higher living standards through planned parenthood; and review of the U.S. immigration policy to ensure above-poverty wages for American citizens. Closer to home, the E&NR is waging a campaign to install energy-saving light bulbs in the WNDC clubhouse and in members' homes.

Some task forces are short-lived, especially those formed to address a specific, immediate concern. Others, like Health and Social Security, and Foreign Policy, endure, seeking solutions to national and international problems. (See Chapter 6, Dorothy Dillon's account of a Foreign Policy Task Force study tour.) The Health and Social Security Task Force keeps the membership informed of relevant issues before the White House, Congress, and the state houses; and supports the administration's Medicare and Medicaid, Welfare Reform, and Social Security legislation.

Still other task forces, like DC/Metro, lie dormant until a political event, such as Mayor Anthony Williams's 1998 election, spark new hope for home rule, urban school initiatives, and voting rights for residents of the District of Columbia. The Campaign Finance Task Force has begun addressing much needed reforms.

The Housing Task Force, one of the club's most durable, resulted from a 1988 seminar that proposed "to first help those in greatest need, the homeless." Former HUD deputy assistant secretary Marilyn Melkonian challenged club members by asserting that "housing is thought of as a right. It is a critical measure of how we are succeeding as a society. But it is not treated as a right. It is a consumer good in a free-market system where ability to pay and social acceptance serve as the filters that determine access." Rising to the secretary's challenge, the task force has, over the years, confronted the inequity: While the nature of housing problems remains the same, the solutions appear to demand more than physical shelter for the socially dependent. As a result, Housing has become the Urban Development and Housing

Task Force, and its advocacy ranges from childcare for low-income and homeless families to youth programs, gun control, and drug-free public housing.

Three task forces—Education and Children's Issues, Telecommunications, and Global Women—are examined in some detail. The Education Task Force, established in 1985, owes its longevity to chair Esther Glasser. Telecommunications addresses the club's urgent need to understand and use computer technology. Its chair is WNDC governor and former Federal Trade Commissioner Mary Gardiner Jones. Global Women, co-chaired by Ellen Overton and Ruth Nadel, was largely inspired by the highly publicized 1995 international women's conference in Beijing.

Esther Glasser

"I took over as chair of the Education and Children's Issues Task Force in 1985," recalled Esther Glasser in a 1999 interview, "soon after the Reagan commission on education issued its report, 'A Nation at Risk: Mediocrity in America's Schools.' The education crisis could no longer be ignored. Our mission was to support quality public education essential to America's competitive, democratic society, and to educate WNDC members on reforms needed to restructure the nation's public schools. The task force began to study the many complex issues; to formulate positions; and to make WNDC heard by legislators at the national, state, and local level.

"Most Americans are simply not aware of the pressing needs for school modernization and construction in urban centers. The problem with many public schools is that the middle class has moved to the suburbs or become enamored of private schools. Changing demographics is also a factor. We have begun to have a large number of students who don't speak English. And families have changed. Single parents and parents holding two jobs don't have time. Many don't speak English, didn't attend American schools, and are intimidated by the school itself. So the children don't have the parental support that encourages success in school.

"The task force takes a holistic approach to remedying the education crisis. We support the club position on gun control. We support Bill Clinton's Year 2000 education agenda: Every child should start school ready to learn and should be attending a safe and drug-free school. The task force encourages increased funding for Head Start. We strongly support the expansion of preschool programs in the DC public school system and elsewhere; and of quality, accessible childcare. Similarly, we have a concern for latchkey children, who are on their own after school. The president is strongly supportive of before- and after-school programs, and so are we....

"Republicans wanted to use the government shut-down as an excuse for eliminating the federal Department of Education. The task force was helpful in that situation, calling and writing Congress and the White House. Secretary of Education Richard Riley has spoken to the membership twice about the importance of maintaining the federal presence in U.S. education, of raising standards, and improving the quality of teacher training.

"We've also supported other groups acting on behalf of education and children. For example, one of the newest initiatives is CHIP, the Children's Health Insurance Program, which is an attempt to reach children who are uninsured. We know that success in school is linked to good health. If early conditions are not identified and corrected, a child can be handicapped by loss of sight or hearing. A task force member with a PhD in public health has joined a DC coalition identifying uninsured children. The WNDC Educational Foundation's Young Woman's Leadership group is also involved in an identification project at Dunbar Senior High School.

"The task force firmly adheres to the principle that education tax dollars should stay within the public schools. When the Bush administration began talking about privatization of the public schools, I, along with many national educators, saw it as a step toward depriving the system of necessary resources for improvement. Schools-for-profit are no guarantee of quality. Nor will a small voucher go far in underwriting a first-class private education. We transmit democratic ideas and values through our public schools. If America is to remain a healthy democracy, we must pay attention to the needs of the public schools.

"The task force advocates improvements in teacher training and mentoring. Surveys show how difficult it is for a beginning teacher to cope with everything that's expected. Holding principals accountable for what goes on in the classrooms means that principals will have to step out of their offices and work with the new staff. We also hope that tomorrow's teachers will be coming out of training institutions that have a more enlightened understanding of what makes an effective teacher. But there is the troublesome issue of salaries. Low pay scales for teachers in early childhood education and daycare centers discourage highly qualified applicants. As education improves, we hope the public will recognize the real value of teachers by paying them what they deserve. It's the old story: If you can read, thank a teacher!

"A diploma has to mean something. One of the sins in public schools has been social promotion, which is, fortunately, falling out of favor. President Clinton's emphasis on national testing started the ball rolling. Many teachers object that 'teaching to the test' narrows what they can include in lesson plans. Advocates of testing say that if a child starts fourth grade in New York City and moves, say, to Peoria, fourth grade in Peoria should look like fourth grade New York. If we ever get nationwide tests—and this is an ongoing struggle, believe me—we will be able to really evaluate the job schools are doing.

"Our task force is looking at two new movements in education: charter schools and magnet schools. Any individual or group, lay or sectarian, can organize a charter school, which is free of many of the restraints imposed by the public school system. The concept is supported by the president and by the Department of Education. Experts say it's too soon to know whether charter schools work. One concern is their lack of accountability. Another is related to the question of separation of church and state.

"Computers are another relatively new introduction to the education field. The goal is to equip individual schools with computers and computer instructors so that children in the lowest grades will become computer literate. The Neval Thomas school, which the club has adopted, has computers. The difficulty has been training the teachers.

"Dropouts and truancy are serious problems. There's a link between the truant and the dropout and some of the juvenile crime. Truants and dropouts are out on the streets, and without any supervision they will get into trouble. But we're a long way from understanding what keeps children in school. Usually, the kid who becomes truant is the kid who is failing in the system; or the system's failing the kid. Frequently, the parent is at work or preoccupied and doesn't even know that the child didn't go to school that day. That's a tough problem.

"Many children qualify for special education. During the Johnson administration a law was passed mandating special education for kids who have learning problems. If DC is an example, this system has failed so far to include a large number of learning-disabled children who are frequently the most destructive children in the system. It's one step forward and two steps backward. Now there seems to be some concern in the courts that we've overreached in our efforts to assist the handicapped.

"I think we, as a club whose members are largely women, will be taking a good look at the issue of gender education. Women now are going in for higher education in greater numbers than men. This is not a wholesome trend.

"A few of our members are mentors or tutors to inner city school kids. We've tried to recruit more, but there are issues of time, commitment, and personal safety. I have a task force mailing list that goes out to about thirty-five people, but it's only when we have a workshop preceding a luncheon speaker that we have an attendance of fifty or more. Otherwise, it's a struggle, really, to get ten people to a task force meeting. Some of the task force members have been with me since the beginning and they are wonderful supporters. We have a couple of retired principals, and people who join the club gravitate towards the Education Task Force if they come out of any kind of education or social work background.

"There is certainly an appreciation of the importance of education in this club. Members may not always be actively involved, but let's not minimize what they can do when they take seriously our pleas to support this, that, and the other legislation. It is the aware public that does this, especially women, whose uppermost interests are their families, their children, and education.

"Recently I attended a demonstration of the use of our Web site to connect us with Congress, and was able to find out what Senator Kennedy's committee was doing on a specific piece of legislation. So now we have that as a valuable tool. And, once again, when the Democratic party meets to draft its platform, we will make our recommendations on education. Maybe the most important thing the task force does is to keep a 'conversation' going between our membership and the legislative bodies that determine the health and welfare of our public education system."

Mary Gardiner Jones

Former Federal Trade Commissioner Mary Gardiner Jones founded WNDC's Telecommunications Task Force. A graduate of Wellesley and Yale Law School, she has also been a teacher, attorney, and entrepreneur, "all with varying degrees of success," she revealed in a 1997 interview. A member of WNDC's governing board, she is currently exploring the potential for administering health care via the Internet.

"The future of WNDC is online," Jones asserted. "To attract young members and to reach a wider segment of the public beyond our membership, we must develop interest in the Internet. Club members must be aware of its virtually limitless potential for communicating and transmitting information. Just one mundane example. If WNDC's entire membership were online, we could annually save thousands of administrative dollars by eliminating stationery, envelopes, stamps, ink cartridges, computer paper, etc. We could simply e-mail notices to members.

"The Internet has been called the great democratizer in our society, and it seems that Democrats should be able to capitalize on that concept. The club's job is to educate. Think of making our political action dispatches available, with a few clicks of a mouse, to the millions of America Online users. We could become noted for our position papers on our Web site. If you want the Democratic position on national childcare or gun riddance, for instance, go to the WNDC Web site. Equally important are the expectations of our future members, retiring baby boomers who will assume that any club, and especially a political club, will have the latest technology. If not, that generation will find us hopelessly out of date and go elsewhere. We've begun bringing the club membership online, but we have a way to go.

"In the fall of 1994 the program committee had been trying to persuade Vice President Al Gore to speak at the club. He has taken such a leadership role in promoting a national agenda for the Internet. We hoped he would address our members on his vision of its future and the benefits it would bring to individual citizens. We never found a mutually convenient time for him to come to the club, so I was asked to develop a daylong forum on the Internet, and this we did in October. The enthusiastic response to the forum led to the creation in November of the Telecommunications—the Telecom—Task Force that enabled the club to take a position on the important public interest issues of access to the Net, privacy on the Net, and online consumer services.

"We mounted a morning seminar the next spring called "A Citizen's Guide to Using the Information Superhighway." That's what we were calling the Internet in those days. After the seminar, Victor Sussman, senior cyberspace editor of *U.S. News and World Report,* spoke at a luncheon on the political and privacy implications of the Internet. Some of those issues aren't resolved today, and with the rapid advances in technology, may never be!

"Our next effort was a symposium in March 1996 devoted to an examination of the new telecommunications bill which was moving through Congress. We explored the issues of privacy and copyright and looked at the competitive aspects of the Telecommunications Act. Then the luncheon speaker explored what the legislation could mean for consumers. The symposium led to an increase in task force membership, and it soon became clear that club members were also very much interested in the 'how to' aspects of computers. So we organized a hands-on computer session, and about thirty WNDC members attended. As a major task force project we equipped the third floor volunteer room with PCs for member and staff use, and offered individual computer lessons. Members generously donated computers, and the club staff did yeoman work upgrading them for online capability. Then the oral history committee contributed a Macintosh to the EF archives, and installed a dedicated line. We made a presentation to the public policy committee on the need for e-mail and a Web site to promote club activities to a much broader audience.

"My interest in telecommunications began in 1967. I was at the Federal Trade Commission, and I'd been on the President's Committee on Science and Technical Information. We'd been concerned about the same issues we're concerned about today: access, privacy, quality of information, copyright, and all those communications issues. I published an article in the AAUW [American Association of University Women] journal on some of the policy issues I could see coming down the road for schools. That got the attention of people in the information field; and Educom, which is the computer network for educational institutions, invited me to participate in their various conferences. I didn't understand their technical language, but I did understand the social policy issues involved, and my role was to ask that kind of question. In the process I learned a lot....

"The vacancy on the Federal Trade Commission in 1964 was a Republican spot. I could qualify in those days as a Republican. Nobody asked me how or why. I had joined my Republican club for social reasons. So when President Johnson asked me if I was a statutory Republican, I could answer yes. I didn't know what it meant, but I knew the answer was yes. It's a five-person commission and no more than three can be members of the same party.

"I must have been one of those fifty women Lyndon Johnson promised to place in high places. He was wonderful, Johnson. He saw *all* his appointees, which Kennedy never did, interviewed them all. And the first time I got interviewed.... I had been talking to President Johnson's appointment secretary, and then I didn't hear a word. So I thought, I'd go on vacation. The day I arrived at my vacation retreat, the man who runs it, who knew me—I'd been there before—came rushing out very excited. Mary, the White House is calling! So I ran in and it *was* the White House. Would it be convenient for me to come down tomorrow?

"Well, is it ever *not* convenient to go to the White House! I turned my little Triumph around and drove back to New York. My apartment had been closed up, and because I was going to be gone for a month, I had absolutely no food. So, in the morning I went down in a little house dress to get breakfast and I locked myself out! Left the key in the apartment. There I was, in my house dress, but I thought it best to just go on to Washington. So I got down to the White House and I sat in the waiting room looking…my hair was not done. Nothing! And I waited and I waited, and pretty soon someone came out and said, Miss Jones, I'm so sorry. The president's tied up. Could I come back at two o'clock? I said, You bet! So I went out and had my hair done. I bought a dress at Garfinkel's and was all properly coiffed and dressed when I got to see him.

"President Johnson was wonderful. He said people would assume his appointing women was political because he was running for election. But he said he just wanted me to know he had enormous respect for women but we don't use their talents. He said, My wife is a very intelligent woman. My mother was a very intelligent woman. My daughters are. We simply don't use women's talents and it's time we do. I think he was sincere. He certainly wasn't grandstanding or politicking for me.

"I was lucky. I saw Lyndon Johnson in his reflective moods and it was wonderful. I'm sure he was a very complex man. He could be very crude at times and probably very bombastic, but I never saw him like that. I saw him when he was really lovely.

"Well, before the White House sent my appointment to the Senate, it got leaked to the press. And then silence for a month. Eventually I did get a telephone call, Would it be convenient…? Yes, it would! So I again came running down from New York, and again I saw President Johnson. He said the White House had received letters about me, calling me an antitrust 'persecutor,' letters complaining that I was impossible to get along with. He guessed they were from the defendants in my cases. The president also said he just wanted me to know what was being said about me because he was sending my name to the Senate the next morning. Then he said he just wanted to make sure that I understood that I might be the only contact some people have with their government and that on me would rest how they react to the government. I mean, he had this real philosophy about what government should be, what his appointees should be like.

"So I was on the commission. I got a recess appointment because by the time he'd gotten around to sending my name up, Congress had adjourned for the Christmas holiday. But again, that was no problem because I wasn't controversial and the senators all leaned over backwards to be nice to a woman. Being a woman at that time was both an advantage and a disadvantage. You stood out, but once you got there, people were polite. So I had no problems.

"In looking back, I realize I was a great beneficiary of the women's movement, but I was never active in it. I was not a joiner and was really quite oblivious to the movement. I was just very busy on the commission and having a *wonderful* experience.

"Being the first woman commissioner on the FTC I got invited by all kinds of consumer groups to give speeches, and I got to speak to all kinds of small consumer groups. In those days, I was an anti-truster. I didn't know anything about consumers. I wouldn't have known a consumer if I fell over one! But I learned very quickly, and I also learned that they were absolutely fascinated by the FTC. The commission brought a lot of complaints about deceptive marketing that were, in theory, for the benefit of consumers. But we'd never asked consumers to participate in any of the hearings that we held. We'd always focused on trying to educate the businessman so that he would conform to the law. It hadn't occurred to us to educate consumers in terms of what their rights were and what they could expect. So when I came back to the commission from my various speaking engagements, I'd have the business cards of women who wanted to be on our mailing list. I wasn't the only one interested in getting women and consumers into the policy-making process of the commission, but because of my experience and contacts, I could assert some leadership. I suggested one day that we invite some of the consumer groups to attend our hearings. I remember one commissioner said, Oh, Mary, not the ladies! And I said, Yes, indeed, if that's who they are! In those early days, consumer leaders were mostly women.

"I hadn't been on the commission more than six months when I went to my chairman and said, I need a wife! He looked at me for a minute and said, You need *what*? I said I needed an extra secretary. I couldn't run my house, travel around making all these speeches, go to hearings, and do the work I needed to do there unless I had help. He was very responsive, saw the need instantly, and gave me an additional secretary.

"Until Ronald Reagan politicized me I had never joined a political party. I had labeled myself as Independent until he came along. But then I couldn't bear it. He wanted to undo everything I believed in, the whole of public service. He didn't care about national government. I mean, even Nixon with all of his terrible failings had never tried to dismantle government. But Reagan was so systematic and I thought it was dangerous. I have to get involved. I'd always voted Democratic, always. I'd never voted Republican, as far back as I can remember. I'd always been for Roosevelt, and

Eleanor was a great role model for me. I had been non-political but always voted Democratic, except for that one lapse when I had joined my Republican club. But that, plus the fact of my Republican upbringing, was what enabled me to get the appointment to the commission; so it was a good lapse. All my friends were intrigued that I filled a Republican spot and, I guess, so was Lyndon Johnson."

Ellen Overton

"My professional interest in women's issues goes back to the mid-'60s," recalled Ellen Overton, co-chair of the Global Women's Task Force, in a 1999 interview. "I wanted to return to work part-time, and there were no part-time jobs. A vocational conference, organized by a committee of Seven Sisters' alumnae, was to be held at the Federal City Tavern in Georgetown. There was such great interest in part-time work that women were lined up around the block to get in. At the same time, and partly as a result of the conference, a group was doing research on a book on part-time opportunities. That group is now a national organization called Wider Opportunities for Women (WOW).

"As a result of the conference and the book, the U.S. Employment Service agreed to work with us to develop part-time employment opportunities. I went to 'work' as a volunteer to help staff the WOW Employment Center. Later, after WOW contracted with several government agencies for workshops on such things as job search strategies, I got involved in that and in getting the Civil Service Commission to accept volunteer work on an application for government employment. I did workshops for government agencies and at local colleges for women reentering the work force.

"Arvonne Fraser, wife of Congressman Donald Fraser from Minnesota, and I were on the WOW board together. Then she became head of the Women's Equity Action League (WEAL) and urged me to eventually become head of volunteers and president of the DC chapter. Arvonne and some other congressional wives were sick and tired of being introduced as 'the wife of.' So they formed a group called the 'Nameless Sisterhood' that started at about the same time as all the consciousness-raising groups. The Nameless Sisterhood met for brown bag lunches and very often we had a speaker to talk about women's issues. We'd go around the room and introduce ourselves without mentioning our husbands. This was a brand new idea in the early '70s.

"Arvonne and I organized 'Advise and Consult.' She advised women on strategies for getting into politics. This was before EMILY's List. I did job search strategy, resumé writing, and hints on filling out the SF-171, that tedious government application for women wanting to enter or reenter the work force. Then we had workshops on how to prepare for an interview and 'dress for success.'

"I graduated magna cum laude and Phi Beta Kappa from Mount Holyoke, went to Yale graduate school, got a job at the Central Intelligence Agency, and then got married. When I was pregnant with my first child in 1956, I had a lot of problems and had to stay in bed several times. Eventually, I decided this wasn't fair to others in my office or to me. The CIA then did a wonderful thing, wonderful for its time: I could have a leave of absence (of course, we didn't have maternity leave in those days), so I knew that if I lost this baby I could go back to my job. I'm convinced that I had my first son because of that peace of mind. Eventually I left the agency to stay home with the children and to help my husband with the social demands of his job, mainly entertaining Middle East dignitaries and their spouses, who seemed to spend most of their time in Garfinkel's!

"In 1976, my husband and I were separated. At that time I was consulting out of my house, working for all kinds of part-time organizations. But I decided I needed a more structured job out of the home with regular hours. Consulting can be frustrating: You win some and you lose some. I applied for all kinds of things. Then a friend, who had been at graduate school with me and was then director of the Women's Program at HEW, called me just before Christmas about a job at the Department of Commerce in the National Oceanic and Atmospheric Administration (NOAA) in Rockville. Four months later I learned that I had gotten the job. I stayed at NOAA for eighteen years and retired in 1995 from their new Office of Sustainable Development.

"As soon as I retired I renewed my interest in global women's issues; that interest was a result of my World War II childhood spent in Romania, England, Switzerland, and the U.S. while traveling on a Liechtenstein passport! I got involved with the international women's conferences. The idea at the United Nations was to have four, one on each continent: Mexico City, Copenhagen, Nairobi, and Beijing. There is only one more, 'Women 2000: Beijing Plus Five,' at the UN in New York. Before Mexico City there were only official government conferences with their official delegates. But by the early '80s, late '70s, maybe, nongovernmental organizations (NGOs) could become accredited by the United Nations to attend and later to participate in the official conferences. I was in Mexico City with the WEAL, and overall, it was a fabulous meeting, a global consciousness-raising experience. By the 1995 conference in Beijing, things were more organized, except maybe in China!

"The Chinese had had only one previous NGO delegation, and the government was really scared about these non-government women from all over the world descending on Beijing. For about a year before Beijing, the State department basically tried to discourage anybody from going. You couldn't go on your own. I joined a tour group out of California. We were going to have fifteen days of touring and then end up in Beijing. The tour group had made hotel reservations, which were canceled twice. Then the Chinese said no, we can't have the NGOs in Beijing. So they built a city from scratch, Huairou, about an hour outside of Beijing. Still, the possibility of attending the conference was on and off, and finally I had to send in my passport to the tour group and apply for a visa through them. Then the Chinese would not grant visas. Then they changed the hotels again, and we didn't know if we were going or where we were staying until just before we left.

"I was very lucky. I ended up in Beijing in some old hotel in a part of the city closest to Huairou. The American delegation had a meeting every morning at the official delegation site in Beijing and they opened it up to any NGO representative who wanted to come. Those of us in hotels in Beijing could get to the morning meetings. But there were women in Huairou who could not get into town and then return because they only ran buses in the morning and in the evening. The rest of the day, tough luck!

"The official U.S. delegation was very good. After they heard about the problem in a morning briefing, three representatives came to Huairou every day, right after lunch, to one of the tents put up for the NGO conference in Huairou. It was called 'Tent City.' So the NGOs could go to the U.S. briefing in Beijing in the morning or they could meet with official delegates in the afternoon in Huairou. There was an amusing story going around that Chinese officials had given the police bed sheets to cover any lesbian NGOs who they feared would run naked through the streets.

"Some of the universal issues we are dealing with in the Global Women's Task Force came from Beijing where a twelve-point Platform for Action had been adopted. While the Beijing conference was still taking place, President Clinton set up the President's Interagency Council on Women so that there would be follow-up in the United States. In the fall of 1995, after we returned from China, and with Hillary [Rodham] Clinton's support, there was a Washington teleconference with sites all over the country. The council, which is made up of top women officials from all relevant U.S. government departments, has regular briefing meetings with NGOs to exchange ideas, and I have been attending those. Since Madeleine Albright became secretary of State, she has become its chair, succeeding Donna Shalala, and the council's office has been moved from the Old Executive Office Building to the State department. So it really does have some clout now.

"At the club, the first thing we tried to do was inform members about the Beijing conference. In October 1995, club members who had been in Beijing held a morning briefing and had a big turnout. Then, in November, Lynn Cutler, a member of the U.S. delegation spoke at lunch about Beijing follow-up activities, and later we had staff members from President Clinton's Interagency Council speak to us. I suppose those meetings were the initial inspiration for the Global Women's Task Force that Ruth Nadel and I started in January 1998. No group at the club was focusing on Beijing follow-up. Also, to have a stronger voice, we wanted to network with other organizations. One example is our effort to ratify CEDAW, the Convention on the

Elimination of All Forms of Discrimination Against Women, which has been ratified by 154 nations, including all of the industrialized world except the United States. It was approved by the House twenty years ago, but is held up in the Senate because of Jesse Helms. Ruth is a great networker and she has been working on a joint ratification effort with the League of Women Voters and the United Nations, and to place the convention on the local agenda of the District of Columbia government. She has been in touch with DC Council member Kathy Patterson, and she is also involved in networking with organizations like Women Connect; the National Council of Women's Organizations; and Interaction, a group that tries to bring NGOs together on common goals. Thanks to her networking, we're getting to be better known.

"In all of our activities, Ruth and I try to include and work with other task forces. It helps both WNDC and the cause when people with like agendas work together and take a firm position on these big issues. When we sign on as members of the Woman's National Democratic Club to meet with women leaders from all over the country and the world, it gives the club a presence."

Ruth Nadel and Ruth Knee (center), co-chairs of the Young Woman's Leadership Project, surrounded by student participants from District of Columbia public schools Dunbar Senior High and the School Without Walls. Photo by Ramonda Wertz.

Chapter 11
THE WNDC EDUCATIONAL FOUNDATION
Raising the Club's Profile

The WNDC Educational Foundation (WNDC-EF) was established in 1991 to promote educational, cultural, and philanthropic activities in metropolitan Washington, DC. The foundation also assists with historic preservation, primarily in the Dupont Circle neighborhood. Unlike club events, which are by invitation only, foundation activities are open to the public, and its 501(c)(3) tax-exempt designation attracts funding from corporate and individual donors.

The Educational Foundation sponsors four major projects: two fellowships awarded annually to women law students; grief counseling and tutoring at the Neval Thomas Elementary School in northeast DC; two higher education scholarships awarded annually to District high school students in EF's Young Woman's Leadership Project; and an oral history and publication program.

Membership in the Washington Historical Society's "Growing Up In Washington" coalition and management of the club's archives and Eleanor Roosevelt Library, with its emphasis on American political history and biography, complete the foundation's major activities. The library and the archives are open to the public.

The legal fellowships were established in 1998 with a $50,000 grant from WNDC member Marian O. Norby. Ms. Norby, who was a secretary in the Truman White House, stipulated that applicants must have worked as a White House secretary or administrative assistant and been accepted at an accredited law school. EF gave consideration to applicants showing an interest in environmental, consumer protection, labor, or other public service law. The first two recipients, Miriam B. Vogel (Georgetown

University Law School) and Lisa S. Wetzel (Wake Forest University Law School), qualified for renewal of their $5,000 fellowships.

Norby funds underwrote the foundation's Web site <www.wndcfoundation.org>, and an interior restoration of WNDC's landmark clubhouse at 1526 New Hampshire Avenue, NW. The funds also provided support for the Eleanor Roosevelt and Human Rights Project, a ten-year effort to produce electronic and print editions of Mrs. Roosevelt's political writings.

The Neval Thomas Elementary School grief counseling and tutoring program aids students of low income, single-parent households (85 percent of the student body) who have been traumatized by violence, divorce, or parental incarceration. The foundation's partnership with the Thomas School at 650 Anacostia Avenue, NE, is sponsored by the Partners in Education program, DC Department of Education.

In December 1996, a Thomas school student was murdered by his mentally unstable mother. The terrible incident affected both students and faculty and was the impetus for EF's initiation of a grief counseling program funded with a $5,000 bequest. EF resources have provided weekly grief counseling sessions and intervention activities, such as field trips to Lorton Penitentiary to expose students to the "Take It From Me" inmate outreach program. The foundation plans to institute professional tutorial support for students with violence-related learning difficulties.

Again working with the District's Education department, EF has selected students from Dunbar Senior High School and The School Without Walls for a Young Woman's Leadership Project (YWLP) designed to raise civic awareness in young eleventh-grade women.

For two years, the foundation brought District students to a series of luncheon lectures at the Woman's National Democratic Club. The students also met with prominent academic and public service leaders and wrote analytical reports on their experiences. EF has raised the level of interest in YWLP by establishing two annual $2,500 merit scholarships for higher education.

A generous gift of stock from Newell Blair, son of WNDC founder Emily Newell Blair, helped purchase computer equipment for the archives and financed the oral history program and publication of this volume. Stock contributions from longtime WNDC member Adelaide Newburger have been designated for outreach programs.

The jewel in the foundation crown is the archives, a unique collection dating from 1922 that chronicles member participation in the Democratic Party and in the women's movement. Audio- and videotapes of club programs, photographs, correspondence, governing board minutes, scrapbooks, oral history transcripts, and other memorabilia comprise the historic collection.

In the 1970s, Margaret "Peg" Colton organized the archives, and she continued to manage them for over twenty years. In 1996, Colton relinquished her files to foundation president, Sandra Bieri, when the club's professional librarian was reorganizing and computerizing the collection. "That was a gift," Bieri recalled.[4]

Margaret "Peg" Colton

"How did I get started on the archives? I can tell you," Peg Colton said in a 1996 interview. "I was asked to take a club position with a great deal of responsibility—I have forgotten whether it was president or vice president—and I said that my husband didn't want me to have a job that had calls at night, so I had to turn down all sorts of presidencies from the PTA to heaven knows what.

"I became recording secretary, probably in the 1960s, and after that I got on the board and I decided to come in and see what was here in the club. I found papers and books and letters and manuscripts all over the place. In those days the club rented rooms, and papers were in bureau drawers and under beds. They were all over the place and I started collecting them. One day I was in a board meeting and there was a very lovely lady there who said several things that made me realize she might be interested in photographs. I went over to her and said, We have so many wonderful photographs in the archives. Would you be interested in cataloging them? Would you like to be in charge of photographs? She said she would, and that was the beginning of my long and wonderful friendship with Toni Linowitz. She also hangs the beautiful art work in the Stevenson dining room.

"I think I began the archives in the mid-'70s, but I would have to look it up. I was a board member then, and the president asked me to be historian. So when I took over I discovered all these wonderful things. Everything you see in here we found in the most unbelievable places. I found them in bookcases. I found them among the silver. I found them in the attic. They were all over the building. All these supplies you see Toni and I bought ourselves. We shopped around and when we needed something we got it, but we couldn't always find what we wanted, so binders and things don't always match. The club minutes are collected and bound by the secretaries. I was recording secretary at one time, so mine are here. We have minutes from the 1920s! Outside of that, Toni and I did every single thing and we have worked together for a long time. For a while, a couple of people came in to help, but I'm not going to live forever and I'd like somebody to train to take my place.

"We've had some very, very fascinating people at the club. I started to tape the past presidents, but I found it very difficult. Do you find the same thing? Some of them I found easy to [tape] and some I found very difficult, but I got as much of it as I could.

---

[4] Transcripts of interviews with Sandra Bieri and Shirley Henderson document the founding and development of the foundation, and are available in the WNDC-EF archives.

It gives the club continuity to have tapes like that, but it's hard to find members willing to go back and search their memories. I only tape them on their experiences at the club and what happened at the time.

"Mostly, I interviewed club presidents, but I talked to a few people like India Edwards. Wasn't that a good tape? She was a grand old lady. She stayed on the board, you know; she had one of those honorary titles. She had no vote, but she came to the board meetings all the time. Boy, she would really make her presence known! She was a strong woman and she put her foot down and got what she wanted. At that time we were considerably younger than she was, and we had definite ideas; and it was very interesting to see that she would accept the difference after a bit of fireworks.

"Oh, I joined the club, I forget exactly when, but it was in the 1940s, about the time the club was getting active again after World War II. Lillian Owen and I must be the oldest members in length of time. Recently we have had several events at the club to which people I haven't seen in twenty or thirty years have come, and it's been like a reunion. We really have had the cream of the Washington wives as members: Trudy Fowler, whose husband was secretary of the Treasury; Jane Wirtz, whose husband was Willard Wirtz, the Labor secretary; and Ann Chapman. Her husband, Oscar, was secretary of Interior. She was the club president, and she was the most beautiful young woman. When I say young, [I mean] young middle-aged woman. She was very beautiful and handled herself very well.

"We really had some very fine presidents and I'm very pleased right now that we have a former president as general manager of the club. Having been president, she knows exactly what we need. The archives were to be put up under the eaves. They wanted to put us on the fourth floor. Someone from the Library of Congress who had heard about the collection called and asked for an an appointment to come and see the archives. It just happened that he came at the time when there was talk of moving the archives, and he said, Under no condition go up there, even though it's air conditioned. He said, The sun will be coming through. Well, we can put a shade there. There will be times when it's too hot up there, and in the summertime there is probably no air conditioning on weekends. Under no conditions put those things up there.

"We had signatures; we have letters. There are things here in these binders that are really, in a way, priceless. Any number are handwritten with important signatures. There are two letters in there to friends of my mother's, and when I came across their names I started to cry; tears came to my eyes. It's so important to me. There are letters from Daisy Harriman to different people, asking them if they wanted to join the club when it was starting. What happened was, after the women got the suffrage they didn't want to lose the momentum and they wanted to start a Democratic club. It was Daisy who went out and recruited influential Democrats.

"The women all called each other Mrs. Harriman and Mrs. Blair and Mrs. Hamlin and Mrs. Jones; and they wore hats. Now you meet the wife of the president of the United States and she calls you Peggy and she expects you to call her Hillary. I find the changes in etiquette, the changes in perception of women, very interesting as I look over these things. But at the same time these women in their plumed and flowered hats got things done, in spite of the fact that everybody laughed at them. Why, the Democrats were out of power in the 1920s, but they wanted to start a club and they wanted to buy a clubhouse and have a corporate seal. It's the most ridiculous thing I've ever heard in all my life, that they were not going to be able to get anywhere with their ideas and plans. As proof, here we are in 1526 New Hampshire Avenue and all of us are very proud of this beautiful historic building."

WNDC past presidents Esther Peterson and Shirley Henderson share a moment of sisterhood. Courtesy WNDC-EF Archives

APPENDIX

WNDC Presidents

Honorary Presidents

Eleanor Roosevelt (Mrs. Franklin D.)
Bess Truman (Mrs. Harry S.)
Jacqueline Kennedy (Mrs. John F.)
Lady Bird Johnson (Mrs. Lyndon B.)
Rosalynn Carter (Mrs. Jimmy)
Hillary Rodham Clinton (Mrs. Bill)

Presidents

Daisy Harriman (Mrs. J. Borden)	1923-26
Natalie S. Jones (Mrs. Andrieus)	1926-28
Emily Newell Blair (Mrs. Harry)	1928-29
Daisy Harriman (Mrs. J. Borden)	1929-31
Fanny F. Herrick (Mrs. Samuel)	1931-33
Huibertje L. Hamlin (Mrs. Charles)	1933-35
Margaret W. Meigs (Mrs. Edward)	1935-37
Etta Ross Hubbard (Mrs. Wilbur)	1937-39
Barbara Brown (Mrs. David Tucker)	1939-40
Mildred Pepper (Mrs. Claude)	1940-41
Virginia Shears (Mrs. Curtis)	1941-43
Elizabeth E. Sayre (Mrs. Francis)	1943-44
Susan V. Clayton (Mrs. William)	1944-45
Grace G. Davis (Mrs. William H.)	1945-47
Daisy Harriman (Mrs. J. Borden)	1947-49
Bertha R. Friant (Mrs. Julien)	1949-50
Emma Morrison (Mrs. Fred W.)	1950-52
Eda S. Brannan (Mrs. Charles F.)	1952-53
Ann Chapman (Mrs. Oscar L.)	1953-55
Alice Hostetler (Mrs. Minier)	1955-56
Marjorie White (Mrs. Mastin G.)	1956-57
Esther Frear (Mrs. J. Allen, Jr.)	1957-58
Lindy Boggs (Mrs. Hale)	1958-59
Constance Casey (Mrs. Joseph E.)	1959-61
Peggy Mann (Mrs. James H.)	1961-63
Mary Keyserling (Mrs. Leon H.)	1963-64
Florence Hoff (Mrs. Irvin)	1964-65
Dorothy Marks (Mrs. Leonard H.)	1965-67
Paula Locker (Mrs. Melville E.)	1967-69
Esther Peterson (Mrs. Oliver)	1969-70
Margo Davis (Mrs. Ross D.)	1970-72
Shirley Koteen (Mrs. Bernard)	1972-74
Mary Munroe (Mrs. Pat)	1974-76
Mary Lou Friedman (Mrs. Edward)	1976-78
Marian Driver (Mrs. William J.)	1978-79
Carol Williams (Mrs. J. D.)	1979-81
Judi Levin (Mrs. Robert N.)	1981-83
Jean R. Jensen (Mrs. Robert)	1983-85
Marelyn Tank (Mrs. Martin L.)	1985-87
Jean R. Jensen (Mrs. Robert)	1987-88
Jane Freeman (Mrs. Orville L.)	1988-89
Amanda F. MacKenzie Hobart	1989-90
Shirley S. Henderson	1990-92
Sacha Millstone	1992-93
Barbara S. Zelenko	1993-95
Joan Chase	1995-97
Ann Goodrich	1997-99
Anna Stout	1999-

Presidents WNDC Educational Foundation

Molly O'Brien • 1991-96   Sandra Bieri • 1996-2000   CynthiaMcCaughan • 2000-

With Hillary Rodham Clinton at WNDC's 75th anniversary celebration, Phyllis Fineshriber displays the needlepoint pillow, "A Bridge to the 21st Century," she designed and stitched for President Bill Clinton, 10 June 1998. Photo courtesy The White House.

BIBLIOGRAPHY & SOURCES

Primary Sources
Primary sources were interviews and conversations recorded by the WNDC Educational Foundation oral history committee, and additional interview tapes and transcripts acquired by the committee.

Interviews
Adams, Frances. Interview with the author. Associates of the American Foreign Service Worldwide (AAFSW) Oral History Collection, 17 April 1991.
Angelos, Mary Catherine. Conversation with the author, 26 February 1996.
Bieri, Sandra. Interview with the author. WNDC-EF oral history program, 13 April 1999.
Blair, Newell. Interviews with the author. WNDC-EF oral history program, 11 March and 24 October 1996.
Boggs, Corinne "Lindy." Interview with the author. WNDC-EF oral history program, 22 December 1995.
Campbell, Elizabeth. Interview with Karin Rindal. WNDC-EF oral history program, 22 May 1996.
Casey, Constance. Interview with Margaret Colton, n.d.[1]
Challinor, Joan. Interview with the author. WNDC-EF oral history program, 4 December 1996.
Chapman, Ann. Interview with the author. WNDC-EF oral history program, 5 February 1996. Interview with Margaret Colton, n.d.
Colton, Margaret. Interview with the author. WNDC-EF oral history program, 25 June 1996.
Darling, Phyllis. Conversation with the author. Hanover, NH, 22 August 1995.
Davis, Margo, Interview with Margaret Colton, n.d.
Dillon, Dorothy. Interview with Coralee Farlie. WNDC-EF oral history program, 14 May 1998.
_____. Interview with Allan Hansen. United States Information Agency (USIA) Alumni Association Oral History Project, 10 May 1988.
Driver, Marian. Interview with Margaret Colton, n.d.
Duncan, Gladys. Biographical data.

---

[5] Undated Colton tapes were recorded in the mid-1970s or early 1980s.

DuPlain, Jan. Interview with Karin Rindal. WNDC-EF oral history program, 8 May 1996.

Edwards, India. Interview with Margaret Colton, n.d.

Fineshriber, Phyllis H. C. Interviews with the author. WNDC-EF oral history program, 23 February and 1 April 1996.

Freeman, Jane. Interview with the author. WNDC-EF oral history program, 7 September 1995.

Freeman, Jo. Conversation with the author. Washington, DC, 7 May 1999.

Friedman, Mary Lou. Interview with Margaret Colton, n.d.

Glasser, Esther. Interview with the author. WNDC-EF oral history program, 6 July 1999.

Goodrich, Anne T. Interview with David Hemming for Glen Whitman oral history project, St. Andrew's Episcopal School, Potomac, MD, 3 February 1988.

Harger, Eone. Interview with the author. WNDC-EF oral history program, 22 April 1999.

Harrison, Cynthia. Conversation with the author. George Washington University, Washington, DC, 14 May 1999.

Henderson, Shirley. Interview with Sandra Bieri. WNDC-EF oral history program, 12 May 1998.

Hight, Elizabeth. Interview with the author. WNDC-EF oral history program, 11 January 2000. Interview with Dr. Thomas Soapes, Franklin D. Roosevelt Library, Hyde Park, NY, 1 November 1978.

Howard, Frances Humphrey. Interview with Peter Jessup. Association for Diplomatic Studies and Training, Arlington, VA, 8 April 1992.

Jensen, Jean. Interview with Margaret Colton, n.d.

Jones, Mary Gardiner. Interview with the author. WNDC-EF oral history program, 26 November 1997.

Keyserling, Mary. Interview with Margaret Colton, n.d.

Kaiser, Hannah. Interview with the author. Associates of the American Foreign Service Worldwide (AAFSW) Oral History Collection, 4 December 1987.

Kidney, Juliet F. Interview with Morris Weisz. Association for Diplomatic Studies and Training, Labor Diplomacy Oral History Project, Arlington, VA, 18 May 1993.

Koteen, Sherley. Interview with the author. WNDC-EF oral history program, 11 August 1999. Interview with Margaret Colton, n.d.

Kramer, Rose. Interview with Susan Ingraham, n.d.

MacKenzie Hobart, Amanda. Interview with the author. WNDC-EF oral history program, 12 November 1997.

Millstone, Sacha. Interview with Nicki Lagoudakis. WNDC-EF oral history program, 11 November 1996.
Munroe, Mary. Interview with Margaret Colton, n.d.
Nadel, Ruth. Conversation with the author, 14 May 1999.
Newburger, Adelaide. Conversation with the author, 19 January 1998.
Norby, Marian. Interview with the author. WNDC-EF oral history program, 28 May 1997.
O'Brien, Maureen. Interviews with Susan Myrick, 16 August 1996, and with the author, 3 June 1998. WNDC-EF oral history program.
Overton, Ellen. Interview with the author. WNDC-EF oral history program, 20 May 1999.
Owen, Lillian. Interview with the author. WNDC-EF oral history program, 18 April 1996.
Peterson, Esther. Interview with Hope Meyers. Associates of the American Foreign Service Worldwide (AAFSW) Oral History Collection, 4 December 1989.
Rauh, Olie. Interview with the author. WNDC-EF oral history program, 7 February 1996.
Reeves, Ola. Interview with the author. WNDC-EF oral history program, 19 November 1997.
Richardson, David. Interview with the author. WNDC-EF oral history program, 20 January 1998.
Seagraves, Eleanor. Conversations with Kathryn Schmidt, 1997. Interview with the author. WNDC-EF oral history program, 18 August 1999.
Simon, Jeanne. Interview with Nicki Lagoudakis. WNDC-EF oral history program, 9 February 1996.
Spingarn, Natalie. Interview with the author. WNDC-EF oral history program, 5 April 1999.
Stewart, Florence. Interview with the author. WNDC-EF oral history program, 1 July 1996.
Tank, Marelyn. Interviews with the author. WNDC-EF oral history program, 25 August 1998 and 5 May 1999.
Uhl-Katcher, Gladys. Interview with Susan Myrick. WNDC-EF oral history program, 23 May 1997.
Wertz, Ramonda. Interview with the author. WNDC-EF oral history program, 7 January 1999.
Wolf, Agnes. Interview with the author. WNDC-EF oral history program, 24 June 1998.
Young, Nancy Beck. Conversation with the author. Washington, DC, 26 May 1995.

Secondary Sources

Books

Beasley, Maurine H., and Holly Shulman, eds. *The Eleanor Roosevelt Encyclopedia.* Forthcoming from Greenwood Press, Westport, CT.

Black, Allida M. *Casting Her Own Shadow: Eleanor Roosevelt and the Shaping of Postwar Liberalism.* New York: Columbia University Press, 1996.

Boggs, Lindy. *Washington Through a Purple Veil: Memoirs of a Southern Woman.* New York: Harcourt Brace & Co., 1994.

Brown, Dorothy M. *Setting a Course: American Women in the 1920s.* Boston: Twayne, 1987.

Catt, Carrie Chapman, and Nettie Rogers Shuler. *Woman Suffrage and Politics.* New York: Charles Scribner's Sons, 1923.

Chadakoff, Rochelle, ed. *Eleanor Roosevelt's My Day: Her Acclaimed Columns 1936-1945.* New York: Pharos Books, 1989.

Carter, Rosalynn. *First Lady from Plains.* Boston: Houghton Mifflin Co., 1984.

Commire, Anne, and Deborah Klezner, eds. *Women in World History.* From Kristie Miller's Daisy Harriman essay, first draft. Forthcoming from Yorkin Publications, Waterford, CT.

Cook, Blanche Wiesen. *Eleanor Roosevelt: Volume One 1884-1933.* New York: Viking, 1992.

_____. *Eleanor Roosevelt: Volume 2 1933-1938.* New York: Viking, 1999.

Davis, Adalyn. *The Woman's National Democratic Club: The Place Where Democrats Meet.* WNDC publication, 1992.

Democratic National Committee Women's Division. *A History of Democratic Women's Move to Leadership.* c. 1979.

Edwards, India. *Pulling No Punches: Memoirs of a Woman in Politics.* New York: G.P. Putnam's Sons, 1977.

Evans, Sara M. *Born for Liberty: A History of Women in America.* New York: The Free Press, 1989.

Fenzi, Jewell with Carl L. Nelson. *Married To The Foreign Service: An Oral History of the Foreign Service Spouse.* New York: Twayne Publishers, 1994.

Freeman, Jo. *A Room at a Time: How Women Entered Party Politics.* Lanham, MD: Rowman & Littlefield, 2000.

Goldberg, Michael Lewis. *An Army of Women: Gender and Politics in Gilded Age Kansas.* Baltimore: The Johns Hopkins University Press, 1997.

Goldsmith, Barbara. *Other Powers: The Age of Suffrage, Spiritualism, and the Scandalous Victoria Woodhull.* New York: Alfred A. Knopf, 1998.

Goodwin, Doris Kearns. *No Ordinary Time: Franklin and Eleanor Roosevelt, The Home Front in World War II.* New York: Simon & Schuster, 1994.

Gould Lewis L., ed. *American First Ladies: Their Lives and Their Legacy.* New York: Garland Publishing Co., 1996.

Gustafson, Melanie, Kristie Miller, and Elisabeth Israels Perry, eds. *We Have Come To Stay: American Women and Political Parties, 1880-1960.* From Kathryn Anderson's essay, "Evolution of a Partisan: Emily Newell Blair and the Democratic Party, 1920-1932;" and Kristie Miller's essay, "Eager and Anxious to Work: Daisy Harriman and the Presidential Election of 1912." Albuquerque: University of New Mexico Press, 1999.

Halberstam, David. *The Fifties.* New York: Villard Books, 1993.

Harriman, Mrs. J. Borden. *From Pinafores To Politics.* New York: Henry Holt and Co., 1923.

Harrison, Cynthia. *On Account of Sex: The Politics of Women's Issues, 1945-68.* Berkeley: University of California Press, 1989.

Johnson, Lady Bird (Claudia T.). *A White House Diary.* New York: Holt, Rinehart and Winston, 1970.

Kemp, Barbara H., and Shirley Cherkasky. *Eleanor Roosevelt's Washington: A Place of Personal Growth and Public Service.* Department of Public Programs, National Museum of American History, Smithsonian Institution. Washington, DC, n.d.

Laas, Virginia Jeans. *Bridging Two Eras: The Autobiography of Emily Newell Blair, 1877-1951.* Columbia: University of Missouri Press, 1999.

Lash, Joseph P. *Eleanor and Franklin.* New York: W.W. Norton & Company, Inc., 1971.

Louchheim, Katie. *By the Political Sea.* New York: Doubleday & Co. Inc., 1970.

Lunardini, Christine. *What Every American Should Know About Women's History.* Holbrook, MA: Bob Adams, Inc., 1994.

McCullough, David. *Truman.* New York: Simon & Schuster, 1992.

Meredith, Ellis, ed. *Democracy at the Cross Roads.* New York: Brewer, Warren & Putnam, 1932.

Miller, Kristie. *Ruth Hanna McCormick: A Life in Politics, 1880-1944.* Albuquerque: University of New Mexico Press, 1992.

Patterson, Jefferson. *Diplomatic Duty and Diversion.* Cambridge, MA: The Riverside Press, 1956.

Peterson, Esther, with Winifred Conkling. *Restless: The Memoirs of Labor and Consumer Activist Esther Peterson.* Washington, DC: Caring Publishing, 1995.

Reeves, Richard. *President Kennedy: Profile of Power.* New York: Simon & Schuster, 1993.

Roosevelt, Eleanor. *This I Remember.* New York: Harper & Brothers, 1949.

Schneider, Dorothy and Carl J. *American Women in the Progressive Era, 1900-1920.* New York: Anchor Books, Doubleday, 1993.

Scott, Anne Firor. *Natural Allies: Women's Associations in American History.* Chicago: University of Illinois Press, 1993.

Shaw, Anna Howard. *The Story of a Pioneer.* New York: Harper & Bros., 1915.

Sicherman, Barbara, and Carol Hurd Green, with Ilene Kantron and Hariette Walker. *Notable American Women: The Modern Period.* Cambridge: The Belknap Press of Harvard, 1980.

Stevens, Doris. *Jailed for Freedom: American Women Win the Vote.* Edited by Carol O'Hare. Troutdale, OR: NewSage Press, 1995.

Swain, Martha. *Ellen S. Woodward: New Deal Advocate for Women.* Jackson: University Press of Mississippi, 1995.

Tugwell, Rexford G. *Off Course: From Truman to Nixon.* New York: Praeger Publishers, 1971.

Ware, Susan. *Beyond Suffrage*: Women in the New Deal. Cambridge: Harvard University Press, 1981.

_____. *Partner and I: Molly Dewson, Feminism, and New Deal Politics.* New Haven: Yale University Press, 1987.

Wecter, Dixon. *The Saga of American Society: A Record of Social Aspiration, 1607-1937.* New York: Charles Scribner's Sons, 1937.

Wheeler, Marjorie Spruill, ed. *One Woman, One Vote: Rediscovering the Woman Suffrage Movement.* Essay 17, "Minnie Fisher Cunningham's Back Door Lobby in Texas: Political Maneuvering in a One-Party State" by Judith N. McArthur. Troutdale, OR: NewSage Press, 1995.

Whithey, Henry F., and Elsie Rathburn Whithey. *Biographical Dictionary of American Architects.* Los Angeles: New Age Publishing Co., 1956.

Wilson, Edith Bolling. *My Memoir.* New York: The Bobbs Merrill Co., 1938.

Ziegler, Edward, and Jeanette Valentine, eds. *Project Head Start: A Legacy of the War on Poverty.* Alexandria, VA: The National Head Start Association, n.d.

_____. *Social Register Washington.* New York: Social Register Association, 1912, 1913, 1930.

_____. *The Social List of Washington.* Washington, DC: Helen Ray Hagner Social Bureau, Inc., 1932.

Articles

Arndt, Jessie Ash. "First Lady Discusses Women's Defense Role." *The Washington Post*, 1 April 1941.

Banister, Marian. "Why I Am a Democrat." *The Bulletin*, July 1926.

Barnes, Bart. "Joseph L. Rauh Jr.: A Life of Activism." *The Washington Post*, 5 September 1992.

Blair, Emily Newell. "Letters of a Contented Housewife." *Cosmopolitan*, c. December, 1909. Western Reserve Historical Society, Cleveland. Emily Newell Blair Family Papers, container 8, folder 59.

_____. "Looking Forward." *The Bulletin*, June 1928.

_____. "Questions Women Are Asking." *Fortnightly Bulletin*, 7 October 1922.

_____. "What Shall We Do With It?" *The Green Book Magazine*. Western Reserve Historical Society, folder 61, n.d.

Bradley, Lenore. "The Uphill Climb: Women in the Truman Administration." *Whistle Stop*, vol. 23, no. 2. Harry S. Truman Library: 1944.

Brown, Rosellen. "[Lindy Boggs] Belle of the Bayou." *The New York Times*, 27 November 1994.

Casey, Constance (daughter). "Mixed Blessings: Memoirs of a Congressman's Daughter." *The Washington Post*, 19 April 1992.

Casey, Phil. "350 Pay Homage Here to Daisy Harriman." *The Washington Post*, 6 September 1967.

Conroy, Sarah Booth. "Plucky Lindy." *The Washington Post*, 24 October 1994.

_____. "75 Years of Sisterhood." *The Washington Post*, 10 November 1997.

Cutlip, Lily. "Democratic Party Group Gives Fete at Woodlawn: First Lady Extends Greetings to 'Queenie.'" *The Washington Herald*, 15 May 1937.

Dolan, Michael. "[Dupont Circle] A Short History of a Very Round Place." *The Washington Post Magazine*, 2 September 1990.

Evans, Ernestine. "Women in the Washington Scene." *Century*, vol. 106, no. 4, August 1923.

Fenzi, Jewell. "75th Anniversary for Woman's National Democratic Club." *Washington History: Magazine of the Historical Society of Washington*, vol. 9, no. 2, Fall/Winter 1997-98.

Free, Ann Cottrell. "Eleanor Roosevelt and the Female White House Press Corps." *Modern Maturity*, October/November 1984.

Gill, Brendan. "A Fast Full Life: The Exceptional Legacy of H. H. Richardson." *The New Yorker*, 1998.

Griffin, Isabel Kinnear. "Mrs. Roosevelt's Press Conferences." *The Democratic Bulletin*, May 1933.

Harriman, Mrs. J. Borden. "Women in Washington." *The Forum*, vol. LXXII, 1924.

Hard, Anne. "Emily Blair, Politician." *The Woman Citizen*, April 1926.

_____. "Friendly Impressions: Mrs. Borden Harriman." *The Woman Citizen*, January 1927.

Kemper, Vicki. "[Esther Peterson] A Citizen for all Seasons." *Common Cause Magazine*, Spring 1995.

Lide, Frances. "Mrs. Roosevelt Will Open Democratic Club's Series on Women's Role in Defense." *The Washington Post*, 30 March 1941.

Louchheim, Katie. "As We Remember Her." *WNDC News*, October 1967.

McCardle, Dorothy. "Along With a Gift: Mrs. Post Gives a Laundry Lesson." *The Washington Post*, 22 November 1966.

McCarthy, Colman. "Joseph Rauh and the Public Interest." *The Washington Post*, 15 September 1992.

McLendon, Winzola. "Women Democrats Inaugurate Social Service Corps." *The Washington Post*, 24 September 1963.

Page, Tim. "Todd Duncan, First Porgy Dies." *The Washington Post*, obituaries, 1 March 1998.

Poe, Vylla. "Mrs. Roosevelt Aids Groups Providing Soldiers' Recreation." Unattributed, 15 May 1941. Eleanor Roosevelt Collection, WNDC archives.

Raver, Anne. "Spreading the Colors of a Great Society." *The New York Times*, 6 May 1993.

[Russell] Jarboe, Jan. "Lady Bird Looks Back." *Texas Monthly*, December 1994.

Schillinger, Liesl. "When Suffrage Was Insufferable: The Jeering of Susan B. Anthony." *The Washington Post*, 3 September 1995.

Shelton, Isabelle. "Send Graduates to Iran, Mrs. Roosevelt Suggests." *The* [Washington, DC] *Evening Star*, 26 May 1959.

Smith, Gretchen. "Mrs. Roosevelt Lauds Courage of the British." Unattributed, 30 November 1942.

Weather report. *The Washington Post*, 24 November 1922.

Wheeler, Linda. "Routing a Ragtag American Army." *The Washington Post*, 12 April 1999.

Yardley, Jonathan. "To Love, Honor and Advise." Book World. *The Washington Post*, 15 August 1999.

_____. "Community Spirit Lacking in Iran: Mrs. Roosevelt Says After Touring Nation." *The Washington Post*, 26 May 1959.

_____. "Congressional Wives Studying The New Deal." *The Washington Herald*, 24 March 1936.

_____. "The Esther Peterson Papers: Ready for Researchers." *News from the Schlesinger Library*, Fall 1999.

_____. "The Membership of Mrs. Duncan Approved." *The Washington Post*, November 1955.

_____. "The New Clubhouse." *The Bulletin*, volume II, no. 5. Washington, DC, May 1927.

_____. "The Picture Story of the Eventful Life of Eleanor Roosevelt, 55 Yesterday." *The Washington Post*, 12 October 1939.

_____. "Mrs. Roosevelt Scouts Fears of Military Clique Ruling U.S." Unattributed, 26 September 1940. Eleanor Roosevelt Collection, WNDC archives.

_____. "Wealthy Society Women Trampled." *Portland (ME) Express*, 20 August 1912. Harriman scrapbook, WNDC-EF archives.

_____. "WNDC Tribute to Late President Kennedy." *WNDC News*, Winter 1963-64.

_____. "Woman's Club To Be Host to Mrs. Roosevelt." Unattributed, 8 June 1943. Eleanor Roosevelt Collection, WNDC archives.

Unpublished Sources

Adair, William. "Survey of Selected Items from the Collections of the Women's [sic] National Democratic Club," 24 July 1991.

Anthony, Susan B., Matilda Gage, and Elizabeth Cady Stanton. 1873 petition to the U.S Congress. National Archives, record group 223, Records of the U.S. House of Representatives, Petitions and Memorials, Committee on the Judiciary, Women's Suffrage (HR 42A-H8.11).

Banzhaf, John F. III. Letter to James E. Mercer, Associate Director, Office of Human Rights, Washington, DC. Re: Banzhaf v. Woman's National Democratic Club, Docket No. 88-518-PA-(N), 10 October 1988.

Blair, Emily Newell. *Gamma's Story*, Book I and Book II. Autobiography of Emily Newell Blair, typescript manuscript "written over a period of years in the 1930s."

_____. Letter to Eleanor Roosevelt, 1 August 1932.

_____. Letter to Harry Blair, 14 November 1927. Western Reserve Historical Society, Emily Newell Blair Family Papers, container 2, folder 16.

_____. Western Union wire to Margaret (Mrs. Edward B.) Meigs resigning WNDC presidency, 13 November 1928.

Boggs, Lindy. Letter to WNDC membership, 6 April 1959.

_____. Letter to WNDC membership, 29 September 1959.

Bradbury, Dorothy E. *Daisy Harriman: Look Back in Awe*. Typescript manuscript, n.d.

Carpenter, Liz. Remarks at the dedication ceremony for a Texas state historical marker commemorating Minnie Fisher Cunningham. New Waverly, TX, 15 March 1992.

Clinton, Hillary Rodham. Remarks at a White House tea for WNDC members, 10 January 1995.

Cunningham, Minnie Fisher. Letters to Emily Newell Blair, 7 January 1927, 12 May 1927.

⎯⎯⎯⎯⎯. Correspondence with Bertie Hamlin. *See* Hamlin, below.

⎯⎯⎯⎯⎯. Letter to Mrs. J. Borden Harriman, 17 September 1926.

⎯⎯⎯⎯⎯. Letter to Mrs. Andreius A. Jones, 18 September 1926.

⎯⎯⎯⎯⎯. Letter to Clem Shaver, 15 April 1927.

Edwards, India. Letter to Margaret Kuh, chair, WNDC Archives and History Committee, 30 September 1975. India Edwards Collection, Harry S. Truman Library, Independence, MO.

Fenzi, Jewell. *WNDC Founders Emily Newell Blair and Daisy Harriman: A Study in Contrasts.* Presented at WNDC speaker luncheon, 16 September 1997, and at the Oral History Association annual meeting, New Orleans, LA, 25 September 1997.

George, Senator Walter F. (D-GA). Letter to Emily Newell Blair, 10 January 1931. Western Reserve Historical Society, Emily Newell Blair Family Papers, container 2, folder 17.

Hamlin, Huibertje. *Memories of Washington from the Age of 7.* Edited 1929-34. Library of Congress Manuscript Division, Hamlin Papers, box 358, folder 10.

⎯⎯⎯⎯⎯. Eight letters exchanged between Bertie Hamlin and Minnie Fisher Cunningham regarding Democratic National Committee support of WNDC, 2 September, 9 September, 13 September, 14 September (letter and telegram), 15 September, 17 September, 21 September (not sent), and Sunday, n.d., 1926. Hamlin folder, Special Collections, WNDC archives.

⎯⎯⎯⎯⎯. Letter to Eleanor Roosevelt declining WNDC presidency, 23 November 1938.

Harriman, Florence Jaffray. Letter to Elizabeth (Mrs. Thomas) Bayard about WNDC founding, 5 July 1922.

⎯⎯⎯⎯⎯. Resignation letter to the governors of the Woman's National Democratic Club, 29 January 1923.

Laas, Virginia. *Breaking Into Politics: Emily Newell Blair and the Democratic Party in the 1920s.* Paper presented at the Mid-America Conference on History, Oklahoma State University, September 1997.

Leavitt, Dorothy. *A History of the Woman's National Democratic Club.* Typescript manuscript, c. 1963.

Manning, Mary. Letter to James E. Mercer re: Banzhaf v. Woman's National Democratic Club, Docket No. 88-518-PA-(N), 20 July 1989.

Mercer, James E. Letter to Gail M. Harmon, Harmon & Weiss. Re: John F. Banzhaf III v. Woman's National Democratic Club, Docket No. 88-518-PA-(N), 27 October 1988.

Minutes of the [WNDC] governing board, 1922-26.

Minutes of the [WNDC] governing board, 19 October 1955.

Minutes of the [WNDC} governing board, 18 March 1959.

Minutes of the [WNDC] governing board, 16 September 1959.

Minutes of the [WNDC] membership business meeting, 18 February 1999.

Minutes of the [WNDC] membership business meeting, 22 June 1999.

Myrick, Susan. *India Edwards*. Paper presented at WNDC speaker luncheon, 16 September 1997, and at the Oral History Association annual meeting, New Orleans, LA, 25 September 1997.

Polan, Glenn K. *Minnie Fisher Cunningham*: A thesis presented to the faculty of Sam Houston State College in partial fulfillment of the requirements for the degree of Master of Arts. Huntsville, TX, August 1968.

Report of the [WNDC] executive committee, 16 September 1959.

Report of the [WNDC] membership committee, 21 October 1959.

Roosevelt, Eleanor. Letter to Florence J. Harriman, 29 July 1922.

Schmidt, Kathryn. *Eleanor Roosevelt as she is seen by the Woman's National Democratic Club*. Paper presented at WNDC speaker luncheon 16 September 1997, and at the Oral History Association annual meeting, New Orleans, LA, 25 September 1997.

Smith, Nancy, archivist, Lyndon B. Johnson Library, Austin, TX. Letter to Myra G. Gutin on Lady Bird's White House activities, 27 January 1982.

Wilcox, Walter D. Letter to Bertie Hamlin on the history of the clubhouse, 21 January 1932.

Wood, Molly M. *An American Diplomat's Wife in Mexico: Gender, Politics and Foreign Affairs Activism, 1907-27*. Unpublished dissertation. Associates of the American Foreign Service Worldwide (AAFSW) Oral History Collection, n.d.

Young, Nancy Beck. *Texas Women, Texas Politics: The Gendered Meanings of Female Grassroots Political Leadership in the Cold War Era*. Unpublished typescript, n.d.

_____. [WNDC] *Committee and Task Force Reports*, 1998-99

_____. *Membership*, typescript article, n.d. WNDC archives.

_____. *Summary of the WNDC Strategic Planning Report*, n.d.

_____. *Woman's National Democratic Club Operations Manual for WNDC Volunteer Leadership*, 1998-99.

Exhibit, Internet, Video Sources

Black, Allida. Videotape. Woman's National Democratic Club speaker luncheon, 8 June 1999.

Boggs, Lindy. Videotape. Woman's National Democratic Club speaker luncheon, 8 December 1994.

Broad, Lou Ann, curator. *From the Right to Vote, the Power to Lead.* Woman's National Democratic Club 75th anniversary exhibit, November 1997.

Kennelly, Barbara. Videotapes. Woman's National Democratic Club speaker luncheons, 9 April 1984 and 3 June 1999.

C-SPAN. Videotape, *Olya Margolin Memorial Seminar,* 13 February 1991. Courtesy of Ben Margolin.

PBS documentary. Videotape, *Great Upset of 1948* (Truman campaign). Courtesy of Marian Norby.

www.nmwh.org. National Museum of Women's History Web site.

INDEX

A

Abell, Bess, 97
abortion, 58-59, 87-88
Albright, Madeleine, 81, 93, 152
All States Bazaar, 62
American Youth Congress, 36
Anthony, Susan B., ix, x
archives, WNDC-EF, 19, 139, 155-159

B

Banister, Marian, 6
Banzhaf, John III, 119, 132
Bayard, Elizabeth, 6
Bayard, Thomas Francis Jr., 6
Bentsen, B. A., 100, 119, 120
Bernstein, Leonard, 98
Bieri, Sandra, 157
Blair, Emily Newell, xii, xiv, 1-5, 6, 7, 14
Blair, Harry Wallace, 2-5
Blair, Newell, 4, 156
Blake, Frances Greenough "Franny," 13-14
Boggs, Corinne Claiborne "Lindy," 65, 66, 67, 75, 82-85
Bonsal, Henrietta, 6
Bonus Army, 25, 27
Boettiger, John, 30
boutique. *See* Sign of the Donkey
"British Occupation." *See* British Service Club
British Service Club, 22, 43-44
Brown, Ron, 124-125
Bulletin, The, 4

C

Cantrill, Ethel, 6
Carpenter, Liz, 18, 117
Carter, Rosalynn, 104, 105;
    First Lady From Plains, 105
Casey, Constance, 47, 68-69
Catt, Carrie Chapman, xii, 18
Central America, study tour of, 80-81
Chiang Kai-shek, Madame, 40
Chapman, Ann, 60, 61-65
child-bearing, 58
Churchill, Winston, 40
Clinton, Hillary Rodham, 115, 137, 162
Clinton, William Jefferson "Bill," 115, 123
Colton, Margaret "Peg," 156-159
committees, 21, 93, 111, 141-142
computers, 146, 147
Congressional Union, xi
Cook, Blanche Wiesen, 33-34
crab cakes. *See* Mikulski, Barbara
Crater's Raiders, 53
Cruz, Arturo, 110
C-SPAN, 106
Cunningham, Minnie Fisher, 4, 5, 17-21

D

Dall, Curtis, 30
Davis, Margo, 88-90
Davis, Susanna "Susie," 64, 65, 66
"Dear Female Democrats," 90
Declaration of Sentiments, ix
Democratic Bulletin, The, 26-27
Democratic Digest, The, 27, 48, 50

Democratic National Committee, 4, 27
  women's division, 45-46, 55,
  103-104
Democratic National Convention
  (1968), 117-118
Democratic Women's Day, 28, 62
Democrats Abroad, 104
Dems for the '90s, 125
Dewson, Mary "Molly," 27, 32, 46
Dillon, Dorothy, 70, 78-81
DNC. *See* Democratic National
  Committee
Dodd, Catherine. *See* Shouse,
  Catherine Filene Dodd
Douglas, Emily, 47, 67
Driver, Marian, 90, 91
Dukakis-Bentsen reception, 119-120
Dukakis, Kitty, 100, 119, 120
Duncan, Gladys, 47, 64-67
Duncan, Todd, 64
Dupont Circle, 91, 99

E

Education and Children's Issues Task
  Force, 143-146
Edwards, Herbert, 44, 50
Edwards, India, 44-50, 56, 76
  Pulling No Punches, 48, 49
802 Connecticut Avenue, 4, 7, 11-12
embezzlement, 101-103
Equal Rights Amendment, xiii, 28,
  53-54, 95
ERA. *See* Equal Rights Amendment

F

fellowships, legal, 155
Ferraro, Geraldine, 107
1520 New Hampshire Avenue,
  130-131

1526 New Hampshire Avenue,
  17-18, 19-20, 21-22, 43, 139. *See
  also* Empire furniture under Bertie
  Hamlin, 76-77
Fineshriber, Phyllis, 114-115, 162
Fraser, Arvonne, 150
Freeman, Jane, 100, 115-121
Friedan, Betty, 59, 72
Funk, Antoinette, 6, 12

G

Gantt, Harvey, 127
gender discrimination, 78
glass ceiling, 79. *See* Shattering the
  Glass Ceiling
Glasser, Esther, 143-146
Global Women's Task Force, 152-153
Golden Lane, 2
governing board, WNDC, 22,
  110-111, 129-130
grief counseling, 156

H

"Hair," 87, 90
Halle, Kay, 95
Hamlin, Charles S., 10
Hamlin, Huibertje "Bertie," 6, 7,
  10-13, 14, 19, 26
  "Empire" furniture, 76-77
Hard, Anne, 7
Harding, Warren G., 1, 2
Harriman, Averell, 8, 10, 77, 105
Harriman, Florence Jaffray "Daisy,"
  xi, 2, 5-10, 11, 12, 14, 19, 47, 65,
  66, 76
Harriman, Jefferson Borden, 8
Harriman, Pamela, 105, 125-127
Head Start. *See* Johnson, Lady Bird
Helm, Edith, 28

INDEX

Henderson, Shirley, 100, 120, 123-132, 160
Hickok, Lorena, 33-34, 46
Hight, Elizabeth "Betty," 28, 36-41
Hight, John, 40-41
Hill, Anita, 136
Hobart, Amanda. *See* MacKenzie, Amanda
Hobby, Oveta Culp, 61
"How Our Laws Are Made," 114-115
How To Cook Reagan's Goose, 108-109
Howard, Janet, 126-127
Howe, Louis, 27, 33
Hull, Cordell, 3, 9
Hull, Frances, 6, 16
Humphrey, Hubert H., 53, 117
Hurst, Florence Jaffray. *See* Harriman, Florence Jaffray "Daisy"

I

inaugural night (1993), 136-137
integration, 47, 64-67, 131, 132. *See also* Special Committee Studying the Space Problem
international women's conferences, 151-153
    Beijing, 151

J

Jackson, Jesse, 127-128
"Jenny for President," 62-63
Jensen, Jean, 101-110
Joan's Den, 96
Johnson, Lady Bird
    garden dedication, 92
    Head Start, 82-84
    Highway Beautification Bill, 82, 116-117
    park benches, 88
    A White House Diary, 82, 88

Johnson, Lyndon Baines, 74, 147-148
Jones, Jesse, 4
Jones, Mary Gardiner, 146-150
    Federal Trade Commission, 147-149
Jones, Natalia, 6, 16, 20

K

Kefauver Committee. *See* Senate Crime Investigating Committee
Kennedy, Jacqueline, 19
Kennedy, John Fitzgerald, 10, 71, 73, 74, 75, 116
Kendrick, Eula, 6, 16
Keyserling, Mary Dublin, 74-77
King, Martin L. Jr., 69, 129
Kirk, Paul, 109-110
Knee, Ruth, 154
Koteen, Sherley, 91-99

L

Lady Bird Special, 82
Lanahan, Frances Scott Fitzgerald, 69
Lash, Joseph, 37
Lash, Trude, 37
League of Women Voters, xii, 1, 2, 19
library, 19
Linowitz, Toni, 157
Louchheim, Katie, 84

M

McAdoo, Nell, 11
McCarthy, Eugene, 117
McCormick, Robert R., 44
McCormick, Ruth Hanna, 3, 4
MacKenzie, Amanda, 124
male members. *See* Newman, Wynn
Margolin, Olya, 114-115
Marian O. Norby Fund, 51, 155

177

Meigs, Margaret, 16, 20
Mercer, Lucy, 35, 36
membership, 47, 113, 118, 133-134, 138, 146
Mikulski, Barbara, crab cakes, 108
Millstone, Sacha, 132-139
Mondale, Joan, 96-98
Mondale, Walter, 89

N

Nadel, Ruth, 152-154
National Federation of Democratic Women, 81, 85, 103
National Organization for Women, 53, 71
National Woman's Party (NWP), xi-xiii
NAWSA (National American Woman Suffrage Association), x, xi, xii, 19
needlepoint, 98, 115
Nesbitt, Henrietta, 31
Neval Thomas School, 155-156
New Deal, 25-28
Newburger, Adelaide, 156
Newman, Wynn, 132
19th Amendment, xii
Norby, Marian O., 50-53, 155.
   See also Marian O. Norby Fund
no-smoking policy, 104
NOW. See National Organization for Women

O

O'Brien, Maureen "Molly," 21-23
Overton, Ellen, 150-153
Owen, Lillian, 46, 158
Owen, Ruth Bryan, 9

P

Page, Harvey, 20
parking, 91
Paul, Alice, xi, xii
Pearson, Drew, 68, 69
Perkins, Frances, 9, 12, 19, 27
Peterson, Esther, 28, 72-74, 94, 160
Planned Parenthood, 87, 88
Post, Marjorie Merriweather, 19
Poston, Gretchen, 96, 98-99
prepaid luncheons, 109
President's Commission on the Status of Women, 71
Progressive Era (1890-1920), xi, 14
Progressive League, 63
public policy committee, 141

R

Rankin, Jeannette, xii
Rauh, Joseph, 64, 115
Rauh, Olie, 64, 87
Rayburn, Sam, 45
Reagan, Ronald, 149
Reeves, Ola, 141
renovations, 20
Richardson, David, 13-14
Rivlin, Alice, 114
Roosevelt, Eleanor, 4, 6, 12, 24-41, 73, 107
   press conferences, 26-27
   WNDC wing and library, 19, 28
Roosevelt, Franklin Delano, 9, 10, 11, 24, 25-36, 40
Roosevelt, Sara Delano, 31-32, 39
Ross, Nellie Tayloe, 7, 27
Rutherford, Lucy. See Mercer, Lucy

S

Sampson, Edith, 47, 67
Seagraves, Eleanor "Ellie," 28, 29-36
Senate Crime Investigating Committee, 56-57
Senate War Investigating Committee, 54
Seneca Falls Convention, ix
1724 I Street, 11-12
sexual revolution, 90
"Shattering the Glass Ceiling," 137
Shaver, Clem, 4, 18
Shouse, Catherine Filene Dodd, 6
Sign of the Donkey, 21
Smeal, Ellie, 112
southern Democrats, 65-66
Snell, Isabelle, 6, 16
Special Committee Studying the Space Problem, 68. *See also* integration
Spingarn, Natalie, 65-67
Stanton, Elizabeth Cady, ix, x
Stevenson, Adlai, 60, 62, 77
Sunday night suppers, 5, 7-8

T

Tank, Marelyn, 110-114
task forces, WNDC, 93-94, 141-153
Telecommunications Task Force, 146-150
Thompson, Malvina "Tommy," 30, 39, 40
Truman, Bess, 44
Truman Committee. *See* Senate War Investigating Committee
Truman, Harry S., 45
    whistle-stop campaign, 51-53
Tugwell, Rexford, 31

U, V, W

Uhl-Katcher, Gladys, 49-50
Vietnam War, 135
Walsh, Thomas J., xii, 7, 8, 9
Watergate, 87, 91-92
whistle-stop campaigns, 50, 51-53, 82
"white pass," 4
Whittemore, Sarah Adams, 20
Wider Opportunities for Women, 150
Wilcox, Walter D., 20
Wilson, Edith Bolling, 12, 14, 20
Wilson, Woodrow, xii, 3, 9, 12
WNDC. *See* Woman's National Democratic Club
WNDC Educational Foundation, 112, 155-159
WNDC News, 113
Wolf, Agnes "Aggie," 54-59
Woman's National Democratic Club, 3, 4, 6, 9, 11, 14, 21-23, 46-48, 84, 113-114
    honorary presidents and past presidents, 161
Women's Bureau, 73, 75
Women's Leadership Forum, 55, 59, 138
Women's National Wilson and Marshall Organization, 9
WOW. *See* Wider Opportunities for Women
Wyeth, Nathan [N. C.], 20

X, Y, Z

Young Women's Leadership Project, 155-156

*An Editorial without Words, The Bulletin, June 1928.
Courtesy of WNDC-EF archives.*

ABOUT THE AUTHOR, THE HISTORIAN & THE EDITOR

The Author

Jewell Fenzi was a diplomatic spouse for thirty years. In 1986, after settling in Washington, DC, she established Foreign Service Spouse Oral History, Inc., and recorded many of the interviews excerpted in her book, *Married To The Foreign Service: An Oral History of the American Diplomatic Spouse* (Twayne Publishers, 1994).

She was a society reporter for *The Honolulu Advertiser* and has written articles for [Department of] *State* magazine; the *Foreign Service Journal*; and *Washington History*, magazine of The Historical Society of Washington, DC. Her *This Is The Way We Cook* book written in Curaçao, Netherlands Antilles, is in its tenth printing.

She is secretary of the WNDC Educational Foundation, chair of the EF oral history program, and is a graduate of the University of California at Berkeley.

The Historian

Dr. Allida Black is research professor of history at The George Washington University, Washington, DC. An authority on Eleanor Roosevelt, she is project director and editor of The Eleanor Roosevelt and Human Rights Project, the first phase of a ten-year effort to produce print and electronic documentary editions of Mrs. Roosevelt's political writings.

Dr. Black is the author of three books, including *Casting Her Own Shadow: Eleanor Roosevelt and the Shaping of Postwar Liberalism*; *Courage In A Dangerous World: The Political Writings of Eleanor Roosevelt*; and *What I Hope To Leave Behind: The Essential Writings of Eleanor Roosevelt*. She teaches courses in recent U.S. political and social history, the Roosevelts, and the modern presidency.

She is a frequent speaker at the Woman's National Democratic Club and a sponsor of the WNDC Educational Foundation's Young Woman's Leadership Project. Dr. Black was an editor and consultant on women's issues for *Democratic Women*. She is a graduate of Emory University, Atlanta, Georgia.

The Editor

Sally Cutler is a Phi Beta Kappa graduate of Smith College, with a master's degree in library science from Catholic University in Washington, DC. She is a freelance editor.